CGI Manual of Style

CGI
Manual
of Style

Robert McDaniel

Ziff-Davis Press
An imprint of Macmillan Computer Publishing USA
Emeryville, California

Acquisitions Editor	Suzanne Anthony
Coordinating Editor	Kelly Green
Editor	Deborah Craig
Technical Reviewer	Jason Wehling
Project Coordinator	Ami Knox
Cover Illustration and Design	Megan Gandt
Book Design	Gary Suen
Word Processing	Howard Blechman
Page Layout	Janet Piercy
Indexer	Julie Kawabata

Ziff-Davis Press, ZD Press and the Ziff-Davis Press logo are trademarks or registered trademarks of, and are licensed to Macmillan Computer Publishing USA by Ziff-Davis Publishing Company, New York, New York.

Ziff-Davis Press imprint books are produced on a Macintosh computer system with the following applications: FrameMaker®, Microsoft® Word, QuarkXPress®, Adobe Illustrator®, Adobe Photoshop®, Adobe Streamline™, MacLink®Plus, Aldus® FreeHand™, Collage Plus™.

Ziff-Davis Press, an imprint of
Macmillan Computer Publishing USA
5903 Christie Avenue
Emeryville, CA 94608

ISBN 1-56276-397-0

Manufactured in the United States of America
10 9 8 7 6 5 4 3 2 1

CONTENTS AT A GLANCE

TABLE OF CONTENTS

Part 1   Introduction to CGI

Part 2   CGI Examples

ACKNOWLEDGMENTS

First and foremost, I want to thank my wife, Vonda, for bearing with me during the past few months. She accepted the reduction in our time together as well as taking on some of the tasks that I no longer had time for. She also continually inspired me when my own motivation waned. She always brings out the best in me.

I also want to thank Suzanne Anthony, Kelly Green, and Deborah Craig for guiding me through this project and introducing me to the world of computer book publishing. All three of you have given me advice in areas where my technical knowledge was of no help.

Finally, I am eternally indebted to those men and women who pass on their knowledge about the Internet through Web pages, online documentation, newsgroup postings, and mailing list e-mails. It was the knowledge I gained from these resources that made this book possible.

INTRODUCTION

Over the past few years, the Internet has emerged from relative obscurity and become a household name. Most of this growth can be attributed to the World Wide Web, which is just one area of the Internet. Before the Web evolved, the Internet was primarily a text-based environment, not known for being particularly accessible. Most people were not interested by this type of text-based setting—many even found it intimidating. What the World Wide Web offered, which the rest of the services on the Internet had not, was a rich multimedia experience. Web pages could incorporate images, sounds, and video, giving Web sites vast audience appeal. The World Wide Web transformed the Internet from a tool for experts and specialists into a user-friendly, exciting, and entertaining environment in which you could get work done or have fun, all with a few mouse clicks or keystrokes.

You are probably already somewhat familiar with the World Wide Web. You most likely have even heard of CGI scripts and are looking for information about how to write your own. But what made you pick up this book? Did you choose it because it's smaller than the others on the shelf? Did you think it would be concise and would present you with exactly the information you need to get started? If so, you won't be disappointed. This book is a brief but thorough introduction to CGI scripting. It can be both simply because you do not need to learn a lot to write CGI scripts.

This book is organized so you can quickly learn what you need to know and get started with your own CGI scripts. It is divided into three parts, each with a specific focus. You don't need to read this book from cover to cover to start writing your own CGI scripts. You only need to read the sections that supply the information you need or that include examples of interest to you.

The first part, which contains three chapters, is an introduction to the nuts and bolts of CGI scripting. The first chapter presents an overview of the Internet, the World Wide Web, HTML, and CGI. It introduces concepts that are important to CGI, such as URLs, HTTP, and the division between client and server computers. If you already have a good grasp of this material and of what CGI is in general, go ahead and skip to Chapters 2 and 3, which supply you with all of the tools you need to begin writing your own scripts. Chapter 2 explains how your script gets data from the Web server and sends output back to the Web browser. Chapter 3 addresses CGI programming issues, such as choosing a programming language, where to place your script files, how to call your scripts from the Web browser, common errors, and security.

The second part of the book includes six chapters that present six practical examples of CGI scripts. These examples reflect some of the most common applications of CGI scripts on the Web. You'll find example form handlers, guest books, shopping carts, access counters, and bulletin boards. There are also some simple examples that demonstrate how to interact with databases and how to animate your Web pages.

At the end of the book is a Quick Reference that lists a number of online resources This section contains a collection of Web URLs, newsgroups, and mailing lists where you can go to for further information on CGI, HTML, HTTP, the World Wide Web, and the Internet. Don't hesitate to explore; that's what using the Web is all about. That's also how you'll find the most up-to-date information available.

Most of the scripts in this book are written in Perl version 5, with one example in C, but no prior knowledge of Perl or C is assumed. The functionality of each code segment is explained thoroughly, allowing you to rewrite the code in your language of choice. However, if your project does not restrict you to a certain language, I highly recommend becoming acquainted with Perl. If you already know any programming language, Perl is easy to learn; it is also very well suited for CGI scripting. If you need help learning Perl, check the resources listed in the Perl section of the Quick Reference at the end of the book.

All of the scripts in this book have been tested on three machines. The first is a DEC Alpha 1000 running the OSF version 3.2 version of UNIX. Because the examples are written in Perl, they contain no machine-specific code and should work equally well under any other UNIX configuration. The DEC Alpha was running Netscape's Communications Server version 1.1 as the Web server. The scripts have also been tested on both a Windows 95 and Windows NT (version 3.51) machine. The Windows 95 machine is a Compaq Deskpro 5120 (120 MHz Pentium machine) with 48MB of RAM. The Windows NT machine is a Gateway 2000 433V (33 MHz 486 machine) with 20MB of RAM. Both Windows machines were using O'Reilly's WebSite version 1.1 as the Web server.

The Internet is in a constant state of flux. Because of this, I highly recommend that you investigate the online resources listed in the Quick Reference for further information after reading this book. I also welcome any comments or questions you may have regarding the content of this book or the Internet in general. You can reach me at robertm@deltanet.com. In the meantime, welcome to CGI scripting!

Introduction to CGI

What Is CGI?

THE WORLD WIDE WEB

WHY USE CGI?

Chapter

1

The Common Gateway Interface, or CGI, is a standard for communication between Web documents and CGI scripts you write. CGI scripting, or programming, is the act of creating a program that adheres to this standard of communication. A CGI script is simply a program that in some way communicates with your Web documents. Web documents are any kind of file used on the Web. They can be HTML documents, text files, image files, or any number of other file formats. The existence of this gateway between programs you write and your Web documents allows you to create much more dynamic and interactive Web pages than you could with HTML alone.

This chapter will help you understand the role of CGI scripting within the World Wide Web and will show why you would want to use it. First, you will be introduced to some of the key elements and terminology of the Web, such as HTTP, URLs, HTML, and CGI. Then you will learn some of the advantages of CGI scripts.

THE WORLD WIDE WEB

Many people have heard of the World Wide Web, but not everyone knows what it is. Even people who use it may have trouble defining it precisely. The World Wide Web is a global collection of interconnected documents on the Internet. Because the World Wide Web has grown explosively and has been advertised so extensively, many people think it is the same thing as the Internet. However, the World Wide Web is only a part of the Internet.

The Internet has been around for over three decades. It began as a Department of Defense program for enabling computers to communicate over great distances without requiring a central server to route the communications traffic. Since those early days, the Internet has grown substantially. Early on it was adopted by the academic community, and more recently it has been commercialized. The federal government no longer funds the Internet directly, leaving private and public telecommunications companies in charge of the major backbones—the major network connections of the Internet. The telecommunications companies charge Internet service providers for connections to the backbone, and Internet service providers in turn charge companies and individuals for their access to the Internet. The Internet itself is nothing more than an enormous number of networked computers all over the world. Like any computer network, the Internet has various software programs running on it, such as e-mail, newsgroups, FTP, gopher, and the World Wide Web.

The World Wide Web, or Web, was born in 1989 at CERN (the European Laboratory for Particle Physics). Since then, it has grown at a phenomenal rate. Today, Web traffic accounts for somewhere between one third and one half of the total traffic on the Internet. Because the Internet consists of many other sources of traffic, many of which have been around for decades, this is an impressive feat.

So, what is the Web? In simple terms, the Web is a part of the Internet that uses the Hypertext Transfer Protocol (HTTP) to display hypertext and images in a graphical environment. Hypertext refers to the ability to present text documents that are interlinked. You might click on a portion of the text in a document and be taken to another section of text in a different document. The Web is based on the concept of hypermedia, which is a superset of hypertext. Think of hypermedia as various forms of media (text, graphics, sound files, and so on) that are interlinked. For example, you could click on a text link in one document and display a graphic image. Figure 1.1 illustrates both a text link and an image link. Clicking on the word "resume" would take you to a page with the actor's résumé, and clicking on the picture itself would take you to a larger version of the same image. In the early days of the Web, text links always had a different color of underlined text, and graphic links were always enclosed within a colored box. Now, however, the current shape of the mouse pointer gives you a better indication of what is and isn't a link. If the mouse pointer changes into a hand with the index finger extended, as shown below the "resume" link in Figure 1.1, the object being pointed to is a link to another document. Documents on the Web are interlinked so you can navigate between them by selecting links. The name World Wide Web alludes to the Web's spiderweb-like nature.

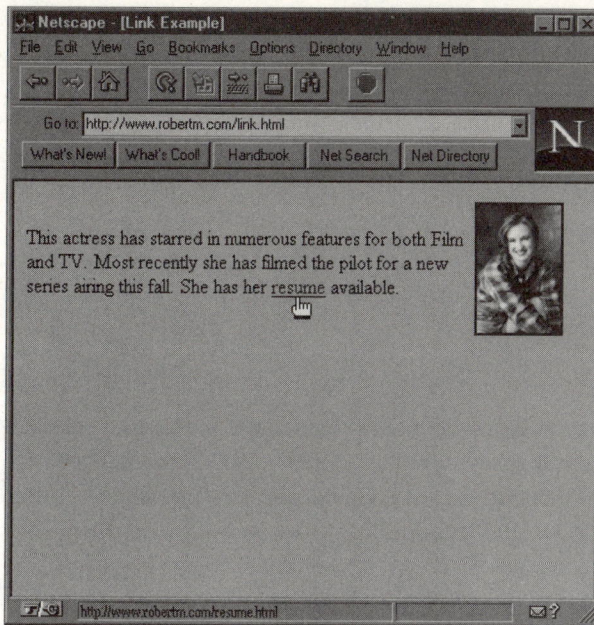

Figure 1.1: An example of a link

CLIENTS AND SERVERS

To understand the World Wide Web and CGI programming, you must understand the division between Web clients and Web servers and how HTTP facili-
tates the interaction between the two. Simply put, a server handles requests
from various clients. For example, suppose you are using a word processing
program to edit files on another computer. Your computer would be the client
because it is requesting the file from another computer. The other computer
would be the server because it is handling your computer's request. With networked computers, clients and servers are very common. A server typically
runs on a different machine than the client, although this is not always the case.
The interaction between the two usually begins on the client side. The client
software requests an object or transaction from the server software, which either handles the request or denies it. If the request is handled, the object is sent
back to the client software. On the World Wide Web, servers are known as Web
servers, and clients are known as Web browsers. Web browsers request documents from Web servers, allowing you to view documents on the World Wide
Web. There's a good chance that you have already used a Web browser. Some of

the most common browsers are Netscape's Navigator, Microsoft's Internet Explorer, and NCSA's Mosaic. Like most software companies that distribute Web browsers, these companies also distribute Web server software.

The process of viewing a document on the Web starts when a Web browser sends a request to a Web server. The Web browser sends details about itself and the file it is requesting to the Web server in HTTP request headers. The Web server receives and reviews the HTTP request headers for any relevant information, such as the name of the file being requested, and sends back the file with HTTP response headers. The Web browser then uses the HTTP response headers to determine how to display the file or data being returned by the Web server. (There's more information on these headers in Chapter 2.)

> **Note:**   This discussion barely scratches the surface of what is actually happening, but it is enough for our study of CGI scripting. If you want more details on HTTP headers, check Chapter 2 as well as the "Useful Web Pages" section of the Appendix.

When a Web browser requests a CGI script from a Web server, the server starts the CGI script and passes the HTTP request headers to it. The information stored in the request headers is available for your script to use. Normally, when a CGI script is finished executing, the output is passed back to the Web server, which formats an HTTP response header and sends the information to the Web browser. It is possible, however, for your CGI script to format the HTTP response header and send the data directly to the Web browser. You can use this approach to reduce the work load of your Web server.

Whether the Web browser is requesting a file or a CGI script, the browser has to know the location of the Web server and the name of the file in order to make the request. With the millions of documents on the Web, you might wonder how the Web browser knows exactly where to look for the file you want to see. You probably also realize that many files on the Web have the exact same name. So how do the Web browsers get the correct document? Each file on the Web has a unique identifier that not only sets it apart from other documents but also describes where it is located. These unique identifiers are called uniform resource locators, or URLs.

UNIFORM RESOURCE LOCATORS

The uniform resource locator (URL) is like an address for Web documents. Every document on the Web has a unique URL, and each part of the URL provides specific information about the location of the document it addresses. Here are some examples of URLs:

```
http://www.thepalace.com/palace-faq.html
http://www.yahoo.com
http://www.thepalace.com/cgi-bin/directory.pl
ftp://ftp4.netscape.com/pub/MacJavaB1/Mac2.0JavaB1.hqx
```

Each URL has three basic parts: the protocol, the server machine, and the file being requested.

The protocol is everything up to the colon and the first two slashes. The protocol for the first three of the preceding examples is http (hypertext transfer protocol) and the protocol for the last one is ftp (file transfer protocol). For a Web browser, the most common protocols are http://, ftp://, gopher://, and news://.

Following the protocol, between the double slashes and the first single slash, is the name of the machine you want to access. This name can be either the domain name of the machine, as in all of the examples, or the IP address. Just as every document on the Internet has a unique identifier, every machine on the Internet must also. This identifier is a number known as the IP (Internet Protocol) address. An example of an IP address is 206.17.52.2. Because names are easier for people to remember than numbers, IP address can be aliased to domain names. For example, the domain name www.thepalace.com points to the machine with the IP address 206.17.52.2. Sometimes you may see a colon and a number following the machine name, as in www.abletree.com:8080. This means that the server you are accessing on the www.abletree.com machine is using the port 8080 instead of the default port, which for Web servers is port 80.

After the protocol and the name of the server machine, the URL contains the name of the file being requested. This name often includes subdirectories on the server machine. If no subdirectories are included, the server looks in the document root, which it believes to be the highest-level directory. In the first example URL, the file palace-faq.html is in the document root on the www.thepalace.com machine. The fourth example is the address for a file called Mac2.0JavaB1.hqx in the pub/MacJavaB1 subdirectory of the ftp4.netscape.com machine.

The second and third examples illustrate special occurrences of URLs. The second example, http://www.yahoo.com, does not specify a file to retrieve. Most of the time, when no file is specified, the Web server automatically looks for a file called index.html and returns that file. If index.html does not exist, the Web server returns a list of files contained in that directory, which in this example is the document root. Many Web servers also allow you to specify a default file to return for URLs formatted in this manner. This default file you specify can be a CGI script, which gives you a great deal of control over what documents are available to certain Web browsers and Internet domains. The third example, http://www.thepalace.com/cgi-bin/directory.pl, looks like the first and fourth example, but with one key difference. The directory cgi-bin does not have to be a subdirectory of the document root. Most Web servers allow you to specify a location for the cgi-bin directory, which is outside of the document root. Also, when a Web server receives a request for a file contained in the subdirectory cgi-bin, it knows that the file is a CGI script and will run it and return only the output from the script. The cgi-bin directory is discussed in more detail in Chapter 3.

So, each document on the Web has a unique URL, but what are these documents? Well, they can actually be any kind of file, such as graphic images, executable programs, text files, word processor documents, and spreadsheets. Any file can be sent by a Web server. However, only a limited number of file types can be displayed in a Web browser. Text, GIF images, and JPEG images are the only files that most Web browsers can display. If a Web server sends a file that the browser cannot display, the user can either start a helper application to display the file or save the file to the hard drive. Most of the documents you encounter on the Web will be text files containing HTML.

HTML

Hypertext Markup Language, or HTML, is a subset of the Standard Generalized Markup Language (SGML), a language that specifies document types and how to display the various types. HTML consists of various tags that describe to the Web browser how to display the information contained within the document. Every hypertext document on the World Wide Web is published in either HTML or SGML. What follows is an example of the contents of an HTML file. Figure 1.2 shows how the Netscape Navigator browser would display that HTML page.

```
<HTML>
<HEAD>
<TITLE>HTML Example</TITLE>
</HEAD>
<BODY>
<H1>This is my HTML page</H1>
This is a simple html page.<BR>
It has a few <I>html tags</I> to <B>illustrate</B> html.
<P>So, let's get on to CGI!
<HR>
</BODY>
</HTML>
```

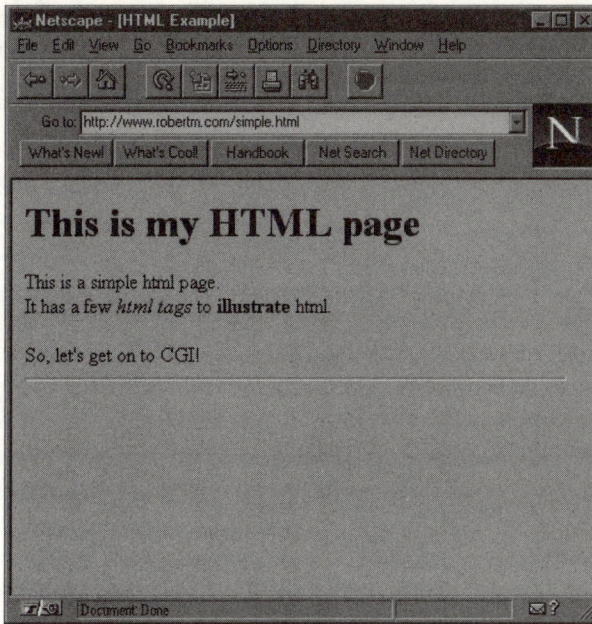

Figure 1.2: The HTML example in a browser window

HTML is very important to CGI scripts. It is from within HTML documents that most CGI scripts get called. Also the information returned from a CGI script is usually either in HTML format or is a pointer to an HTML document. Because of this close interaction between CGI and HTML, it is helpful to be familiar with HTML before learning CGI scripting. This book does not teach HTML scripting, and it assumes a basic understanding of HTML tags. But don't be too concerned if you do not already know HTML. The examples in this book, like the one a moment ago, will only contain basic HTML, which should be fairly self-explanatory. For help learning HTML, try *HTML3 Manual of Style* by Larry Aronson (Ziff-Davis Press, 1995) or consult the "Useful Web Pages" section of the Appendix for a list of online resources.

CGI

Remember, CGI stands for Common Gateway Interface. As its name implies, it is a gateway between the Web server and your CGI script. It enables the CGI program that you write to receive input from and send output to a Web browser. You can write CGI programs in almost any programming language. If you already know how to program, CGI will be very easy for you to learn. To get started, you just need to know how data is passed back and forth between the Web server and your program. But because CGI is not a programming language, you need to know one to write CGI scripts.

The way CGI works is quite easy as well. Let's take a simple CGI script and execute it from a Web browser. Here is the contents of first-one.pl.

```
#!/usr/local/bin/perl
print "Content-type: text/html\n\n";
print "<H1>Simple CGI Script</H1>\n";
print "This is my first CGI script!\n";
```

Note: Most of the examples in this book are written in Perl 5 and run on a UNIX system. They have also been tested on a Windows system. If you are trying these examples on a Windows machine, be sure to remove the #!/usr/local/bin/perl line, which is specific to UNIX environments. If you don't know Perl, don't worry. The examples will either be easy or there will be a line-by-line explanations of the code within the text. For instance, this example just prints three lines of text to standard out (stdout), which is the default location to which a program sends its output. In most cases standard out is the monitor. However, for CGI scripts, standard out is sent to the Web server and then on to the Web browser.

Because Perl is an interpreted language, you can just place the preceding code in a text file, save it as first-one.pl, and run the program with the Perl 5 interpreter. For UNIX systems, this means making the file first-one.pl executable. You can also run this file on Windows and Macintosh systems by using the Perl 5 interpreter available for those systems.

For now, place the file first-one.pl in the cgi-bin directory of your Web server. cgi-bin is a naming convention for Web servers running on UNIX systems. Windows users will have something similar, such as cgi-shl for Windows 95 or NT machines running the WebSite™ Web Server by O'Reilly & Associates, Inc. You will learn about another option for file placement in Chapter 3. After you have placed the file in the cgi-bin directory, go to your Web browser and load the file by opening the URL http://www.robertm.com/cgi-bin/first-one.pl. Figure 1.3 shows the result in my browser window.

Note: The domain name www.robertm.com in the preceding URL is specific to my machine. All the examples in the book will reference that domain. For your URL, you need to use the domain name or IP address of the machine on which you are working. If you don't know this information, ask your system administrator.

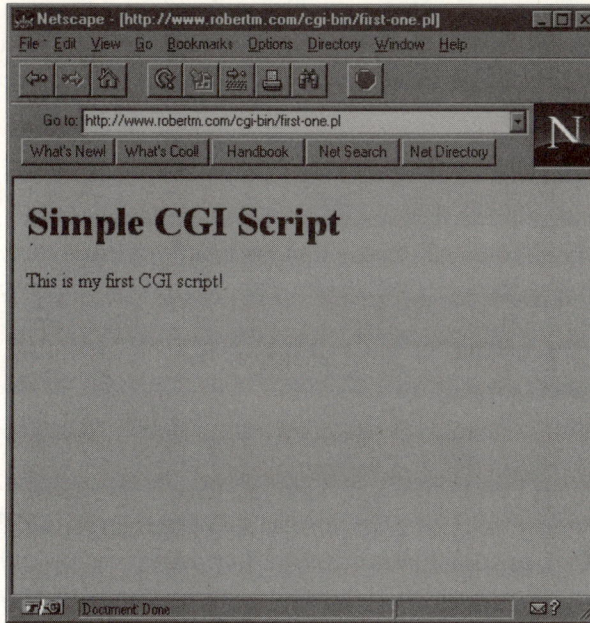

Figure 1.3: Results of first-one.pl script

Let's take a look at what is happening behind the scenes when you call this script from your browser. First, the browser sends an HTTP request for the first-one.pl file in the cgi-bin directory on the www.robertm.com machine. The Web server on the www.robertm.com machine receives the request and finds the file on the system. Because the request is for a document in the cgi-bin directory, the Web server knows that it is a CGI script, and executes it. At this point, the script takes over. It executes its three lines and sends the output, stdout in this case, to the Web server. The Web server receives the data and checks the header the CGI script returned. The header in the preceding script is the Content-type: text/html line. (Valid headers are discussed in detail in Chapter 2.) This header tells the Web server that the data it received from the CGI script is just HTML. The Web server then forms an HTTP response header and sends the header and the CGI output to the Web browser that called it.

As you can see in the preceding example, only the line

```
print "Content-type: text/html\n\n";
```

in the CGI script is CGI specific. The other two lines simply output the HTML that is displayed in the browser. The HTML would be exactly the same if it were in an HTML file on the Web server. When you begin writing CGI scripts, you will discover that only a small amount of your code has to deal with the CGI. The rest of the code is specific to the task you want to accomplish.

WHY USE CGI?

You may have noticed that the preceding CGI example could just as easily been a simple HTML file. In fact, you don't gain any advantage from making it a CGI script. So why use CGI? Well, for the preceding example, you wouldn't. It is just a simple example CGI script. As you learn CGI, however, you will see that it allows you to extend the functionality of Web documents to produce dynamic and interactive pages.

DYNAMIC WEB PAGES

Recall that the World Wide Web is divided into Web browsers and Web servers that use HTTP to communicate, and that most Web pages are written in HTML. But HTML pages are always static. They do not change unless you edit the file and alter the contents. CGI, however, allows you to create very dynamic documents. A CGI script can draw from up-to-date information to form the Web page that is displayed in the browser. For example, you can use CGI to create documents that display current data such as the time, date, and number of accesses to that page. With HTML alone, it would be impossible to display this information in real time.

CGI can also interface with a database to make dynamic documents. If your database included a lot of information that you wanted to make accessible via the Web, it would be a laborious project to convert all of the data into HTML pages. Then, every time the data in your database changed, you would have to edit every HTML page containing the information that had changed. For a large database, this process would be very time consuming and error prone. There would also be limits on how the user could search through the data. Every possibility for search results would have to be an HTML page created and maintained by you. CGI makes this process much easier. All of the data can remain in your database, where you maintain it as you always have. When a user requests information from your database through the Web pages you create, your CGI script extracts the relevant data and displays it in the browser. You can even allow the user to change to the data by adding, deleting, or modifying records.

As mentioned, you can set up your Web server to use a CGI script for the default document returned to the user when just your domain name is entered as the URL. This approach allows you to send different documents depending on the type of browser being used or the domain from which the request originated, giving you some control over which users see your data. You can also make a script return different data virtually every time it is called. In this way, your home page would always be different for all users, every time they accessed it.

INTERACTIVE WEB PAGES

CGI scripts also provide a mechanism for making Web pages interactive. By using the <FORM> tag in HTML, you can receive data directly from the user who is viewing your Web pages. All of this data can be sent to a CGI script that can then act upon it. For example, you could create a simple navigation control for your entire Web site using a drop-down list containing the names of all the Web pages on your site. The user would simply select which page he or she wanted to view, and the CGI script would return it.

Bulletin boards are another way you can use CGI to create interactive Web pages. You can write scripts that will display all of the messages posted so far and allow the user to post new messages. You could make the page very simple, with just a list of messages, or you could make it a Usenet-style message area, with replies to messages underneath the original posting.

CGI lets you do all this and more. For the most part, the only limit is in your own ability to program. If the data you want to display can be formatted with HTML, you can output it from your CGI script.

The Elements of the Common Gateway Interface

PASSING DATA TO YOUR CGI SCRIPT

RETURNING THE RESULTS

Chapter

2

Chapter 1 explained what CGI is and how it fits into publishing on the World Wide Web. This chapter describes how data is passed between your Web server and your CGI script. You will discover where to look for the data you need and how to pass the results of your script back to the Web server. You will even learn how to send data from your CGI script directly back to the Web browser, bypassing the server altogether.

Remember, the Common Gateway Interface is simply a way of passing data between your Web browser/server and your CGI script. This chapter presents all of the tools you need to begin writing CGI scripts. So, let's start with how the Web server passes data to your CGI script and then move on to returning your results to the Web browser.

PASSING DATA TO YOUR CGI SCRIPT

You don't need to do much to ensure that your CGI script receives the necessary data from your Web server. The CGI has already defined how this is done and the task is performed automatically every time your Web server executes a CGI script. All of the relevant data sent to the server from the Web browser, such as form input, plus the HTTP request headers are sent from the server to the CGI script in either environment variables or by standard input (stdin), which is the default location at which your program receives input. Because this task is done for you, all you have to know is where to look for the information you need.

ENVIRONMENT VARIABLES

When a Web browser requests a CGI script from a Web server, the server starts the CGI program in what is termed a *stateless environment*. What this means is that the CGI script is running in its own state or environment. It does not inherit values from the environment that the Web server is running under. This is important because many Web browsers can be requesting the same CGI script at the same time, and the Web server can start many copies of the same script. Each version of the script that is running concurrently must run independently from all the other scripts, otherwise conflicts may arise. Because the Web server sets up a new environment for your CGI script, it places almost all of the information available to the script in environment variables. Table 2.1 lists the CGI environment variables.

Table 2.1: CGI Environment Variables

Variable	Meaning
AUTH_TYPE	Contains the authentication method used to validate the Web browser, if any is used. An example of an authentication method is a username/password scheme.
CONTENT_LENGTH	The length of the user-provided content from the Web page requesting the CGI script, which is sent via the user's Web browser. Because the user-provided content is passed to the CGI script as a string, this value is in bytes, with each byte representing one character.
CONTENT_TYPE	Contains the type of the data that accompanies the browser's request for the CGI script. Examples are text/html or image/jpeg.
GATEWAY_INTERFACE	Holds the version of the Common Gateway Interface being used. For version 1.1 of the CGI specification, this variable would be CGI/1.1.
PATH_INFO	Holds additional path information for the CGI script. This is usually the virtual path to another document in the document root that the CGI script will use. This value is set from the information appended to the URL requesting the CGI script. See PATH_TRANSLATED for an example.

Table 2.1: CGI Environment Variables (Continued)

Variable	Meaning
PATH_TRANSLATED	Holds the physical path as translated from the virtual path provided in the PATH_INFO variable. For example, suppose the document root was the www subdirectory of the /usr directory. For the URL http://www.robertm.com/cgi-bin/calculate.pl/cgi-data.txt, the PATH_INFO variable would be /cgi-data.txt and the PATH_TRANSLATED would be /usr/www/cgi-data.txt.
QUERY_STRING	Contains the user-provided data when the request method is GET. This data is appended along with a question mark to the referenced URL. For example, in the URL http://www.robertm.com/cgi-bin/answer.pl?state=CA, the QUERY_STRING would be "state=CA."
REMOTE_ADDR	Stores the IP address of the machine running the Web browser requesting the CGI script.
REMOTE_HOST	Stores the domain name of the machine running the Web browser requesting the CGI script. If this information is unavailable to the Web server, REMOTE_ADDR will be set and REMOTE_HOST will not be set.
REMOTE_IDENT	Stores the user's login name only if the Web server supports identification.
REMOTE_USER	Stores the username the Web browser specified for authentication. This is only set if the server supports authentication and the CGI script is protected.
REQUEST_METHOD	Contains the request method used to request the CGI script. This can contain any of the valid HTTP request methods such as GET, HEAD, POST, PUT, and so on.
SCRIPT_NAME	Stores the virtual path and name of the CGI script being executed. This is used for self-referencing URLs.
SERVER_NAME	Contains the name, either domain name or IP address, of the machine running the Web server.
SERVER_PORT	Contains the port number on which the Web browser sent the request to the Web server.

Table 2.1: CGI Environment Variables (Continued)

Variable	Meaning
SERVER_PROTOCOL	Contains the name and version of the protocol being used to make the request for the CGI script. In most cases, this will be the HTTP protocol and will look something like HTTP/1.0.
SERVER_SOFTWARE	Stores the name and version of the Web server software that executed the CGI script. For example, for the Netscape Communications Server version 1.1, the variable would be set to Netscape-Communications/1.1.

In addition to the CGI environment variables, the Web server makes available all the HTTP request headers received from the Web browser. These are also placed in environment variables, all of which have the prefix HTTP_. Table 2.2 lists the HTTP request header environment variables.

Table 2.2: HTTP Request Header Environment Variables

HTTP Request Header	Meaning
HTTP_ACCEPT	Contains a comma-separated list of media types the browser can accept in response from the Web server. Examples are audio/basic, image/gif, text/*, */*. The last two examples contain the wildcard *, which is a stand-in for any string of characters. text/* means that all forms of text can be accepted; */* means that the browser will accept any content type.
HTTP_ACCEPT_ENCODING	Contains the valid encoding methods the browser can receive in response from the Web server. Examples are x-zip, x-stuffit, and x-tar.
HTTP_ACCEPT_LANGUAGE	Contains the browser's preferred language for a response from the Web server. However, responses in any language not specified in this variable are allowed. An example is en_UK, which is the English of the United Kingdom.

Table 2.2: HTTP Request Header Environment Variables (Continued)

HTTP Request Header	Meaning
HTTP_AUTHORIZATION	Contains authorization information from the Web browser. Its value is used for the browser to authenticate itself with the Web server. There is not a single specific format for possible values of this field, and new formats may be added. One example is the user/password scheme, where the value, in my case, would be user robertm:mypassword.
HTTP_CHARGE_TO	Formats for this field are still undetermined. However, it is available to contain information for the account that is to be charged for the costs of receiving the requested data.
HTTP_FROM	Contains the name of the requesting user as supplied by the Web browser in an e-mail address format. Some examples are robertm@deltanet.com and rmcdanie@primenet.com.
HTTP_IF_MODIFIED_SINCE	Can contain a value specified in a valid ARPANET date standard, such as Weekday, DD-Mon-YY HH:MM:SS TIMEZONE. This field can be used in conjunction with the GET method to return the requested document only if it has changed since the date specified.
HTTP_PRAGMA	Holds the value of any special directives for the Web server. For instance, a proxy Web server has one valid value for a pragma request header, no-cache, which means that the proxy server should always request the document from the real Web server instead of returning a nonexpired cached copy.
HTTP_REFERER	Contains the URI (uniform resource identifier, which is a superset of URLs) of the document that contained the link to the currently requested document. An example would be http://www.thepalace.com/web-pages.html.
HTTP_USER_AGENT	Contains the name of the Web browser software that requested the document. An example is Mozilla/2.0 (Win95; I), which would be the user agent for the Netscape 2.0 browser for Windows 95.

Clearly there are many environment variables available to your CGI script. For the most part, you will only use a few of these. Of course, your objective will determine which variables you need for your project. Listing 2.1 shows a CGI script that displays the values of the CGI and HTTP request header environment variables.

Listing 2.1: The display.pl CGI Script

```perl
#!/usr/local/bin/perl

print "Content-type: text/html\n\n";
print "AUTH_TYPE = $ENV{'AUTH_TYPE'}<BR>\n";
print "CONTENT_LENGTH = $ENV{'CONTENT_LENGTH'}<BR>\n";
print "CONTENT_TYPE = $ENV{'CONTENT_TYPE'}<BR>\n";
print "GATEWAY_INTERFACE =
       $ENV{'GATEWAY_INTERFACE'}<BR>\n";
print "PATH_INFO = $ENV{'PATH_INFO'}<BR>\n";
print "PATH_TRANSLATED = $ENV{'PATH_TRANSLATED'}<BR>\n";
print "QUERY_STRING = $ENV{'QUERY_STRING'}<BR>\n";
print "REMOTE_ADDR = $ENV{'REMOTE_ADDR'}<BR>\n";
print "REMOTE_HOST = $ENV{'REMOTE_HOST'}<BR>\n";
print "REMOTE_IDENT = $ENV{'REMOTE_IDENT'}<BR>\n";
print "REMOTE_USER = $ENV{'REMOTE_USER'}<BR>\n";
print "REQUEST_METHOD = $ENV{'REQUEST_METHOD'}<BR>\n";
print "SCRIPT_NAME = $ENV{'SCRIPT_NAME'}<BR>\n";
print "SERVER_NAME = $ENV{'SERVER_NAME'}<BR>\n";
print "SERVER_PORT = $ENV{'SERVER_PORT'}<BR>\n";
print "SERVER_PROTOCOL = $ENV{'SERVER_PROTOCOL'}<BR>\n";
print "SERVER_SOFTWARE = $ENV{'SERVER_SOFTWARE'}<BR>\n";
print "HTTP_ACCEPT = $ENV{'HTTP_ACCEPT'}<BR>\n";
print "HTTP_ACCEPT_ENCODING =
       $ENV{'HTTP_ACCEPT_ENCODING'}<BR>\n";
print "HTTP_ACCEPT_LANGUAGE =
       $ENV{'HTTP_ACCEPT_LANGUAGE'}<BR>\n";
print "HTTP_AUTHORIZATION =
       $ENV{'HTTP_AUTHORIZATION'}<BR>\n";
print "HTTP_CHARGE_TO = $ENV{'HTTP_CHARGE_TO'}<BR>\n";
print "HTTP_FROM = $ENV{'HTTP_FROM'}<BR>\n";
print "HTTP_IF_MODIFIED_SINCE =
       $ENV{'HTTP_IF_MODIFIED_SINCE'}<BR>\n";
print "HTTP_PRAGMA = $ENV{'HTTP_PRAGMA'}<BR>\n";
print "HTTP_REFERER = $ENV{'HTTP_REFERER'}<BR>\n";
print "HTTP_USER_AGENT = $ENV{'HTTP_USER_AGENT'}<BR>\n";
```

Note: Once again, to run this program on a Windows machine, remove the line #!/usr/local/bin/perl.

Place this code in a file called display.pl in your cgi-bin directory. You can then run it from your Web browser by a URL in the form http://www.robertm. com/cgi-bin/display.pl. Remember, www.robertm.com is specific to my machine. In its place you need to specify the domain name or IP address of the machine running your Web server. Also, try running this script with different Web browsers and on different machines, or maybe even create an HTML page that has a link to the script, and notice how the values of the environment variables change.

STANDARD INPUT

Under most circumstances, all the information your script needs will be contained in the environment variables. However, in some cases the Web server passes data to your CGI script by using standard input. When a Web browser requests a CGI script from a Web server with the request method of POST, which is most often used with forms in HTML, the user-provided data, if any, is sent via standard input. The Web server still assigns values to most of the environment variables discussed earlier. In fact, when the user-provided data is sent via standard input, you should always check the value of CONTENT_LENGTH before working with the data sent since the Web server does not send an EOF (End Of File) at the end of the data.

URL ENCODING

Whether the Web server sends the user-provided data via standard input or by assigning it to the QUERY_STRING environment variable, the data is always sent as one long string of name/value pairs that is URL encoded. This encoding consists of changing all spaces to plus signs (+) and converting certain special characters into hexadecimal. Before working with the data, you need to decode the string and separate the name/value pairs.

Each name/value pair consists of a field name and value separated by an equal sign (=). The field name is usually taken from the NAME attribute in one of the <INPUT>, <TEXTAREA>, or <SELECT> tags of an HTML form, and the value is usually data entered by the user submitting the form. The name/value pairs are separated by an ampersand sign (&). In Perl, a useful function called split separates a string into substrings at intervals that you specify. Below is an example of how you can split the name/value pairs. Each name/value pair is first placed into an array. Then the name and value are separated and placed into an associative array, with the name acting as the key and the value being assigned to the array element. By the way, an associative array is an array that is indexed by strings rather than integers. For associative arrays, the index is referred to as the key. So, for name{'first'}=Robert, the array is name, the key is first, and the value is Robert.

Listing 2.2 splits up the name/value pairs, but remember that the query string is URL encoded as well. You must decode the contents of the string in addition to splitting the name/value pairs. Listing 2.3 adds the code within the foreach loop that changes all equal signs (=) to spaces and replaces hexadecimal codes with their character equivalents.

Listing 2.2: Perl Code to Split Name/Value Pairs

```perl
# This line places each name/value pair as a separate
# element in the name_value_pairs array.
@name_value_pairs = split(/&/, $user_string);

# This loops over each element in the name_value_pairs
# array, splits it on the = sign, and places the value
# into the user_data associative array with the name as the
# key.
foreach $name_value_pair (@name_value_pairs) {
  ($name, $value) = split(/=/, $name_value_pair);

  # If the name value pair has already been given a value,
  # as in the case of multiple items being selected, then
  # separate the items with a " : ".
  if (defined($user_data{$name})) {
    $user_data{$name} .= " : " . $value;
  } else {
    $user_data{$name} = $value;
  }
}
```

Listing 2.3: Perl Code to URL Decode User-Provided Data

```perl
# This line changes the + signs to spaces.
$user_string =~ s/\+/ /g;

# This line places each name/value pair as a separate
# element in the name_value_pairs array.
@name_value_pairs = split(/&/, $user_string);

# This loops over each element in the name_value_pairs
# array, splits it on the = sign, and places the value
# into the user_data associative array with the name as the
# key.
foreach $name_value_pair (@name_value_pairs) {
  ($name, $value) = split(/=/, $name_value_pair);

  # These two lines decode the values from any URL
```

Listing 2.3: Perl Code to URL Decode User-Provided Data (Continued)

```
# hexadecimal encoding. The first section searches for a
# hexadecimal number and the second part converts the
# hex number to decimal and returns the character
# equivalent.
$name =~
    s/%([a-fA-F0-9][a-fA-F0-9])/pack("C",hex($1))/ge;
$value =~
    s/%([a-fA-F0-9][a-fA-F0-9])/pack("C",hex($1))/ge;

# If the name value pair has already been given a value,
# as in the case of multiple items being selected, then
# separate the items with a " : ".
if (defined($user_data{$name})) {
  $user_data{$name} .= " : " . $value;
} else {
  $user_data{$name} = $value;
}
}
```

You might wonder why the entire string is not hexadecimal URL decoded before it is split, even though plus signs are replaced with spaces at this stage. Some of the special characters that are converted to hexadecimal when URL encoding takes place are the +, &, and = signs. If these were changed before the string was split or plus signs were converted to spaces, any of these special characters could alter where a value is split or what value is actually displayed, causing incorrect results. This is why hexadecimal encoding is done. It enables your CGI script to distinguish between when a symbol is typed by the user or is being used for a special purpose. For example, the name/value separator & would not be changed to hexadecimal whereas a & symbol typed by the user would be changed.

The code samples in both Listings 2.2 and 2.3 are not complete, ready-to-execute CGI scripts. Rather, they are just examples of the lines of code that perform the URL decoding. Chapter 4 will incorporate these lines of code into a subroutine for use within the examples in this book.

RETURNING THE RESULTS

Whenever a CGI script is called, it needs to return a result to the Web server, which then sends it to the Web browser that requested it. A CGI script also has the option of bypassing the Web server and returning the result directly to the Web browser. Whether the results are being sent to the Web server or directly to the Web browser, the CGI script must specify a valid header.

When a CGI script completes execution, it typically sends its results back to the Web server via standard output. The Web server receives the results, formats the proper HTTP response header, and returns all of the data to the Web browser. The first thing the CGI script must return to the browser is a parsed header.

PARSED HEADERS

Every CGI script must precede any data returned to the Web server with a parsed header. A parsed header is the lines of code output by your CGI script that get parsed by the Web server. This parsed header is in the same format as an HTTP header and can contain any of the CGI variable names listed in Table 2.1. Parsed headers must always be immediately followed by a blank line. Any lines in the parsed header that are not directives to the Web server are sent back to the Web browser as part of the HTTP response header. The current version of CGI, version 1.1, specifies three server directives, which are shown in Table 2.3.

Table 2.3: Server Directives for Parsed Headers

Directive	Meaning
Content-type	Specifies to the Web server the MIME type of the data being returned by the CGI script.
Location	Contains either the virtual path or the URL of a document that your CGI script wants returned to the Web browser requesting your script.
Status	Returns to the Web server an HTTP status line, which will then be returned to the Web browser. Status lines consist of a three-digit status code and the reason string. Examples are 404 Not Found and 403 Forbidden.

Here's an example of a parsed header being returned in a CGI script:

```
#!/usr/local/bin/perl

print "Content-type: text/html\n\n";
```

BYPASSING THE SERVER

Most Web servers allow you to send the output from your CGI script directly back to the Web browser rather than through the Web server. For the Netscape Communications server, you can activate this feature by preceding the name of your CGI script with nph-.

When your CGI script sends its output directly back to the Web browser, it has to specify a nonparsed header that must contain the proper HTTP response headers. Table 2.4 lists the HTTP response headers.

Table 2.4: HTTP Response Headers

HTTP Response Header	Meaning
ALLOWED	Specifies to the requesting browser which request methods are allowed. Examples are GET, HEAD and PUT.
CONTENT-ENCODING	Specifies which encoding method is used. Examples are x-zip, x-stuffit, and x-tar.
CONTENT-LANGUAGE	Specifies the language the returning document is in. An example is en, which is English in one of its forms.
CONTENT-LENGTH	Specifies the size in bytes of the returning data.
CONTENT-TRANSFER-ENCODING	Specifies the encoding of the data between the Web server and the Web browser. The default is binary.
CONTENT-TYPE	Contains the type of the data being transferred. Examples are text/html and image/gif.
COST	Will contain the cost of the retrieval of the object being requested. The format of this header has not yet been specified.
DATE	Contains a creation date of the requested object in a valid ARPANET format.
DERIVED-FROM	Can contain a version number for the requested object, allowing for version control of editable documents.
EXPIRES	Contains an expiration date for the requested information, after which the document should be retrieved again. This header is used primarily for caching mechanisms and is in an ARPANET date format.
LAST-MODIFIED	Contains the date when the requested object was last modified. This header is in an ARPANET date format.
LINK	Holds information about the document being returned. You can use it to specify information such as the inclusion of another URL within the returned document or the creator of the returned object.
MESSAGE-ID	Contains a unique identifier for the HTTP message.

Table 2.4: HTTP Response Headers (Continued)

HTTP Response Header	Meaning
PUBLIC	Fairly similar to the ALLOW response header. However, it specifies the request methods that anyone can use, not just the requesting browser. Examples for this header are GET, HEAD, and TEXTSEARCH.
TITLE	Contains the title of the document being returned. For an HTML file, this is equivalent to the value contained within the <TITLE></TITLE> tags.
URI	Gives the URI (uniform resource identifier) where the requested object can be found. This will not always be the URL the user entered in the Web browser requesting the returned object. However, it will point to an object that should be the same as the one being returned, with some degree of variance. An example is http://www.robertm.com/Group-one/section1.htmlvary=language, version which gives a URI with the same document, which might vary in language or version.
VERSION	Defines the version of an object that can be changed. Its format is currently undefined.

You do not need to provide every HTTP response header to have a valid nonparsed header. For example, a CGI script with a valid nonparsed header would look like this:

```
#!/usr/local/bin/perl

print "HTTP/1.0 200 OK\n";
print "Server: Netscape-Communications/1.1\n";
print "Content-type: text/html\n\n";
```

Writing CGI Scripts

Choosing a programming language

Testing and debugging your script

Configuring the server

Calling your CGI script

Security

In the previous chapter, you learned how your CGI script receives data from the Web server and how to return your script's results to the Web browser. You now have the all the knowledge you need to begin writing useful CGI scripts. So let's get started.

This chapter lays the foundation that you need to write, debug, and run your CGI scripts. The first piece of this foundation is choosing a programming language in which to write your scripts. You learn what to look for when selecting a language and which languages are the most popular. You also pick up a few pointers on testing and debugging and common mistakes that you can avoid. After you have finished coding and debugging, you learn how to configure your Web server and how to call your CGI script. Finally, you learn a bit about security for both the data that is being transmitted and the system on which your script is running.

CHOOSING A PROGRAMMING LANGUAGE

Before starting your script, you need to choose which programming language to use. For most projects, choosing a language is largely a matter of preference. While die-hard UNIX gurus will rely on one of the UNIX shells, C, or Perl, a Windows user might prefer a DOS batch file or Visual Basic. The choice is up to you, but you must choose a language that will produce a program that is executable on the system hosting the Web server. This means that if your Web server is on an Apple Macintosh system, you cannot use a scripting language— such as a UNIX shell program—that does not run on that Apple Macintosh.

Although this is the only restriction, it should not be your sole consideration. You benefit from choosing a language that is familiar to you, that is commonly used by other CGI scripters, that is a good match for your specific system, and that can perform the operations needed to accomplish the objective for writing the script.

COMMON LANGUAGES

Most CGI scripts are written in AppleScript, C, C++, Perl, TCL, any UNIX shell, or Visual Basic. These are not the only languages in use, but they are by far the most common. Although you can use any language you wish, there are two good reasons to consider using one of the common ones.

First, it will be faster to program CGI scripts because of shared code. Many people on the World Wide Web have already written CGI scripts for common tasks. Several have made their scripts freely available for others to use. You can usually find these scripts by searching through the various script repositories on the Web. There is a list of many of these script archives in the "Script Archive" section of the Appendix. Form handlers, access counters, and shopping carts—which are explained with examples in Chapters 4 and 5—are just a few examples of the types of scripts to be found in these script archives. Most of the scripts even give you permission to alter the code to suit your particular needs. As you can imagine, most of these scripts are written in the common languages mentioned earlier, so you will be better equipped to use them if you know one of these languages. These script archives also contain many useful library routines for parsing form data and returning valid headers.

Second, if you use one of the common CGI scripting languages it is easier to get help with debugging. If you are having trouble with one of your scripts, you may need to get help. On the Internet, there are a few ways of posing questions and getting knowledgeable advice without having to pay large consulting fees. You can post questions and read responses in USENET newsgroups or mailing lists. If you are using one of the popular languages, more people will be able to help you with any problems that crop up.

A FIT FOR YOUR PLATFORM

When choosing which programming language to use, you should take into consideration what platform it will run on. Most of the common languages are available for all of the platforms for which there are Web servers. The most obvious example of one that is not is AppleScript. Clearly, if your Web server does not run on an Apple machine, you shouldn't write your CGI scripts in AppleScript, even if that is your favorite language. However, if your Web server runs on an Apple Macintosh, AppleScript is a powerful choice because it allows easier interaction with other programs on the Macintosh than C or C++. So, choose a language that will work on your system, and make your job the easiest.

APPROPRIATE FOR THE PROBLEM

Finally, make sure that the language you choose is appropriate for the task at hand. For simple form handling, any of the common languages work well, but when you start developing more complicated scripts, such as accessing a database, Perl is clearly a better choice than a UNIX shell. However, C is better than Perl when you need to do a lot of sorting very quickly, because C is compiled and Perl is interpreted. Keep in mind what you need to accomplish when selecting the programming language, and choose appropriately.

TESTING AND DEBUGGING YOUR SCRIPT

Like other programs, CGI scripts should be thoroughly tested before you make them available for the whole Internet to use. The simplest way to do this is by splitting the debugging task into two areas: the logic of the program and the interface. Testing the logic of the program is no different than testing a normal program. Does it do what you intended it to do? To find out, imagine that your CGI script is a regular program. Test it by executing it from the command line (or however you run your programs) and make sure it works correctly. Then, after the logic is correct, insert the CGI-specific code that interfaces with the Web browser and server—such as reading the environment variables and returning the correct header. To test the interface, you may want to use a combination of command-line execution (with Simulation of Environment Variables) and browser execution (running it from within the browser). Once you are ready to test the script from within the browser, you need to configure the Web server to run CGI scripts. This may already be done for you. If not, see the section "Configuring the Server" later in this chapter.

COMMAND-LINE EXECUTION

After you have written your CGI script, you should try to run it from the command line. The command line is the old text-only terminal interface in which the user is prompted for text input and the computer responds to the commands the user types. Two examples of a command-line interface are the DOS shell and the UNIX shell. To run your script from the command line, just type the name of the script file at the command prompt and press Enter.

The main purpose of running your script from the command line is to catch any logical errors. At this point you can check for syntax errors and runtime errors as well as verifying that the program does what you want. To verify that your program does what it should, you may need to assign values to the environment variables to simulate running from a browser.

SIMULATE VARIABLES

When you are debugging your code from the command line, the environment variables discussed in Chapter 2 will not be set. To verify that your program performs correctly, you may need to simulate the environment variables that would be set if you were running it from a Web server. You can do this easily by assigning values to the necessary environment variables in a section of temporary code in your script. After you are done debugging your script, just comment out or remove these lines of code.

COMMON PROBLEMS

One of the most common error messages received with CGI scripts is, "Server Error, document returned invalid header." This error is usually the result of not specifying a valid header to be returned to the Web server. Remember, all data returned to the server must have a valid header. The header has to be properly formatted with spaces and punctuation, as described in the previous chapter. Often the extra blank line between the Content-Type Parsed header line and the actual start of the data is missing. If you have double-checked your code and the proper header is being returned but you are still receiving the Server Error, check for an abnormal termination of your script. If the script "crashed" during execution, the Web server would receive the crash message instead of the header and would interpret this message as an invalid header.

On UNIX systems, CGI scripts often do not execute as a result of incorrect file permissions on the script file. The script file must not only be executable on the command line, but must be executable by the Web server. If the user ID under which the Web server is running is not the owner or in the group of the script file, the script must be "world-executable," which is a file permission status for files on UNIX systems. Check your file system and Web server documentation for more information about user IDs and file permissions.

For Windows systems using Perl, the most common problem is with the perl.exe executable. Unlike the UNIX system, all Perl programs on the Windows system must be executed running the Perl interpreter and passing the name of your Perl program file as a parameter. For example, to execute the file first.pl, you would type

```
c:\perl\perl.exe first.pl
```

at the command prompt of a DOS shell and press Enter. You could also type just

```
perl first.pl
```

if the path to the perl.exe file is in your PATH statement in your autoexec.bat file.

Knowing this, your first thought might be to execute your Perl CGI script by using a URL in the form

```
http://www.robertm.com/cgi-bin/perl.exe?first.pl
```

which will work. However, this can be a major security risk because your Perl interpreter is in a directory that is available to the entire World Wide Web. This security risk has been exploited on many machines.

There are two ways to overcome this security risk. One is to use a wrapper program, which is another program that will reside in the cgi-bin directory and call the Perl interpreter in a secure manner. A much easier solution, however, is to create an association. In Windows, an association is based upon the file name extension. For example, most Windows systems consider all files with the .txt extension to be text files that are opened with the Windows program Notepad. (In other words, .txt files are "associated" with Notepad.) Double-clicking on a file called readme.txt in a Windows environment will start the Notepad program and open the file readme.txt within Notepad. Similarly, you can create an association between the Perl interpreter and files with the .pl extension. This strategy allows you to leave your perl.exe program in another directory on your machine and call your CGI script with URLs in the form http://www.robertm.com/cgi-bin/first.pl. Consult your Windows documentation for instructions on how to create the association.

Finally, when executing the script from within your browser, always make sure that the script file is in the correct location for the Web server. The Web server must know that the file being requested is a CGI script. Otherwise, it will simply display the contents of the script file in the user's browser. On most systems, CGI scripts reside in a special directory, the cgi-bin directory. When the Web server receives a request for a file in the cgi-bin directory, it knows that the file is a script that it should execute. Many Web servers have an option that allows them to recognize files with the .cgi extension as script files. If this option is enabled, the CGI scripts can be in any directory under the document root, but must have a .cgi extension. For more information on the cgi-bin directory and the .cgi extension, see the next section.

CONFIGURING THE SERVER

After you have run your CGI script from the command line, you will want to run it from within a Web browser. Before you can do this, however, you need to configure your Web server to handle requests for CGI scripts. By default, the Web server returns any requested file to the Web browser that requested it.

For your CGI scripts, the script contents would be displayed in the browser window rather than the script being executed. If you configure the Web server to recognize CGI scripts, whenever a browser requests a script file the server will automatically run the script instead of returning the file to the browser. If your Web server already has working CGI scripts, you do not need to configure the server to get your CGI scripts to work.

Web server software makes use of configuration files to store specifics about the Web site, such as the location of the documents (known as the document root), the port number on which to listen, and the location of CGI scripts. (There are many other settings in the server configuration files. Check the documentation for your server for a complete list of the settings.) If you have Web space on someone else's server (your Internet service provider's server, for instance), you need to consult that system's webmaster for details on where to place your CGI scripts. If you run your own server, check the documentation for details on how to specify a cgi-bin directory or enable the .cgi extension.

CGI-BIN

Most Web servers store all CGI scripts in a single directory. This directory is called cgi-bin (sometimes it's called cgi-win for Windows machines). The cgi-bin directory can be anywhere on the system, as long as the Web server has access to it. Your Web server's configuration file must specify the full path name to the cgi-bin directory so the server can find it. Once the Web server is configured to recognize the cgi-bin directory, you execute your scripts by referencing the cgi-bin directory as if it were at the document root level. For example, suppose your domain is inter.net and your Web site is at http://www.inter.net/. To run the funtimes.pl script in the cgi-bin directory, you would type

```
http://www.inter.net/cgi-bin/funtimes.pl
```

THE .CGI EXTENSION

Most Web servers let you specify a file name extension (typically .cgi) to designate which files are CGI scripts. If you enable this feature on your Web server, you can store your CGI scripts in any directory on your Web site, not just in the cgi-bin directory. This allows you to keep your script files with the HTML files they work with. If the .cgi designation is recognized, you could call the funtimes.cgi script in the /football directory by typing

```
http://www.inter.net/football/funtimes.cgi
```

CALLING YOUR CGI SCRIPT

By now you have learned how to test your script from the command line. You know that you need to configure your server, and you know where to put your CGI script files. Now you need to think about how you want to call your script from your HTML file. In most cases, what you want to accomplish dictates how you call the script. When you need to handle form input, for instance, you have to specify the name of the CGI script within the <FORM> tag. The other methods for calling your CGI script—in the anchor tag (<A>), in the image tag (<IMG>), and with Server Side Includes (more on these in the section "Calling a CGI Script in Server Side Includes" later in this chapter)—also require that you specify the name of the CGI script within the HTML tag.

CALLING A CGI SCRIPT IN THE <FORM> TAG

If you are writing a script to handle form input, you place the name of the CGI script in the ACTION attribute of the <FORM> tag, as shown here:

```
<FORM METHOD=POST ACTION="/cgi-bin/formhandle.pl">
```

> **Note:**   It is assumed that you already know how to write the HTML code for a form. If not, consult the forms section of an HTML book. If you are already somewhat familiar with this topic, but need to refresh your memory, the HTML is presented briefly in Chapter 4.

Intuitively, the value of the ACTION attribute is what action the browser will perform when the form is submitted. You can use any valid URL as the ACTION for a form. When the form is submitted, the browser sends the Web server a request for that item. If the item is a CGI script, the script is executed and all of the data that was entered in the fields of the form are sent via the QUERY_STRING environment variable or standard input. For other URLs, such as an HTML or GIF file, the document is returned to the browser. In the preceding example, the browser is requesting a CGI script, formhandle.pl, which the Web server will execute. Here is the HTML code you would use if you were using the .cgi extension for your CGI scripts.

```
<FORM METHOD=POST ACTION="formhandle.cgi">
```

CALLING A CGI SCRIPT IN THE <A> TAG

You can also call CGI scripts by assigning them to the HREF attribute of the <A> tag, like this

```
<A HREF="/cgi-bin/clicked.pl">Click Here</A>
```

or

```
<A HREF="clicked.cgi">Click Here</A>
```

> **Note:** The rest of the examples in this book reflect scripts stored in the cgi-bin directory of the Web server. Keep in mind that you can implement the same scripts by using the .cgi extension if that option is enabled on your server.

When clicked, the links defined by the preceding lines of HTML code cause the Web server to execute the referenced CGI script (in this example, the clicked.pl or clicked.cgi script).

Recall from Chapter 2 that the value for QUERY_STRING is the user-provided information when the request method is GET. One way the user can pass this information via the GET method is to append a question mark followed by the data to the URL requesting the CGI program. Here is an example of appending the information to a CGI script request in the HREF attribute of the <A> tag.

```
<A HREF="/cgi-bin/clicked.pl?file=clicked.html">Click Here</A>
```

As the programmer, you can use this method to pass parameters to your program by URL encoding a string of name/value pairs on the command line. In the preceding example, the name of an HTML file is being passed to the clicked.pl script via the QUERY_STRING environment variable.

In most cases, this approach will not be very useful. Remember, the line of HTML is hard-coded in the HTML page, unless the page is generated dynamically (there will be some examples of this in Chapter 5). It will always be the same value, no matter who is clicking on the page. However, this approach can be useful in some applications, such as the shopping cart examples in Chapter 5.

CALLING A CGI SCRIPT IN AN IMG TAG

You can also call CGI scripts from within the <IMG> HTML tag. If you place the path to a CGI script as the value to the SRC attribute, the Web server will execute the CGI script and return the output as the source for the image. Your CGI script must return output that is in a graphic format, either by directly returning the ASCII description of an image or by redirecting the Web server to the location of the graphics file. For example, here is a line of HTML code that calls the CGI script cgi-image.pl:

```
<IMG SRC="/cgi-bin/cgi-image.pl">
```

Here is the contents of cgi-image.pl, which simply redirects the Web server to a graphic file:

```
#!/usr/local/bin/perl

print "Location: /graphics/image1.gif\n\n";
```

As you probably know, this is not a practical use of the feature. You could achieve the exact same effect simply by referencing the image1.gif file in the SRC attribute of the <IMG> tag. However, being able to dynamically return an image file lets you create graphic images at runtime or vary the image file that is displayed.

CALLING A CGI SCRIPT IN SERVER SIDE INCLUDES

Most Web servers can enable a feature known as Server Side Includes. Server Side Includes are Web server commands that reside within the HTML of an HTML document. When the Web server parses the HTML file, it executes all the Server Side Include commands and places the results in the place of the command. Server Side Includes allow you to include another item within your Web page simply by adding an HTML tag. These included items can be many different things, such as another HTML document, an image file, or a CGI script. All Server Side Include statements are in the form

```
<!--#command tag1="value1" tag2="value2" -->
```

To execute a CGI script from within a Server Side Include, you use the exec command. The exec command has two valid tags, cmd and cgi. The cmd tag executes the associated value with /bin/sh (the UNIX Bourne shell). The cgi tag calls the CGI script whose virtual path is the associated value. Here is the line of HTML code that executes and includes the output from the CGI script include-me.pl:

```
<!--#exec cgi="/cgi-bin/include-me.pl" -->
```

SECURITY

Security is an important and sometimes overlooked issue with CGI scripts. As the author and user of CGI scripts, you must understand that both the data being transmitted and the machine the Web server is running on are vulnerable to unauthorized access.

VULNERABILITY OF DATA

Many CGI scripts are used in conjunction with form input. These scripts gather data from the person using the Web browser, interpret that data, and pass information back to the browser. The data en route to either the script or the browser passes through many machines as it travels across the Internet. Under most circumstances, someone with access to these other machines can view this information.

Most of the time, the data will pass between the browser and your script unnoticed and untouched. However, keep in mind that the information is vulnerable. For this reason, it is best not to send and receive sensitive data that you do not want someone other than the intended recipient to view. Several companies are working on providing greater security for data being transmitted on the Web. The Netscape Commerce Server and the Secure Mosaic Server are the only ones readily available at the moment. These are two versions of Web servers that enhance the security of the data while it is in transit.

VULNERABILITY OF YOUR SERVER

When a Web browser requests a CGI script from your Web server, that script is run on your machine. Anytime someone else runs a CGI script on your machine, there is the potential for abuse. If you do not take precautions when writing your scripts, your machine may be open to invasion by unauthorized individuals.

For example, suppose you wrote a simple HTML page with a form for the user to enter his or her name. When the user submits that form, your CGI script receives the data the user entered and outputs it within an HTML page. On the surface, that seems harmless enough, and it usually is. If you have Server Side Includes enabled, however, this could be a major security risk. Suppose the user entered something like

```
<!--#exec cmd="cat /etc/passwd" -->
```

Remember that the value of the cmd attribute is executed by /bin/sh on UNIX systems with the results being sent back to the browser. In this case, the browser could receive the contents of the password file for the system.

As long as you know that your server is vulnerable, you can protect your machine and still safely run your CGI scripts. In the previous example, you could place a line of code in your CGI script that checked for Server Side Include statements, alleviating that risk.

Part 2

CGI Examples

Handling Forms

HTML FORM BASICS

PROCESSING THE FORM INPUT

Handling form input is one of the most common uses of CGI scripts today. This is in large part due to the numerous uses for forms. A form is just a group of HTML tags that generate such elements as input fields, list boxes, check boxes, radio buttons, and push buttons. Forms allow the user viewing your Web page to interact with you or your Web site by supplying information or making a selection.

In this chapter, you will set up a feedback form that allows the user viewing your pages to send you messages. This will be a simple example of a form and the CGI script needed to handle the input from the form. Because you create forms with HTML and process them with CGI scripts, this chapter briefly reviews the HTML code for creating forms. Again, if you are not already familiar with the HTML of a form or with the concepts of input fields, list boxes, check boxes, radio buttons, and push buttons, you should consult a book on HTML such as *HTML3 Manual of Style* by Larry Aronson (Ziff-Davis Press, 1995).

HTML FORM BASICS

Forms are defined in the HTML specification and not in CGI. CGI simply provides the means for handling the input received from a form. To create a form, you just use the <FORM> tag and the associated <INPUT>, <SELECT>, and <TEXTAREA> tags. A basic form can consist of as little as a single button. However, most forms contain many more elements. This section briefly presents the HTML form tags <FORM>, <INPUT>, <SELECT>, and <TEXTAREA>, and the relevant attributes for the tags.

THE <FORM> TAG

All HTML forms begin with the <FORM> tag and end with the </FORM> tag. The <FORM> tag commonly takes two attributes: METHOD and ACTION. A third defined attribute, ENCTYPE, is not commonly used and is not necessary for the examples in this book.

The METHOD attribute tells the Web server how to send the data to the CGI script. Values for the METHOD attribute are GET and POST. Most commonly, the POST value is assigned to METHOD. Recall from Chapter 2 that the location of the user-supplied data varies depending on this value. For the GET method, the user data is URL encoded and placed in the QUERY_STRING environment variable. The POST method also URL encodes the data, but sends it via standard input.

The value of the ACTION attribute tells the Web server what action to perform when the form is submitted. A form is submitted when the user viewing the Web page either clicks on the submit push button (more on this in "The <INPUT> Tag" below) or presses the Enter key when there is only a single input field. Once the form is submitted, the data is URL encoded and sent to the Web server by either the GET or POST method. The Web server receives the data and checks the value of the ACTION attribute.

The ACTION attribute can have any valid URL for its value. For our purposes, this value will always be the location of our CGI script. For example, let's call the CGI script for the feedback form feedback.pl. If you placed this form in the cgi-bin directory of your Web server, the ACTION attribute would be set to /cgi-bin/feedback.pl. Between the <FORM> and </FORM> tags are all other elements of the form, such as the <INPUT>, <SELECT>, and <TEXTAREA> tags. For the example feedback form, the beginning form tag would be <FORM METHOD=POST ACTION= "/cgi-bin/feedback.pl">.

THE <INPUT> TAG

<INPUT> tags reside between the <FORM> and </FORM> tags and are the most versatile element tags of the form. With the <INPUT> tag, you can create check boxes, radio buttons, single-line input fields, and submit and reset push buttons. The <INPUT> tag does not have a closing tag and has six attributes, which are described in Table 4.1.

Like many visual elements, these HTML tags are better shown than explained. Listing 4.1 displays the HTML code that creates an example of each type of input element. Figure 4.1 shows how these input elements appear in the Netscape browser.

Table 4.1: <INPUT> Tag Attributes

Attribute	Values
TYPE	This attribute determines what form the input field will take. The possible values are
	text: Creates a single-line text input field. This is the default value for the <INPUT> tag.
	password:Similar to text, except all entered values are represented on screen as asterisks.
	hidden: Creates a field that is invisible to the user. This is used to pass information that the user does not need to see or modify on to the form handler CGI script.
	checkbox:Creates a single check box, which can be either on (checked) or off (unchecked)
	radio: Similar to checkbox in that it creates an option that can be either on or off. However, when several radio buttons have the same value of the NAME attribute, only one radio button can be on (checked) at a time.
	submit: Creates a push button that, when clicked, causes the form to be submitted (performs the action).
	reset: Generates a push button that, when clicked, resets the elements of the form to their default values.
NAME	The value for this attribute is sent to the server as the name for the name/value pairs. For example, if the user typed robertm@ deltanet.com in a single-line text input field with "email" as the name attribute, the Web server would receive email=robertm@ deltanet.com. When you create a group of radio buttons, all the buttons must have the same value for the NAME attribute.
VALUE	For text and password elements, this attribute holds an initial value for the field to contain. For checkbox and radio elements, this attribute holds the value that is sent to the Web server when the element is selected. If the VALUE attribute is not specified for checkbox and radio elements, the Web server receives "on" as the value for the selected elements. For submit and reset elements, this attribute holds the value used for the label of the button. For example, creating a submit button with the VALUE attribute equal to "Send" yields a push button labeled "Send."

Table 4.1: <INPUT> Tag Attributes (Continued)

Attribute	Values
CHECKED	This attribute does not take a value and is only used with check-box and radio elements. It makes the initial state of the element checked.
SIZE	This attribute is only for use with the text and password elements; it defines the physical size, in characters, of the input element. The default value is 20, which creates an input field 20 characters wide.
MAXLENGTH	This attribute is only for text and password elements. It defines the maximum number of characters the input element will receive.

Listing 4.1: Examples of Input Elements

```
<FORM METHOD=POST ACTION="/cgi-bin/example.pl">
Single Line Entry Field: <INPUT TYPE=text NAME=text VALUE="Default
value" SIZE=30>
<P>Password Entry Field: <INPUT TYPE=password NAME=password SIZE=10
MAXLENGTH=8>
<P>Check Box: <INPUT TYPE=checkbox NAME=checkbox CHECKED>
<P>Radio Buttons - Yes <INPUT TYPE=radio NAME=radio VALUE=yes> No
<INPUT TYPE=radio NAME=radio VALUE=no>
<P>Submit Pushbutton: <INPUT TYPE=submit VALUE=Send>
<P>Reset Pushbutton: <INPUT TYPE=reset VALUE=Reset>
</FORM>
```

The feedback form you will create in this chapter uses several input fields, but all of them are of the text type. Some of the examples in Chapter 5 contain other <INPUT> tag elements. The feedback form in this chapter only needs an input field for the user's name, e-mail address, and the submit push button. Here are these three input fields:

```
<B>Name-Address</B><BR><INPUT NAME="name" SIZE=42>
<P><B>E-mail Address</B><BR><INPUT NAME="email" SIZE=42>
<P><INPUT TYPE="submit" VALUE="Send">
```

The first two lines create 42-character single-line text entry fields for the name and e-mail address. The final line creates the submit push button and gives it the value "Send" for the label. Because the <INPUT> tag elements do not include labels (that is, some text describing what you want the user to enter in that field), this code includes text labels for the name and e-mail fields.

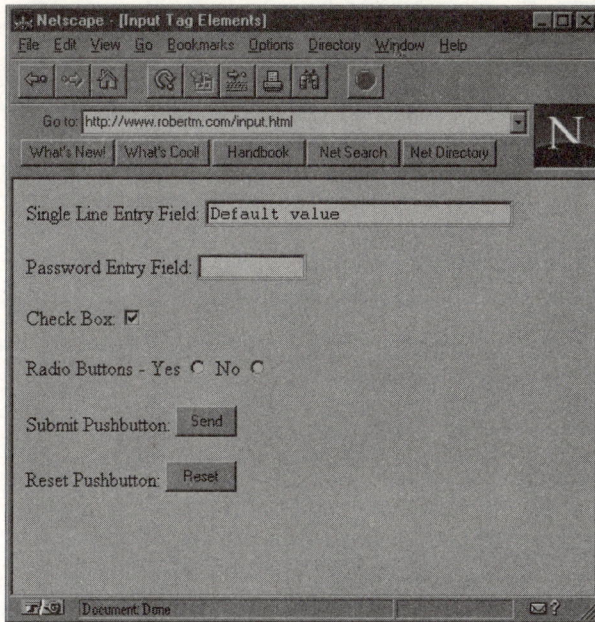

Figure 4.1: The <INPUT> tag elements

THE <SELECT> TAG

The <SELECT> tag allows you to create scrollable lists or drop-down lists. A scrollable list is a list of items that you can scroll through and from which you can select single or multiple items. A drop-down list is similar to a scrollable list, but it only displays one item unless you drop down the list by pressing on it. You can only select one item from a drop-down list.

The <SELECT> tag has three attributes: NAME, SIZE and MULTIPLE, as described in Table 4.2.

Table 4.2: <SELECT> Tag Attributes

Attribute	Values
NAME	This attribute is similar to the NAME attribute of the <INPUT> tag. The value for this attribute is sent to the server as the name for the name/value pairs. For example, in a scrollable list with the NAME attribute set to "flavor" with two options selected, vanilla and chocolate, the Web server would receive "flavor=vanilla" and "flavor=chocolate".

Table 4.2: <SELECT> Tag Attributes (Continued)

Attribute	Values
SIZE	This attribute determines how many options are displayed for the scrollable list. If SIZE is set to 1, which is the default if the SIZE attribute is not present, the list will be a drop-down list. Otherwise, it will be a scrollable list displaying the number of options defined in SIZE. If the MULTIPLE attribute is present, the list will always be displayed as a scrollable list, regardless of whether the SIZE attribute is set to 1.
MULTIPLE	This attribute does not take any values. If present, it allows multiple options to be selected.

The <SELECT> tag has both beginning and ending tags, <SELECT> and </SELECT>. Within these tags, you specify the list options by using the <OPTION> tag. The <OPTION> tag does not have a closing tag and has only one attribute, SELECTED, which makes the associated option selected in the default form. For example, Listing 4.2 shows the HTML for a drop-down list of numbers from one to three. Listing 4.3 shows the HTML for a scrollable list with ice cream flavors. Notice that more than one ice cream flavor can be chosen, and that vanilla is always initially selected. Figure 4.2 shows how the Netscape browser will display these HTML examples.

Listing 4.2: Example <SELECT> Drop-down List

```
<FORM METHOD=POST ACTION="/cgi-bin/example.pl">
<SELECT NAME="number" SIZE=1>
<OPTION>one
<OPTION>two
<OPTION>three
</SELECT>
</FORM>
```

Listing 4.3: Example <SELECT> Scrollable List

```
<FORM METHOD=POST ACTION="/cgi-bin/example.pl">
<SELECT NAME="flavor" SIZE=3 MULTIPLE>
<OPTION>Chocolate
<OPTION SELECTED>Vanilla
<OPTION>Strawberry
<OPTION>Chocolate Chip
<OPTION>French Vanilla
<OPTION>Peach
</SELECT>
</FORM>
```

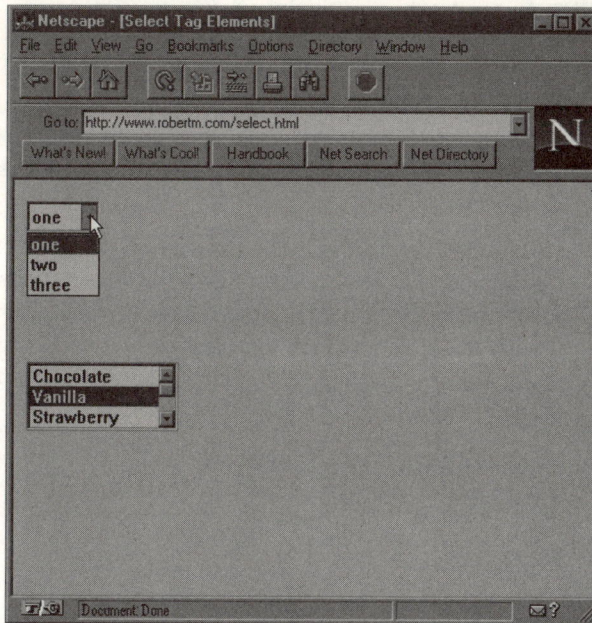

Figure 4.2: <SELECT> examples

The feedback form will not use any <SELECT> tags.

THE <TEXTAREA> TAG

You use the <TEXTAREA> tag to place a multiline text input area in the form.
It has both beginning and ending tags, <TEXTAREA> and </TEXTAREA>.
Table 4.3 describes the four attributes the <TEXTAREA> tag can take.

Table 4.3: <TEXTAREA> Tag Attributes

Attribute	Values
NAME	As with the NAME attribute of the <INPUT> and <SELECT> tags, the value for this attribute is sent to the server as the name for the name/value pairs. For example, in a text area with the NAME attribute set to "comments" containing the string "I think it is a great product!" the Web server would receive "comments=I think it is a great product!".
ROWS	The value for this attribute defines the number of rows for the text area entry field. This only defines the physical height, in characters, of the box, not the number of rows the user can enter into the box.

Table 4.3: <TEXTAREA> Tag Attributes (Continued)

Attribute	Values
COLS	The value for this attribute defines the number of columns for the text area entry field. Again, this is the physical width, in characters, of the box, not the number of characters the user can enter.
WRAP	This attribute is a Netscape extension to the <TEXTAREA> tag. A Netscape extension is a tag or attribute that works under certain versions of the Netscape Navigator browser, but does not work under all browsers. It is not a part of the current HTML specification, but it may be added in later versions of HTML. The WRAP attribute can take one of three values: *Off:* This default setting makes the TEXTAREA field work exactly as it would without the WRAP attribute (no wrapping). *Virtual:* This value causes the data being entered into the TEXTAREA field to wrap when it reaches the width of the box. However, when the data is sent to the Web server, wrapped lines are sent as a single line. *Physical:* This value also causes the data being entered into the TEXTAREA field to wrap when it reaches the width of the box. When the data is sent to the Web server, however, new line characters are sent at all of the wrap points.

Any text between the <TEXTAREA> and </TEXTAREA> tags is used as the default text for the text area box. What follows is the HTML for a text area box with some default text. Figure 4.3 shows how the Netscape browser would display that HTML.

```
<FORM METHOD=POST ACTION="/cgi-bin/example.pl">
<TEXTAREA NAME="comments" ROWS=4 COLS=40 WRAP=PHYSICAL>
Place your comments here.
</TEXTAREA>
</FORM>
```

The feedback form in this chapter uses one <TEXTAREA> field. You do not need default contents for the text area box, but you will include a label. Here is the <TEXTAREA> HTML for the feedback form.

```
<P><B>Comments</B><BR><TEXTAREA NAME="comments" ROWS=10
COLS=38></TEXTAREA>
```

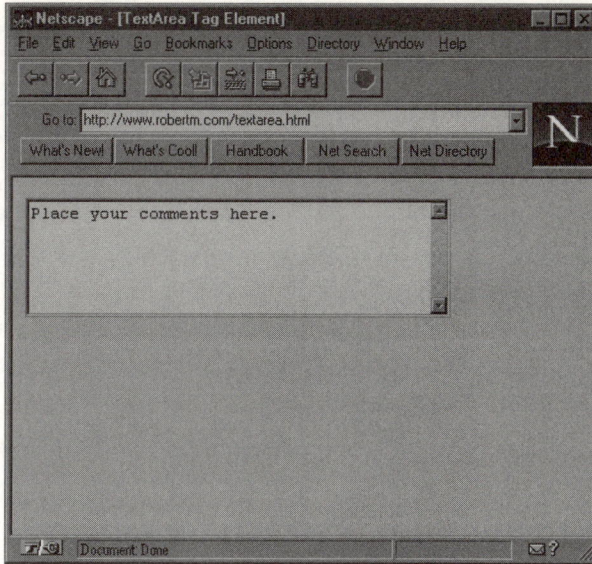

Figure 4.3: <TEXTAREA> example

PUTTING TOGETHER THE FEEDBACK FORM

Now you know all of the HTML you need for your feedback form. The next step is to combine the various parts of the form and place them in an HTML file. Let's name the file feedback.html (or feedback.htm if you cannot use a four-digit file name extension). Listing 4.4 contains the contents of the feedback.html file, and Figure 4.4 illustrates what the form looks like when displayed by the Netscape Web browser.

PROCESSING THE FORM INPUT

Now that the HTML for the feedback form is completed, you must create the feedback.pl CGI script that will receive the data sent by the user through the form in the Web browser. Once the feedback.pl script has received the data from the Web server, it must decode the information. Then it takes the data and places it in an e-mail message. Finally, the script returns the user to the home page of your Web site.

Listing 4.4: HTML for Feedback Form

```
<HTML>
<HEAD>
<TITLE>Feedback Form</TITLE>
</HEAD>
<BODY>
<H1>Feedback</H1>
<FORM METHOD=POST ACTION="/cgi-bin/feedback.pl">
<B>Name</B><BR><INPUT NAME="name" SIZE=42>
<P><B>E-mail Address</B><BR><INPUT NAME="email" SIZE=42>
<P><B>Comments</B><BR><TEXTAREA NAME="comments" ROWS=10
COLS=38></TEXTAREA>
<P><INPUT TYPE="submit" VALUE="Send"></FORM>
</BODY>
</HTML>
```

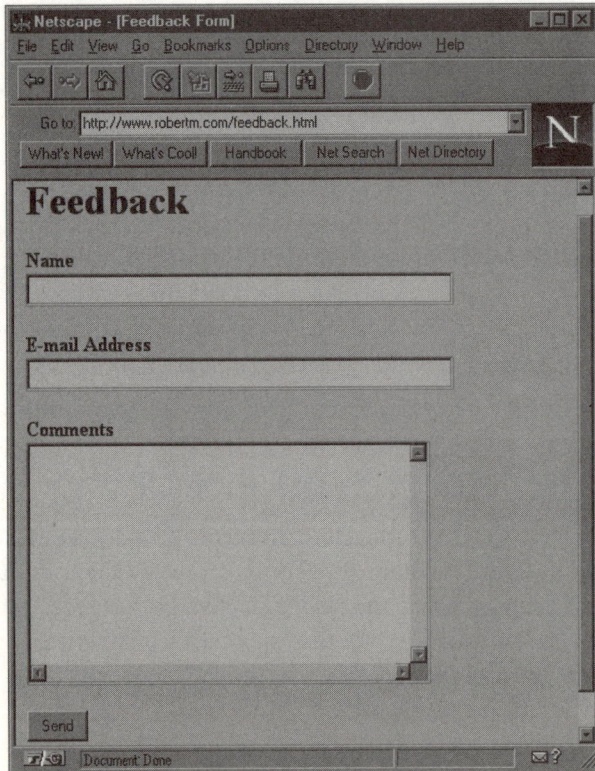

Figure 4.4: The feedback form

DECODING THE INPUT

Remember, when user-supplied data is sent to a CGI script it is URL encoded. Therefore, the first thing the script must do is to decode this data. Chapter 2 included the lines of code for doing so. Let's take the code from Listing 2.3 and place it in a subroutine called User_Data. A subroutine in Perl is just a function that you can call by using the ampersand followed by the function name, as in &User_Data;. In Perl, the definitions of subroutines usually sit at the end of the file. So, your feedback.pl file will contain a call of the User_Data subroutine and the User_Data subroutine definition. Listing 4.5 shows what you have so far for the feedback.pl.

Listing 4.5: First Part of feedback.pl

```perl
#!/usr/local/bin/perl

# Decode the user data and place it in the
# data_received associative array.
%data_received = &User_Data();

sub User_Data {
  local (%user_data, $user_string, $name_value_pair,
        @name_value_pairs, $name, $value);

  # If the data was sent via POST, then it is available
  # from standard input. Otherwise, the data is in the
  # QUERY_STRING environment variable.
  if ($ENV{'REQUEST_METHOD'} eq "POST") {
    read(STDIN,$user_string,$ENV{'CONTENT_LENGTH'});
  } else {
    $user_string = $ENV{'QUERY_STRING'};
  }

  # This line changes the + signs to spaces.
  $user_string =~ s/\+/ /g;

  # This line places each name/value pair as a separate
  # element in the name_value_pairs array.
  @name_value_pairs = split(/&/, $user_string);

  # This code loops over each element in the name_value_pairs
  # array, splits it on the = sign, and places the value
  # into the user_data associative array with the name as the
  # key.
  foreach $name_value_pair (@name_value_pairs) {
    ($name, $value) = split(/=/, $name_value_pair);
```

Listing 4.5: First Part of feedback.pl (Continued)

```perl
# These two lines decode the values from any URL
# hexadecimal encoding. The first section searches for a
# hexadecimal number and the second part converts the
# hex number to decimal and returns the character
# equivalent.
$name =~
    s/%([a-fA-F0-9][a-fA-F0-9])/pack("C",hex($1))/ge;
$value =~
    s/%([a-fA-F0-9][a-fA-F0-9])/pack("C",hex($1))/ge;

# If the name/value pair has already been given a value,
# as in the case of multiple items being selected, then
# separate the items with a " : ".
if (defined($user_data{$name})) {
    $user_data{$name} .= " : " . $value;
} else {
    $user_data{$name} = $value;
}
}
return %user_data;
}
```

E-MAILING THE INPUT

After the user's input is decoded, the data is ready to be worked with. For the purposes of this example, let's have the CGI script send the information via e-mail. This requires an SMTP mail server to send the e-mail message. (SMTP stands for Simple Mail Transfer Protocol.)

The way you interface with the SMTP mail server varies depending on whether you're using Windows or UNIX. So, let's create two subroutines, one for e-mailing on a Windows machine and one for e-mailing on a UNIX machine. Each takes a single argument, a string that contains the information that you want e-mailed. Because you will be using the same string regardless of which subroutine you call, let's write the code to put the string together first.

From where you left off in the previous section, your feedback.pl script has the user data in the associative array %data_received. If you just output this array to your e-mail message, the data would be one long string containing all of the information. To make that data easier to read, you can break it up into separate lines by using the following code.

```perl
foreach $key (sort keys(%data_received)) {
    $mail .= "$key:\n";
    foreach (split(" : ", $data_received{$key})) {
```

```
    $mail .= "$_\n\n";
  }
}
```

This code contains two loops. The outer one loops over each array element. Recall that an associative array is indexed by elements known as keys. So, to loop over the entire array, you have to loop over all of the keys. You do this by using the Perl keys() function, which returns all of the keys for the associative array argument between the parentheses. Each key is then assigned to the $key variable. Once inside the outer loop, the key value gets added to the $mail string along with the \n character, which is the new line character. The inner loop then checks the value of each array element for the " : " (space colon space) characters. Recall from the User_Data subroutine that these characters are used to separate multiple values assigned to a single name—as with the flavors example in Listing 4.3. By splitting up the array on these characters, you can place each value on its own line.

The line $mail .= "$_\n\n"; puts the values of the name/value pairs into the string that will be sent via e-mail. The .= is an assignment operator that means the same as $mail = $mail + (something else). In other words, it appends the information on the right side to the current contents of the $mail variable. You have to use this operator because you are placing all of the name/value pairs in the same variable. On the right side of the assignment operator, you place the $_ variable and two "\n" characters. The $_ variable is a special Perl variable that in this context is holding the value information of the current name/value pair. For example, the string Chocolate : Vanilla has two values. During the inner loop, the $_ variable would first be assigned Chocolate, which would get appended to the $mail string, and then assigned Vanilla, which would also be appended to the $mail string.

If you don't know Perl, this example should help to clarify what is happening. The feedback form has three input areas: the name input field, the e-mail input field, and the comments text area. For this example, you can set the contents of the name field to Robert McDaniel, the e-mail field to robertm@ deltanet.com, and the comments text area to Hi there. So, after calling the &User_Data(); subroutine, the %data_received associative array would have the following three elements:

```
$data_received{'name'}=Robert McDaniel
$data_received{'email'}=robertm@deltanet.com
$data_received{'comments'}=Hi there
```

The outer loop starts the formatting by looping over all of the sorted key values. So, the first value of the $key variable would be comments, followed by e-mail and then name. The $mail variable would first be set to comments:\n, and then the inner loop would start. Because the value of comments does not contain any " : "substrings, the loop only executes once with the $_ variable set to Hi there. This string and two \n's are then appended to the $mail string. At the end of the first iteration of the loop, the $mail variable is the following:

```
$mail=comments:\nHi there\n\n
```

After the next iteration, in which $key is set to email, the $mail variable is the following:

```
$mail=comments:\nHi there\n\nemail:\nrobertm@deltanet.com\n\n
```

Finally, after the final iteration of the outer loop, the variable $mail is the following:

```
$mail=comments:\nHi
there\n\nemail:\nrobertm@deltanet.com\n\nname:\nRobert McDaniel\n\n
```

When the string is finally printed into an e-mail message, the contents of the message will be

```
comments:
Hi there

email:
robertm@deltanet.com

name:
Robert McDaniel
```

E-mailing on a UNIX system   Now that you have the message formatted for e-mail, you can send it. If you're running UNIX, you will use the program sendmail as your SMTP server. Sendmail allows you to send the user's data in an output stream, so all you have to do is open the output stream, print the e-mail header necessary for sendmail, print the message string, and close the output stream. Listing 4.6 contains the Perl code for accomplishing these tasks. Because there is also a Windows version, I placed the code in a subroutine called Unix_Email.

The Perl code to call this subroutine would be

```
&Unix_Email($mail);
```

Listing 4.6: Unix_Email Subroutine

```
sub Unix_Email {
  local ($message) = @_;

  open(MAIL, "|/usr/sbin/sendmail -t") || die "Content-type:
text/text\n\nCan't open /usr/sbin/sendmail!\n";
  print MAIL "To: robertm\@robertm.com\n";
  print MAIL "From: httpd\@robertm.com\n";
  print MAIL "Subject: From you Feedback Form\n";
  print MAIL "$message\n\n";

  return close(MAIL);
}
```

This line calls the subroutine with a parameter, namely the $mail string you just finished formatting. The Unix_Email subroutine received this parameter from the special Perl array variable @_. So, the line

```
local ($message) = @_;
```

just declares a local variable $message and assigns to it the value of the $mail variable used as the parameter. The line containing the open statement opens a new stream, which in this case is an output stream to the sendmail program. The path /usr/sbin/sendmail is the path to the sendmail program on my computer; your path may be different. The rest of the line causes the CGI script to exit if a stream to sendmail cannot be opened. The four print statements all send their output to the MAIL stream, which you just opened. The first three print lines print the header that sendmail needs to send the e-mail message. The final print statement outputs the $message variable, which contains the string that you formatted earlier. This string will be the body of the e-mail message.

E-mailing on a Windows system   If you are running Windows, you can use a program called WinSMTP for your SMTP server. WinSMTP has a command-line utility called WRMail that allows you to send a message from your CGI script. Unlike sendmail, WinSMTP cannot stream the output to WRMail. Instead you have to write the contents of the e-mail message to a file and then e-mail the file with WRMail. This involves a couple of extra steps, such as creating a unique file name, creating the file, and deleting the file after you are done. You will place this code in a subroutine called Windows_Email, the Perl code for which is shown in Listing 4.7.

Most of this code should be fairly straightforward. The first section creates the file name by using the last several digits of the results of the time function (which returns the number of nonleap seconds since January 1, 1970) with a

Listing 4.7: The Windows_Email Subroutine

```perl
sub Windows_Email {
  local ($message) = @_;

  # Create the file name
  $filename = substr(time, 3);
  srand(time||$$);
  $filename .= "." . int(rand(999));

  # Create the file
  open(MAILFILE, ">$filename") || die "Content-type:
text/text\n\nCan't open the output file $filename!\n";
  print MAILFILE $message;
  close(MAILFILE);

  # E-mail the file
  system("c:\\winsmtp\\wrmail -r -t\"From Your Feedback Form\" -
shttpd\@robertm.com -f$filename robertm\@robertm.com");

  # Delete the file
  system("del $filename");

}
```

randomly generated extension between 0 and 998. Because this program could be executed several times at almost the exact same moment, you must take these precautions to guarantee a unique file name. The second section outputs the contents of the $message string into the file. As you see, to create a new file, you just open an output stream to the file. Finally, the code sends the e-mail by calling the WRMail program with the necessary parameters, as specified in the program's documentation, and deletes the temporary file.

RETURNING A REPLY

After the information has been received and processed, the CGI script should send something to the user's browser to indicate that the action has completed. For the feedback.pl example, send your home page back to the user's browser. Because this HTML page already exists, you can just send the location of the file rather than sending all of the HTML tags and text. Here is the line of Perl code that returns the home page to the user's browser.

```perl
print "Location: http://www.robertm.com\n\n";
```

Now all the pieces of the feedback form are completed. Listing 4.4 contains the complete HTML for the feedback form. The previous few sections presented all of the code for the feedback.pl CGI script. Listing 4.8 supplies the entire feedback.pl script so you can see it all in one place.

Listing 4.8: The feedback.pl Script

```perl
#!/usr/local/bin/perl

# Decode the user data an place it in the
# data_received associative array.
%data_received = &User_Data();

foreach $key (sort keys(%data_received)) {
  $mail .= "$key:\n";
  foreach (split(" : ", $data_received{$key})) {
    $mail .= "$_\n\n";
  }
}


# If you want to run this program on a Windows
# machine, comment out the &Unix_Email($mail); line (add a # at
# the beginning) and uncomment the &Windows_Email($mail);
# line. Also remember to remove the first line!
&Unix_Email($mail);
#&Windows_Email($mail);

print "Location: http://www.robertm.com\n\n";

sub Unix_Email {
  local ($message) = @_;

  open(MAIL, "|/usr/sbin/sendmail -t") || die "Content-type:
  text/text\n\nCan't open /usr/sbin/sendmail!\n";
  print MAIL "To: robertm\@robertm.com\n";
  print MAIL "From: httpd\@robertm.com\n";
  print MAIL "Subject: From you Feedback Form\n";
  print MAIL "$message\n\n";

  return close(MAIL);
}

sub Windows_Email {
  local ($message) = @_;

  # Create the file name
```

Listing 4.8: The feedback.pl Script (Continued)

```perl
$filename = substr(time, 3);
srand(time||$$);
$filename .= "." . int(rand(999));

# Create the file
open(MAILFILE, ">$filename") || die "Content-type:
text/text\n\nCan't open the output file $filename!\n";
print MAILFILE $message;
close(MAILFILE);

# E-mail the file
system("c:\\winsmtp\\wrmail -r -t\"From Your Feedback Form\" -
shttpd\@robertm.com -f$filename robertm\@robertm.com");

# Delete the file
system("del $filename");

}

sub User_Data {
  local (%user_data, $user_string, $name_value_pair,
        @name_value_pairs, $name, $value);

 # If the data was sent via POST, then it is available
 # from standard input. Otherwise, the data is in the
 # QUERY_STRING environment variable.
 if ($ENV{'REQUEST_METHOD'} eq "POST") {
   read(STDIN,$user_string,$ENV{'CONTENT_LENGTH'});
 } else {
   $user_string = $ENV{'QUERY_STRING'};
 }

 # This line changes the + signs to spaces.
 $user_string =~ s/\+/ /g;

 # This line places each name/value pair as a separate
 # element in the name_value_pairs array.
 @name_value_pairs = split(/&/, $user_string);

 # This code loops over each element in the name_value_pairs
 # array, splits it on the = sign, and places the value
 # into the user_data associative array with the name as the
 # key.
 foreach $name_value_pair (@name_value_pairs) {
   ($name, $value) = split(/=/, $name_value_pair);
```

Listing 4.8: The feedback.pl Script (Continued)

```perl
# These two lines decode the values from any URL
# hexadecimal encoding. The first section searches for a
# hexadecimal number and the second part converts the
# hex number to decimal and returns the character
# equivalent.
$name =~
  s/%([a-fA-FØ-9][a-fA-FØ-9])/pack("C",hex($1))/ge;
$value =~
  s/%([a-fA-FØ-9][a-fA-FØ-9])/pack("C",hex($1))/ge;

# If the name/value pair has already been given a value,
# as in the case of multiple items being selected, then
# separate the items with a " : ".
if (defined($user_data{$name})) {
  $user_data{$name} .= " : " . $value;
} else {
  $user_data{$name} = $value;
}
}
return %user_data;
}
```

Other Form Examples

A GUEST BOOK

A SHOPPING CART

Chapter 5

I n Chapter 4, you learned the basics about handling form input and created a simple CGI script for handling a feedback form. This chapter continues the discussion of forms by presenting two more examples, the guest book and the shopping cart (both of which are defined in their respective sections). Along with feedback forms, guest books and shopping carts are among the most popular uses of forms and form handlers.

A GUEST BOOK

A Web site guest book is the online equivalent of guest books you may have seen at art galleries, museums, bed and breakfasts, or retail stores. In these establishments, a guest book consists of a blank book in which guests may enter their names and addresses. If you flipped back through the book, you would see information about many people who had visited that location.

For your online guest book, you want the user to be able to view previous entries. You also want that user to be able to enter his or her own information to the top of the list. Why the top of the list? Well, with paper guest books, the page is usually turned to the most recent entry, so that guests can easily add their names to the end of the list. With online guest books, if you added the newest guest to the end of the list, this listing would be the last thing a user would see. Users signing in would have to scroll though the entire list just to see their entries in the book.

You can accomplish all of these requirements with a single CGI script. Your guest book script will display the information of previous visitors and process the form submission of current visitors. When your script receives a new entry to the guest book, it will add the entry to the top of your guest book list and display the current list to the user.

SETTING UP THE SIGN-IN FORM

As with the feedback form example in Chapter 4, you first need to set up the sign-in form that the user will fill out to add his or her entry to your guest book. To do this, you must decide what information to request from the user. For this guest book example, you will ask for the user's name, e-mail address, home page URL, city, state, and country. You can capture all of these items by using the single-line text input element. You will also include a text area in which the user can add any comments. The HTML for this guestbook.html (guestbk.htm if your system limits you to an eight-character file name and a three-character file name extension) file would be the following:

```
<HTML>
<HEAD>
<TITLE>Guest book Sign In</TITLE>
</HEAD>
<BODY>
<H1>Guest book Sign In</H1>
To sign our guest book, please fill out the fields below. If you do not want to
provide some of the information, just leave those fields blank, but keep in mind
that you must include your name to be added to the guest book.
<FORM METHOD=POST ACTION="/cgi-bin/guestbook.pl">
<P><B>Name</B><BR><INPUT NAME="name" SIZE=42>
<P><B>E-mail Address</B><BR><INPUT NAME="email" SIZE=42>
<P><B>Home Page URL</B><BR><INPUT NAME="url" SIZE=42>
<P><B>City</B><BR><INPUT NAME="city" SIZE=20>
<P><B>State</B><BR><INPUT NAME="state" SIZE=2>
<P><B>Country</B><BR><INPUT NAME="country" SIZE=20>
<P><B>Comments</B><BR><TEXTAREA NAME="comments" ROWS=10 COLS=38></TEXTAREA>
<P><INPUT TYPE="submit" VALUE="Sign In"> <INPUT TYPE="reset" VALUE="Reset">
</FORM>
</BODY>
</HTML>
```

Figure 5.1 shows how the sign-in form will appear in Netscape.

Note: This HTML code contains all of the necessary elements for gathering the information you need. However, for the sake of simplicity, and because this is a book on CGI scripting and not Web page design, this HTML code does not generate a great looking Web page. For your actual Web page, I would recommend using some other elements (graphics and HTML tags like the <TABLE> tag) to improve the design.

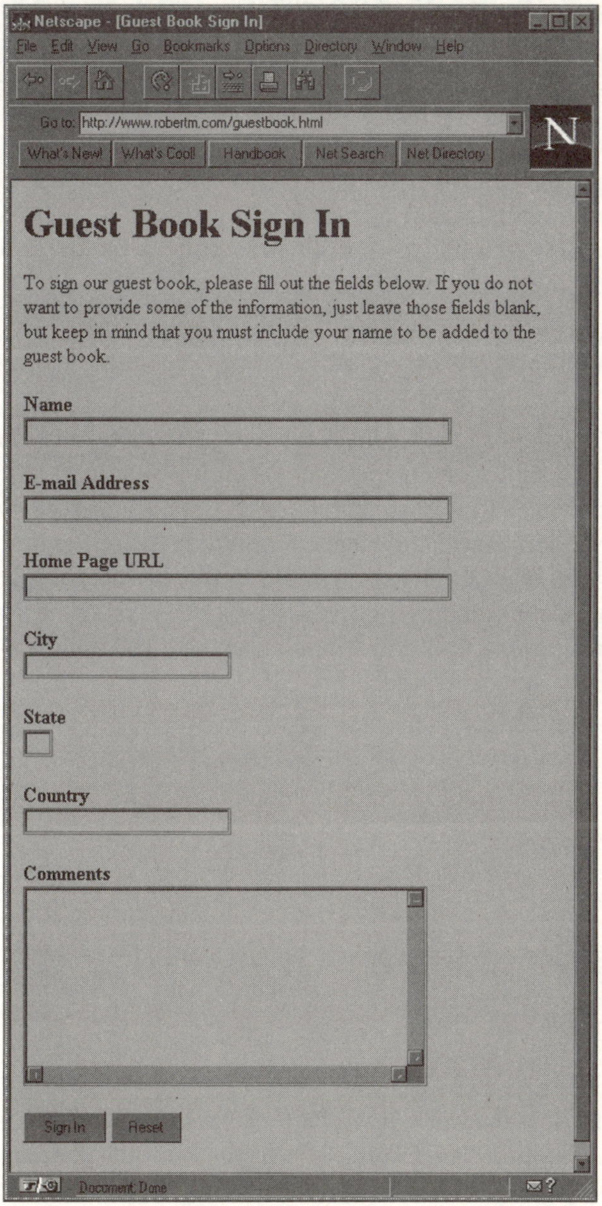

Figure 5.1: The guest book sign-in form

HANDLING THE INPUT FROM THE SIGN-IN FORM

With the sign-in form complete, you can start working on the CGI script for handling the guest book. The first thing to do is to receive the input from the sign-in form, process it, and then write it to your guest book file. The guest book file is a text file that holds all of the user sign ins. When you receive a sign in, you place the new information at the top of the guest book file.

As in the form example from Chapter 4, you first need to receive the data from the user's browser and decode it. To do so, you can use the same User_Data subroutine that you used in the preceding chapter.

```
# Decode the user data an place it in the
# data_received associative array.
%data_received = &User_Data();
```

In this example, unlike the feedback form in Chapter 4, you write this information to a file, later displaying the contents of this file as part of a HTML page. Remember from Chapter 3 that if Server Side Includes are enabled for your Web server, someone could enter a Server Side Include as one of the entries of your guest book and have the results of that directive displayed in his or her Web browser. You can prevent this possibility by parsing the user's input for Server Side Include directives and removing any that you find. You will do this by creating a new subroutine called No_SSI.

```
sub No_SSI {
  local (*data) = @_;

  foreach $key (sort keys(%data)) {
    $data{$key} =~ s/<!--(.|\n)*-->//g;
  }
}
```

This subroutine receives one parameter, the associative array that contains the user's input data. It then loops over each element in the array checking for Server Side Include directives. The line

```
$data{$key} =~ s/<!--(.|\n)*-->//g;
```

is what actually does the work. It is a Perl regular expression that performs the search and substitution. The leading "s" tells the Perl interpreter to replace everything between the first and second slashes with the material between the second and third slashes. In this case, the pattern <!--(.|\n)*--> will match any properly formatted Server Side Include, which will be replaced with nothing (in other words, will be deleted) because there is nothing between the second and third slashes. The "g" at the end of the line tells the Perl interpreter to change all occurrences instead of only the first one it finds.

You now have the user's data properly decoded and any Server Side Includes removed. The next thing to do is to enter the information into your guest book file. You do this by placing all of the elements of the user's information into a single string, with HTML tags. This string is then added to the first line of the guest book file.

When you set up the guest book form, you told users they had to enter their names. That was the only mandatory field. To make sure this field has a value, you will place an if statement around the code to enter the entry into the guest book file. This if statement checks whether the user's name has been entered. (Actually, it only checks whether the string is not blank. The user could enter any valid string.) If there is a value, the user's information is placed in the $new_guest string and that string is added to the beginning of the guest book file. If the user did not enter a valid string for the name field, he or she is prompted to do so.

```
if ($data_received{"name"} ne "") {
  $new_guest = "<B>Name:</B> $data_received{\"name\"}<BR>\n";
  $new_guest .= "<B>Data:</B> $date<BR>\n";

  $new_guest .= "<B>E-Mail:</B> <A
HREF=\"mailto:$data_received{\"email\"}\">$data_received{\"email\"}</A><BR>\n" if
$data_received{"email"} ne "";
  $new_guest .= "<B>Home Page URL:</B> <A
HREF=\"$data_received{\"url\"}\">$data_received{\"url\"}</A><BR>\n" if
$data_received{"url"} ne "";
  $new_guest .= "$data_received{\"city\"}, " if $data_received{"city"} ne "";
  $new_guest .= "$data_received{\"state\"} " if $data_received{"state"} ne "";
  $new_guest .= "$data_received{\"country\"}<BR>\n" if $data_received{"country"}
ne "";
  $new_guest .= "<B>Comments:</B> $data_received{\"comments\"}\n" if
$data_received{"comments"} ne "";

  $new_guest .= "<P><HR><P>\n";

  open(GUESTBOOK,"$guestbookfile") || die "Content-type: text/text\n\nCannot open
$guestbookfile";
  @guestbook = <GUESTBOOK>;
  close(GUESTBOOK);

  unshift(@guestbook, $new_guest);
  open(GUESTBOOK,">$guestbookfile") || die "Content-type: text/text\n\nCannot
open $guestbookfile";
  print GUESTBOOK @guestbook;
  close(GUESTBOOK);
```

```
} else {
  print "Content-type: text/html\n\n";
  print "<H1>Sign-In Unsuccessful</H1>\n";
  print "You must enter your name to be added to the guest book.";
}
```

Notice how each of the first lines within the if statement are in the form

```
$new_guest .= "some string" if $data_received{"some element"} ne "";
```

By adding the fields in this manner, you only add the specified element if the user entered a value for it. For example, the line that adds the user's city is

```
$new_guest .= "$data_received{\"city\"}, " if $data_received{"city"} ne "";
```

This line appends the name of the city, $data_received{"city"}, to the string $new_guest if the user entered a string in the city field of the guest book form.

After all of the user's information and HTML tags have been appended to the variable $new_guest, the guest book file is opened, the contents of the file are placed within the array @guestbook, and the file is closed. The name of the guest book file is stored in the $guestbookfile string. The code for placing the path and file name of the guest book file within the $guestbookfile string is shown in Listing 5.1 at the end of this section. The line

```
unshift(@guestbook, $new_guest);
```

makes the string $new_guest the first element of the @guestbook array, moving all other contents over one index in the array. The guest book file is then opened again and the contents of the @guestbook array are printed to the file, overwriting any previous contents.

Notice the difference between the first and second open statements. The file name in the second open statement is preceded by the greater than (>) character. To Perl this means that the file is being opened for output. When a file is opened with this status, all of the previous contents of the file are overwritten. The less than (<) character means to open the file for input, and >> means to append to the file. If none of these special characters are specified, the file is opened for input, as is the case with the first open statement in the example.

If the user did not enter a valid string for the name field of the guest book form, the else portion of the if...else statement is executed. The code in this section prints a response to the user's Web browser stating that he or she needs to enter a value for the name field.

When the user does enter a correct value for the name field and all of the code under the if block is executed, the user's data is added to the guest book file. However, in the preceding example no information is sent back to the user's Web browser. Because the user just entered information for your guest book, it would be appropriate to now display the contents of your guest book with the new entry at the top. Because you have to have the code for displaying the guest book in another part of your guest book script (for when the user just wants to display the guest book without adding an entry first), the best way to do this is to call a subroutine that displays the guest book. (If you didn't call a subroutine, you would have to place the code for displaying the guest book in multiple places in your script file.) All you need to add to the previous code is the line

```
&Display_Book($guestbookfile);
```

immediately after the second close(GUESTBOOK); statement.

DISPLAYING THE CONTENTS OF THE GUEST BOOK

As mentioned, you still need a subroutine that displays the contents of the guest book file. Because you already placed all relevant HTML tags along with the guest book entries, you just need to print the contents of the file preceded with and followed by the appropriate HTML header and footer. You do this with the following code:

```
sub Display_Book {
  local ($guestbookfile) = @_;
  local (@guestbook);

  open(GUESTBOOK,"$guestbookfile") || die "Content-type: text/text\n\nCannot open
$guestbookfile";
  @guestbook = <GUESTBOOK>;
  close(GUESTBOOK);

  print "Content-type: text/html\n\n";
  print "<HTML><HEAD><TITLE>My Guest Book</TITLE></HEAD><BODY>";
  print "<H1>My Guest Book</H1>";
  print @guestbook;
  print "</BODY></HTML>";
}
```

This subroutine opens the guest book file, places all of the contents in the array @guestbook, prints the parsed header and preceding HTML tags, prints the contents of the @guestbook array (which is the contents of the guest book file), and prints the ending HTML tags.

PUTTING IT ALL TOGETHER: THE GUESTBOOK.PL SCRIPT

Now you have all the pieces of the guest book script. All that you need to do is to put them together. At the beginning of this section you learned that you can do the entire guest book with one script. You may be thinking, "Don't we need two scripts, one to display the guest book and one to add entries to the guest book?" Well, even if you aren't thinking that, the answer is no. When a CGI script is called, it is called with a certain method, such as GET or POST. If no method is specified, as when the script is called from an <A> tag, the method defaults to GET. You can use this fact to your advantage. Remember that when the user signs in with the guest book form, the method is POST. So, all you have to do is check which method is used. If it is POST, the user is trying to sign the guest book. If it is GET, the user is trying to view the guest book. To make your guest book script more readable, you can place the code for adding the user's data to the guest book in a subroutine called Add_Guest. Then check the method that was used and call the appropriate subroutine. If the method is POST, you call the Add_Guest subroutine; otherwise call the Display_Book subroutine to just display the guest book. To accomplish this, use the Perl statement

```
$ENV{"REQUEST_METHOD"} eq "POST" ?  &Add_Guest($file) : &Display_Book($file);
```

This statement checks the conditional—everything before the question mark (?). If the conditional is true, it executes the expression between the question mark and the colon (:). If the conditional is false, the expression after the colon is executed.

Listing 5.1 contains the Perl code for the completed guest book script, and Figure 5.2 shows how Netscape would display the contents of the guest book. If you are using guestbook.pl on a Windows machine, remember to remove the #!/usr/local/bin/perl line. Also, for both Windows and UNIX machines, you need to change the path to the guestbook.dat file to the correct path for your machine. Windows users need the path to look something like

```
$file = "c:\\robertm\\guestbook.dat";
```

A SHOPPING CART

A shopping cart is a CGI script that enables your users to create a list of items they want to purchase from inventory displayed on your Web pages. The shopping cart CGI script is analogous to a store's shopping cart. With a real shopping cart, you walk through the store, placing items in the cart. When you are finished shopping, you pay for everything at once at the check stand. Likewise, with the shopping cart script you can browse through Web pages, placing items in

Listing 5.1: The guestbook.pl File

```perl
#!/usr/local/bin/perl

$file = "/users/robertm/guestbook.dat";
$date = localtime(time);

$ENV{"REQUEST_METHOD"} eq "POST" ?  &Add_Guest($file) :
&Display_Book($file);

sub Add_Guest {
  local ($guestbookfile) = @_;
  local (%data_received, $new_guest, @guestbook);

  # Decode the user data and place it in the
  # data_received associative array.
  %data_received = &User_Data();

  &No_SSI(*data_received);

  if ($data_received{"name"} ne "") {
    $new_guest = "<B>Name:</B> $data_received{\"name\"}<BR>\n";
    $new_guest .= "<B>Data:</B> $date<BR>\n";

    $new_guest .= "<B>E-Mail:</B> <A
HREF=\"mailto:$data_received{\"email\"}\">$data_received{\"email\"}</A>
<BR>\n" if $data_received{"email"} ne "";
    $new_guest .= "<B>Home Page URL:</B> <A
HREF=\"$data_received{\"url\"}\">$data_received{\"url\"}</A><BR>\n" if
$data_received{"url"} ne "";
    $new_guest .= "$data_received{\"city\"}, " if
$data_received{"city"} ne "";
    $new_guest .= "$data_received{\"state\"} " if
$data_received{"state"} ne "";
    $new_guest .= "$data_received{\"country\"}<BR>\n" if
$data_received{"country"} ne "";
    $new_guest .= "<B>Comments:</B> $data_received{\"comments\"}\n" if
$data_received{"comments"} ne "";

    $new_guest .= "<P><HR><P>\n";

    open(GUESTBOOK,"$guestbookfile") || die "Content-type:
text/text\n\nCannot open $guestbookfile";
    @guestbook = <GUESTBOOK>;
    close(GUESTBOOK);
```

Listing 5.1: The guestbook.pl File (Continued)

```perl
    unshift(@guestbook, $new_guest);
    open(GUESTBOOK,">$guestbookfile") || die "Content-type:
text/text\n\nCannot open $guestbookfile";
    print GUESTBOOK @guestbook;
    close(GUESTBOOK);

    &Display_Book($guestbookfile);

  } else {
    print "Content-type: text/html\n\n";
    print "<H1>Sign-In Unsuccessful</H1>\n";
    print "You must enter your name to be added to the guest book.";
  }
}

sub Display_Book {
  local ($guestbookfile) = @_;
  local (@guestbook);

  open(GUESTBOOK,"$guestbookfile") || die "Content-type:
text/text\n\nCannot open $guestbookfile";
  @guestbook = <GUESTBOOK>;
  close(GUESTBOOK);

  print "Content-type: text/html\n\n";
  print "<HTML><HEAD><TITLE>My Guest Book</TITLE></HEAD><BODY>";
  print "<H1>My Guest Book</H1>";
  print @guestbook;
  print "</BODY></HTML>";
}

sub No_SSI {
  local (*data) = @_;

  foreach $key (sort keys(%data)) {
    $data{$key} =~ s/<!--(.|\n)*-->//g;
  }

}

sub User_Data {
  local (%user_data, $user_string, $name_value_pair,
         @name_value_pairs, $name, $value);

  # If the data was sent via POST, then it is available
```

Listing 5.1: The guestbook.pl File (Continued)

```perl
# from standard input. Otherwise, the data is in the
# QUERY_STRING environment variable.
if ($ENV{"REQUEST_METHOD"} eq "POST") {
  read(STDIN,$user_string,$ENV{"CONTENT_LENGTH"});
} else {
  $user_string = $ENV{"QUERY_STRING"};
}

# This line changes the + signs to spaces.
$user_string =~ s/\+/ /g;

# This line places each name/value pair as a separate
# element in the name_value_pairs array.
@name_value_pairs = split(/&/, $user_string);

# This code loops over each element in the name_value_pairs
# array, splits it on the = sign, and places the value
# into the user_data associative array with the name as the
# key.
foreach $name_value_pair (@name_value_pairs) {
  ($name, $value) = split(/=/, $name_value_pair);

  # These two lines decode the values from any URL
  # hexadecimal encoding. The first section searches for a
  # hexadecimal number and the second part converts the
  # hex number to decimal and returns the character
  # equivalent.
  $name =~
    s/%([a-fA-F0-9][a-fA-F0-9])/pack("C",hex($1))/ge;
  $value =~
    s/%([a-fA-F0-9][a-fA-F0-9])/pack("C",hex($1))/ge;

  # If the name/value pair has already been given a value,
  # as in the case of multiple items being selected, then
  # separate the items with a " : ".
  if (defined($user_data{$name})) {
    $user_data{$name} .= " : " . $value;
  } else {
    $user_data{$name} = $value;
  }
}
return %user_data;
}
```

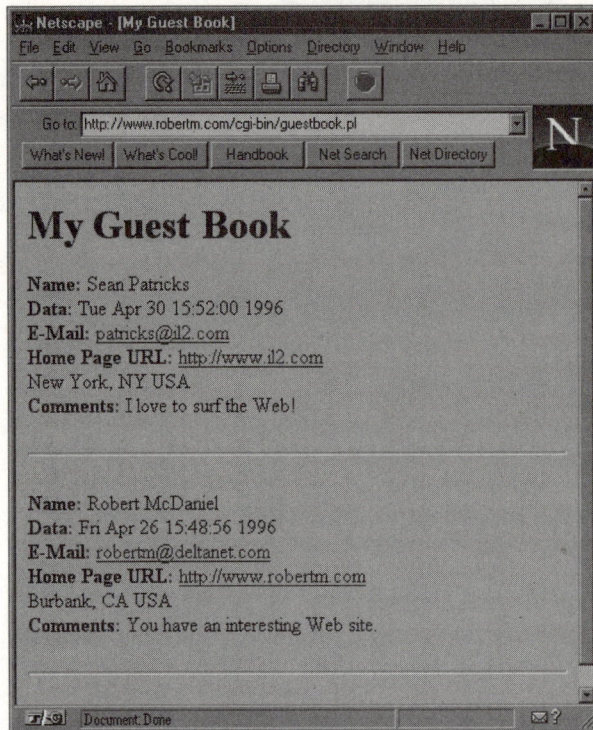

Figure 5.2: Example contents of the guest book

your virtual shopping cart. When you're done shopping, you can purchase all the items in your cart at the virtual checkout counter. If you did not have a shopping cart CGI script, you would have to buy the items one at a time.

When maintaining a shopping cart, the main difficulty is identifying which shopping cart belongs to which user. If your shopping cart script cannot keep track of each user's shopping cart, items will be put in the wrong carts and users will end up buying incorrect items. There are two basic ways you can keep track of shopping carts—with temporary files and a cart number or with the Netscape cookie (which is described in a moment). This section first develops a shopping cart script that uses temporary files as the shopping carts. After that you learn about the Netscape cookie and use a revised shopping cart script that makes use of the cookie. In both of these examples, you develop a shopping cart for the store Virtual Stationers, which has three categories of products: paper, envelopes, and writing instruments.

THE FILE-BASED SHOPPING CART

In the file-based shopping cart, you construct a CGI script that creates a unique file for every user. Within this file, you store the names and quantities of the items the user selects from your Web pages. The user must be able to add items, view the items, and modify or delete items within the file. The shopping cart CGI script must generate the HTML pages for each user.

You might wonder why the HTML pages must be generated from your CGI script. These HTML pages contain forms that have an input field that allows the users to indicate how many items to add to their shopping carts. When a user enters a number and presses the Add Items to Cart push button, these items and quantities are sent to your CGI script for addition to the user's shopping cart. But how do you identify which shopping cart belongs to that user? Normally, the user's Web browser does not send any unique information as part of the HTTP header that accompanies the POST request of the form. So, there is no information to use as a unique identifier. This means you have to create a unique identifier and assign it to each user who has a shopping cart. This unique identifier can be any name, number, or combination of characters, as long as you can guarantee that only one user at a time will receive that identifier.

In addition, you still have to get the user's Web browser to send this unique identifier every time the user presses one of the push buttons on your forms. To have this identifier included with the information sent from the user's Web browser, you must include it as a hidden field of the form. That way, when the form is submitted, the unique identifier is sent. However, this presents another problem. How do you get a user's unique identifier in a hidden field of the HTML page sent to that user's Web browser? If you included the line

```
<INPUT TYPE=hidden NAME="cart_no" VALUE="32719">
```

in your HTML page (where cart_no is the unique identifier), every user requesting your HTML page would have the cart_no 32719. Remember, HTML pages are static. Every user will see the same page. The only way around this problem is to have the HTML pages created by your CGI script.

When a user first visits your Web site, you assign a unique identifier for a cart_no. Then, every other page that that user requests is generated from your shopping cart script. This way, when the user requests another page, you can have the link send the cart_no to your CGI script, which will then place that cart_no in the HTML page it sends back to the user's Web browser. For example, when the user wants to go to the Envelopes section of the Virtual Stationers Web site, the HTML code would look like this:

```
<A HREF="/cgi-
bin/shcart.pl?cart_no=82894734.345&page=envelope">Envelopes</A>
```

This URL calls the shopping cart script and passes it the cart_no identifier, which is the unique identifier you are using, and the name of the page that the user is requesting. Within the shopping cart script, the HTML code necessary for the Envelopes Web page is generated and sent back to the user's Web browser.

The HTML Templates When developing the shopping cart, you first need to decide how the HTML pages will look. These pages—which display the inventory the user can select from—could be generated entirely from your CGI script. However, to minimize the HTML tags in your CGI script, you will keep most of the HTML tags in separate files with .tmpl (for template) extensions (use .tml if your system restricts you to a three-character file name extension). When the user requests one of these Web pages, your CGI script will read in the template file, change the cart_no value to the unique number for that user, and send the HTML code to the user's Web browser. So, when you create these template files, you need to leave a placeholder for the cart_no value. If you use a placeholder, the value can easily be found and replaced in your CGI script. For example, Listing 5.2 shows the template file for the Virtual Stationers home page and Figure 5.3 displays the vshome.tmpl file as it would appear when your shopping cart script sends it to a user's Web browser for display.

Listing 5.2: The vshome.tmpl File

```
<HTML>
<HEAD>
<TITLE>Virtual Stationers</TITLE>
</HEAD>
<BODY>
<H1>Virtual Stationers</H1>
Your source for paper, envelopes, and writing instruments.
<P>
<UL>
<LI><A HREF="/cgi-bin/shcart.pl?cart_no=XXXX&page=paper">Paper</A>
<LI><A HREF="/cgi-
bin/shcart.pl?cart_no=XXXX&page=envelopes">Envelopes</A>
<LI><A HREF="/cgi-bin/shcart.pl?cart_no=XXXX&page=writing">Writing
Instruments</A>
</UL>
</BODY>
</HTML>
```

Notice how the value for cart_no is XXXX. This is the placeholder mentioned earlier. In the Display_Store_Page subroutine, which will be developed in the next section, this template would be read into an array, all of the XXXX

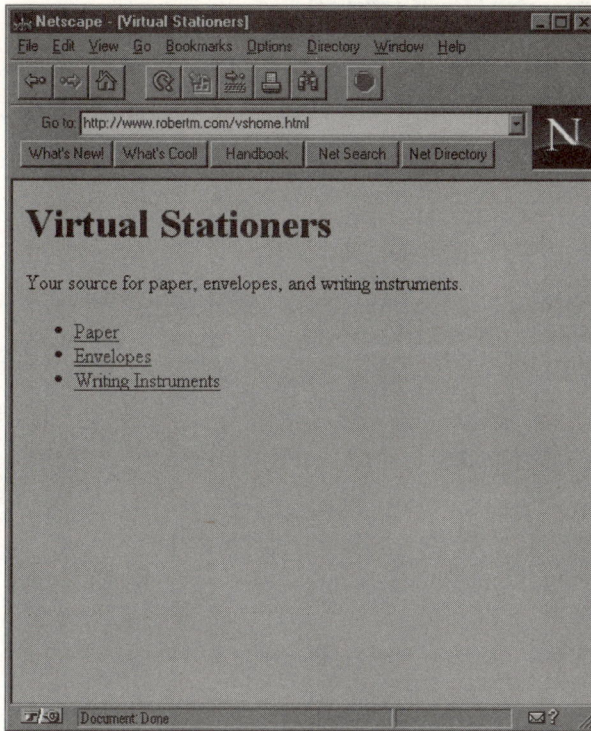

Figure 5.3: The vshome.tmpl file

values would be changed to the user's cart_no, and the array with the HTML code would be sent back to the user's Web browser. By using this same place-holder idea, you can now put together the HTML pages for the paper, envelopes, and writing instruments sections of the Virtual Stationers Web site. Listings 5.3, 5.4, and 5.5 include the HTML for these pages. Figures 5.4, 5.5, and 5.6 show how these listings would appear in Netscape.

Listing 5.3: The paper.tmpl File

```
<HTML>
<HEAD>
<TITLE>Virtual Stationers - Paper</TITLE>
</HEAD>
<BODY>
<H1>Virtual Stationers - Paper</H1>
<FORM METHOD=POST ACTION="/cgi-bin/shcart.pl">
```

Listing 5.3: The paper.tmpl File (Continued)

```
<INPUT TYPE=hidden NAME="cart_no" VALUE="XXXX">
<TABLE BORDER=1>
<TR>
<TH>Item</TH>
<TH>Price</TH>
<TH>Quantity</TH>
</TR>
<TR>
<TD VALIGN=top ALIGN=left>White 20lb bond, 1 Ream (500 sheets)</TD>
<TD VALIGN=top ALIGN=right>$5</TD>
<TD VALIGN=top ALIGN=left><INPUT TYPE=text NAME="White 20lb, 1
Ream::5" SIZE=4></TD>
</TR>
<TR>
<TD VALIGN=top ALIGN=left>White 20lb bond, 1 Case (10 Reams)</TD>
<TD VALIGN=top ALIGN=right>$35</TD>
<TD VALIGN=top ALIGN=left><INPUT TYPE=text NAME="White 20lb, 1
Case::35" SIZE=4></TD>
</TR>
<TR>
<TD VALIGN=top ALIGN=left>Canary 20lb bond, 1 Ream (500 sheets)</TD>
<TD VALIGN=top ALIGN=right>$6</TD>
<TD VALIGN=top ALIGN=left><INPUT TYPE=text NAME="Canary 20lb, 1
Ream::6" SIZE=4></TD>
</TR>
<TR>
<TD VALIGN=top ALIGN=left>Canary 20lb bond, 1 Case (10 Reams)</TD>
<TD VALIGN=top ALIGN=right>$40</TD>
<TD VALIGN=top ALIGN=left><INPUT TYPE=text NAME="Canary 20lb, 1
Case::40" SIZE=4></TD>
</TR>
<TR>
<TD VALIGN=top ALIGN=left>Blue 20lb bond, 1 Ream (500 sheets)</TD>
<TD VALIGN=top ALIGN=right>$6</TD>
<TD VALIGN=top ALIGN=left><INPUT TYPE=text NAME="Blue 20lb, 1 Ream::6"
SIZE=4></TD>
</TR>
<TR>
<TD VALIGN=top ALIGN=left>Blue 20lb bond, 1 Case (10 Reams)</TD>
<TD VALIGN=top ALIGN=right>$40</TD>
<TD VALIGN=top ALIGN=left><INPUT TYPE=text NAME="Blue 20lb, 1
Case::40" SIZE=4></TD>
</TR>
</TABLE>
```

Listing 5.3: The paper.tmpl File (Continued)

```
<P>
<INPUT TYPE=submit NAME="submit" VALUE="Add Items to Cart">
<INPUT TYPE=submit NAME="submit" VALUE="View Cart Contents">
<INPUT TYPE=submit NAME="submit" VALUE="Checkout">
<P>
[ <A HREF="/cgi-
bin/shcart.pl?cart_no=XXXX&page=envelopes">Envelopes</A> | <A
HREF="/cgi-bin/shcart.pl?cart_no=XXXX&page=writing">Writing
Instruments</A> ]
</FORM>
</BODY>
</HTML>
```

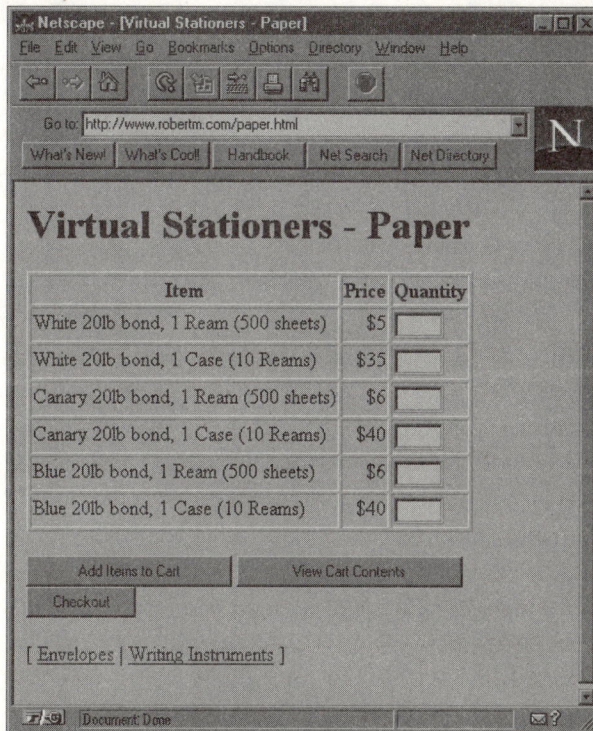

Figure 5.4: The paper page

Listing 5.4: The envelope.tmpl File

```
<HTML>
<HEAD>
<TITLE>Virtual Stationers - Envelopes</TITLE>
</HEAD>
<BODY>
<H1>Virtual Stationers - Envelopes</H1>
<FORM METHOD=POST ACTION="/cgi-bin/shcart.pl">
<INPUT TYPE=hidden NAME="cart_no" VALUE="XXXX">
<TABLE BORDER=1>
<TR>
<TH>Item</TH>
<TH>Price</TH>
<TH>Quantity</TH>
</TR>
<TR>
<TD VALIGN=top ALIGN=left>#10 White (500)</TD>
<TD VALIGN=top ALIGN=right>$5</TD>
<TD VALIGN=top ALIGN=left><INPUT TYPE=text NAME="#10 White (500)::5"
SIZE=4></TD>
</TR>
<TR>
<TD VALIGN=top ALIGN=left>#10 Window (500)</TD>
<TD VALIGN=top ALIGN=right>$6</TD>
<TD VALIGN=top ALIGN=left><INPUT TYPE=text NAME="#10 Window (500)::6"
SIZE=4></TD>
</TR>
<TR>
<TD VALIGN=top ALIGN=left>6x9 Padded Mailer (10)</TD>
<TD VALIGN=top ALIGN=right>$7</TD>
<TD VALIGN=top ALIGN=left><INPUT TYPE=text NAME="6x9 Padded Mailer
(10)::7" SIZE=4></TD>
</TR>
<TR>
<TD VALIGN=top ALIGN=left>9x12 Clasp (100)</TD>
<TD VALIGN=top ALIGN=right>$6</TD>
<TD VALIGN=top ALIGN=left><INPUT TYPE=text NAME="9x12 Clasp (100)::6"
SIZE=4></TD>
</TR>
<TR>
<TD VALIGN=top ALIGN=left>10x13 Clasp (100)</TD>
<TD VALIGN=top ALIGN=right>$8</TD>
<TD VALIGN=top ALIGN=left><INPUT TYPE=text NAME="10x13 Clasp (100)::8"
SIZE=4></TD>
</TR>
```

Listing 5.4: The envelope.tmpl File (Continued)

```
</TABLE>
<P>
<INPUT TYPE=submit NAME="submit" VALUE="Add Items to Cart">
<INPUT TYPE=submit NAME="submit" VALUE="View Cart Contents">
<INPUT TYPE=submit NAME="submit" VALUE="Checkout">
<P>
[ <A HREF="/cgi-bin/shcart.pl?cart_no=XXXX&page=paper">Paper</A> | <A
HREF="/cgi-bin/shcart.pl?cart_no=XXXX&page=writing">Writing
Instruments</A> ]
</FORM>
</BODY>
</HTML>
```

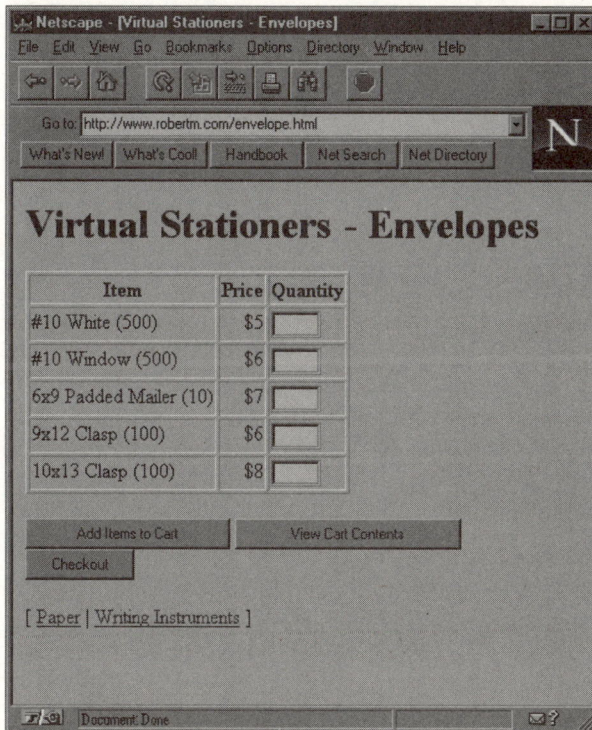

Figure 5.5: The envelopes page

Listing 5.5: The writing.tmpl File

```
<HTML>
<HEAD>
<TITLE>Virtual Stationers - Writing Instruments</TITLE>
</HEAD>
<BODY>
<H1>Virtual Stationers - Writing Instruments</H1>
<FORM METHOD=POST ACTION="/cgi-bin/shcart.pl">
<INPUT TYPE=hidden NAME="cart_no" VALUE="XXXX">
<TABLE BORDER=1>
<TR>
<TH>Item</TH>
<TH>Price</TH>
<TH>Quantity</TH>
</TR>
<TR>
<TD VALIGN=top ALIGN=left>Ballpoint pen, black (12)</TD>
<TD VALIGN=top ALIGN=right>$1</TD>
<TD VALIGN=top ALIGN=left><INPUT TYPE=text NAME="Ballpoint pen, black
(12)::1" SIZE=4></TD>
</TR>
<TR>
<TD VALIGN=top ALIGN=left>Ballpoint pen, blue (12)</TD>
<TD VALIGN=top ALIGN=right>$1</TD>
<TD VALIGN=top ALIGN=left><INPUT TYPE=text NAME="Ballpoint pen, blue
(12)::1" SIZE=4></TD>
</TR>
<TR>
<TD VALIGN=top ALIGN=left>Highlighter, yellow (2)</TD>
<TD VALIGN=top ALIGN=right>$1</TD>
<TD VALIGN=top ALIGN=left><INPUT TYPE=text NAME="Highlighter, yellow
(2)::1" SIZE=4></TD>
</TR>
<TR>
<TD VALIGN=top ALIGN=left>#2 Pencil (12)</TD>
<TD VALIGN=top ALIGN=right>$2</TD>
<TD VALIGN=top ALIGN=left><INPUT TYPE=text NAME="#2 Pencil (12)::2"
SIZE=4></TD>
</TR>
</TABLE>
<P>
<INPUT TYPE=submit NAME="submit" VALUE="Add Items to Cart">
<INPUT TYPE=submit NAME="submit" VALUE="View Cart Contents">
<INPUT TYPE=submit NAME="submit" VALUE="Checkout">
<P>
```

Listing 5.5: The writing.tmpl File (Continued)

```
[ <A HREF="/cgi-bin/shcart.pl?cart_no=XXXX&page=paper">Paper</A> | <A
HREF="/cgi-bin/shcart.pl?cart_no=XXXX&page=envelopes">Envelopes</A> ]
</FORM>
</BODY>
</HTML>
```

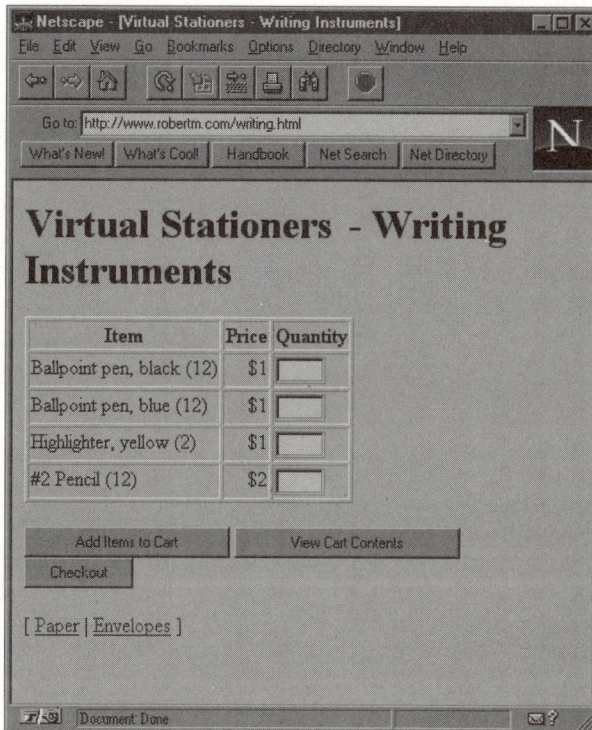

Figure 5.6: The writing instruments page

All three of these HTML pages include a quantity form that allows users to select how many items to add to their shopping carts. Each form also contains a hidden field with the cart_no value. This hidden field passes the cart_no to the CGI script if the user submits the form by pressing one of the three buttons on the page—Add Items to Cart, View Cart Contents, and Checkout. When users request a quantity of items to be added to their shopping carts, notice that the name/value pairs getting sent to the script are in the format "item description::price=quantity."

The last HTML template file you need is the file for displaying the shopping cart's contents to the user. This file is slightly different from the previous templates. It will be empty to begin with, because the contents will vary depending on the specific user's cart contents. Also, it replaces the Add Items to Cart and View Cart Contents push buttons with the Make Changes push button. Listing 5.6 contains the HTML code for the template file that displays the cart's contents and Figure 5.7 shows how this would look when a user has a few items selected.

Listing 5.6: The display.tmpl File

```
<HTML>
<HEAD>
<TITLE>Virtual Stationers - Contents of Your Shopping Cart</TITLE>
</HEAD>
<BODY>
<H1>Virtual Stationers</H1>
<H2>Contents of Your Shopping Cart</H2>
<FORM METHOD=POST ACTION="/cgi-bin/shcart.pl">
<INPUT TYPE=hidden NAME="cart_no" VALUE="XXXX">
<TABLE BORDER=1>
<TR>
<TH>Item</TH>
<TH>Price</TH>
<TH>Quantity</TH>
<TH>Item Subtotal</TH>
</TR>
</TABLE>
<P>
<INPUT TYPE=submit NAME="submit" VALUE="Make Changes">
<INPUT TYPE=submit NAME="submit" VALUE="Checkout">
<P>
[ <A HREF="/cgi-bin/shcart.pl?cart_no=XXXX&page=paper">Paper</A> | <A
HREF="/cgi-bin/shcart.pl?cart_no=XXXX&page=envelopes">Envelopes</A> |
<A HREF="/cgi-bin/shcart.pl?cart_no=XXXX&page=writing">Writing</A> ]
</FORM>
</BODY>
</HTML>
```

The File-Based Shopping Cart Script   Now that you've created the HTML templates, you need to write the shopping cart script. This script must assign the unique cart_no to each user; display the Web pages; and add, display, and modify the contents of the user's shopping cart. To make the script easier to

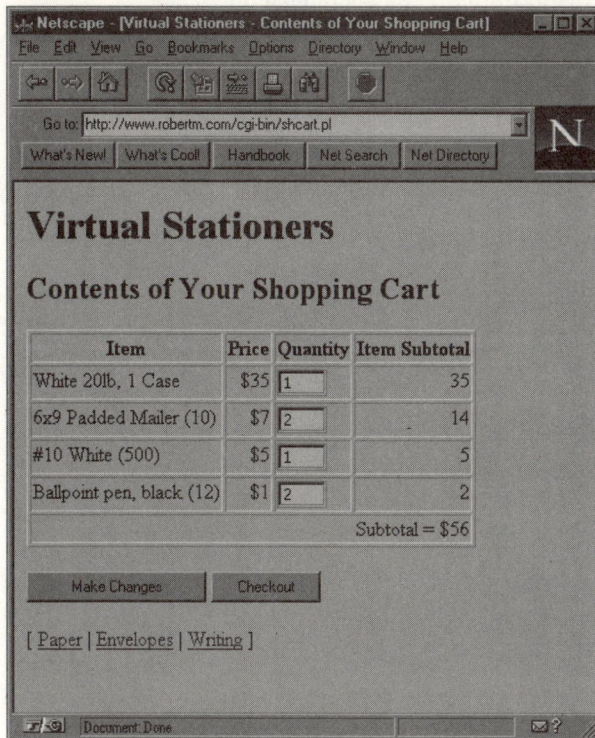

Figure 5.7: The display page

read, write, and debug, it's best to create a subroutine for each one of these actions. The subroutines for the shopping cart script are Display_Store_Page, Assign_Cart_Number, Add_Items_To_Cart, Display_Cart_Contents, Modify_Cart_Contents, and Checkout.

The Display_Store_Page Subroutine The Display_Store_Page subroutine is the function that parses the template files you created earlier, replaces the cart_no place holder with the correct cart number for the user, and returns the HTML page to the user's Web browser. Listing 5.7 includes the Perl code for the Display_Store_Page subroutine.

Listing 5.7: The Display_Store_Page Subroutine

```
sub Display_Store_Page {
  local (%data) = @_;
```

Listing 5.7: The Display_Store_Page Subroutine (Continued)

```perl
# Windows users need to change the '/'s below to
# '\\'s. For example '/vshome.tmpl' would be
# '\\vshome.tmpl' for Windows machines.
local (%products) =
    ( 'home', $path . '/vshome.tmpl',
      'paper', $path . '/paper.tmpl',
      'envelopes', $path . '/envelope.tmpl',
      'writing', $path . '/writing.tmpl', );
local (@template);

$data{'cart_no'} = &Assign_Cart_Number unless $data{'cart_no'};
$data{'page'} = 'home' unless $data{'page'};

open(TEMPLATE, "$products{$data{'page'}}") || die "Content-type:
text/html\n\nCannot open templates!";
@template = <TEMPLATE>;
close(TEMPLATE);

foreach (@template) {
  s/XXXX/$data{'cart_no'}/ge;
}

print "Content-type: text/html\n\n";
print @template;

}
```

Most of this subroutine should look familiar. It starts by receiving the user-supplied data as a parameter and places the data into the %data associative array. Then some other local variables are declared. The associative array %products has the name of the Web pages as the keys and the path to the associated template as the values. The variable $path is a global variable that will be set at the beginning of the shopping cart script. Listing 5.12 at the end of this section demonstrates where this variable will be set. After the local variables are declared, you should check whether the user has already been assigned a cart number. The line

```perl
$data{'cart_no'} = &Assign_Cart_Number unless $data{'cart_no'};
```

reads like "Assign a cart number to the variable $data{'cart_no'} unless it already has a value." The next line checks whether a page has been specified. If this subroutine is called and no page is specified, it will display the home page.

The next few lines open the appropriate template file and read in the contents to the @template array. Then each element of the @template array is checked for the cart_no placeholder XXXX, which is replaced with the real cart_no. Next the parsed header and the modified contents of the @template array are sent back to the Web browser.

The Assign_Cart_Number Subroutine   The Assign_Cart_Number subroutine is only called from the Display_Store_Page subroutine. Its function is to assign a unique cart number to any user who does not already have one. It also deletes old shopping carts that are no longer in use. Listing 5.8 contains the Perl code for the Assign_Cart_Number subroutine.

Listing 5.8: The Assign_Cart_Number Subroutine

```perl
sub Assign_Cart_Number {
  local ($cart_no);

  # Windows users need to change the "ls $path/carts |" string
  # to "dir $path\\carts |".
  open(FILES, "ls $path/carts |") || die "Content-type:
text/html\n\nCannot list existing carts!";

  while (<FILES>) {
    chop;
    unlink $_ unless -M $_ < 1;
  }
  close(FILES);

  srand(time|$$);
  $cart_no = time . "." . int(rand(999));

  # Windows users must change the string ">$path/carts/$cart_no"
  # to ">$path\\carts\\$cart_no".
  open(CART, ">$path/carts/$cart_no") || die "Content-type:
text/html\n\nCannot open new cart!";
  close(CART);
  return $cart_no;
}
```

The first open statement just lists all the shopping carts currently in the carts directory. The carts directory is the subdirectory you create to store all of the shopping carts. Essentially, the string "ls $path/carts |" ("dir $path\\carts |" for Windows machines) is executed and the results are sent on the input stream FILES. The while loop checks each file received from the FILES stream, deleting it unless it was last modified less than a day ago. In other words, all shopping carts that haven't been touched for over a day are deleted. This keeps your directory from filling up with shopping carts that are no longer in use.

The next lines should look familiar. They are similar to the lines used to assign a file name for the Windows version of feedback.pl in Chapter 4. They create a unique cart number by using the current date and a random one- to three-digit extension.

The second open statement creates the shopping cart file by opening the file for output. Recall from the guest book example that the > operator preceding the file name means to open the file for output. If the file does not already exist, as is the case here, it is created. After the file is created, the output stream to the file is closed and the cart number is returned.

The Add_Items_To_Cart Subroutine The user selects items from the store's Web pages by placing a quantity value (a number greater than 0) in the Quantity field of the form. The user than adds the selected items to his shopping cart by pressing the Add Items to Cart push button. When the user presses this push button, the shopping cart script will execute and the Add_Items_To_Cart subroutine will be called.

This subroutine must take the items selected, format the information for the shopping cart file, and place it within the file. This can all be accomplished with the Perl code shown in Listing 5.9.

Listing 5.9: The Add_Items_To_Cart Subroutine

```
sub Add_Items_To_Cart {
  local (%data) = @_;
  local ($cart_item, @add_items);

  foreach $key (%data) {
    if (($key ne "cart_no") && ($key ne "submit")) {
      if ($data{$key} > 0) {
        $cart_item = join('::', $key, $data{$key});
        $cart_item .= "\n";
        push(@add_items, $cart_item);
      }
    }
  }

  # Windows users need to change the string
">>$path/carts/$data{'cart_no'}"
  # to ">>$path\\carts\\$data{'cart_no'}".
```

Listing 5.9: The Add_Items_To_Cart Subroutine (Continued)

```perl
 open(CART, ">>$path/carts/$data{'cart_no'}") || die "Content-type:
text/html\n\nCannot open cart!";
 print CART @add_items;
 close(CART);

 &Display_Cart_Contents(%data);
}
```

The foreach loop takes each element received in the %data associative array, which is the user-supplied data, formats it, and places it in the @add_items array. What "formats it" means is to put it in a standard format that you will recognize in your other subroutines. Remember from the earlier HTML templates section that the name/value pairs getting sent to the script are in the format "item description::price=quantity." For example, if the user selected 3 reams of the 20lb white paper, the name/value pair would be "White 20lb, 1 Ream::5=3". So, this foreach loop takes each name/value pair and creates a string that looks like "White 20lb, 1 Ream::5::3\n" for this example. It then places that string into the @add_items array.

After all of the items the user selected are added to the @add_items array, the user's shopping cart is opened. Remember that the >> operator preceding the file name in an open statement means to append to the file. Once the cart file is opened, the items are appended to the file. The routine finishes with a call to the Display_Cart_Contents subroutine, which sends the entire shopping cart contents back to the user's Web browser. So, every time users make an addition to their cart, they see the current contents of the cart.

The Display_Cart_Contents Subroutine   The Display_Cart_Contents subroutine is used when the user selects the View Cart Contents push button as well as at the end of the Add_Items_To_Cart and Modify_Cart_Contents subroutines. It opens the user's shopping cart and displays all of the items in the cart. Because you want the user to be able to modify the quantity of items originally selected, you should place the quantity in an text input field. For the shopping cart display, you also calculate the subtotal of items selected. Listing 5.10 shows the Perl code for the Display_Cart_Contents subroutine.

The first part of this subroutine is similar to the Display_Store_Page subroutine. It opens and reads in the display.tmpl template file and changes the XXXX placeholder to the real cart number stored in the $data{'cart_no'} variable. The second open statement opens the user's shopping cart file and places all of the contents into the array @cart_raw.

Listing 5.10: The Display_Cart_Contents Subroutine

```perl
sub Display_Cart_Contents {
  local (%data) = @_;
  local (@template, @cart_raw, @cart_contents, $item, $price,
         $quantity, $cost, $sub);

  # Windows users need to change the string "$path/display.tmpl"
  # to "$path\\display.tmpl"
  open(TEMPLATE, "$path/display.tmpl") || die "Content-type:
text/html\n\nCannot open template!";
  @template = <TEMPLATE>;
  close(TEMPLATE);

  foreach (@template) {
    s/XXXX/$data{'cart_no'}/ge;
  }

  # Windows users need to change the string
"$path/carts/$data{'cart_no'}"
  # to $path\\carts\\$data{'cart_no'}.
  open(CART, "$path/carts/$data{'cart_no'}") || die "Content-type:
text/html\n\nCannot open cart!";
  @cart_raw = <CART>;
  close(CART);

  $sub = 0;
  foreach (@cart_raw) {
    chop;

    ($item, $price, $quantity) = split(/::/);
    $cost = $price * $quantity;
    $sub += $cost;

    push(@cart_contents, "<TR>\n");
    push(@cart_contents, "<TD VALIGN=top ALIGN=left>$item</TD>\n");
    push(@cart_contents, "<TD VALIGN=top ALIGN=right>\$$price</TD>\n");
    push(@cart_contents, "<TD VALIGN=top ALIGN=left><INPUT TYPE=text
NAME=\"$item\:\:$price\" VALUE=\"$quantity\" SIZE=4></TD>\n");
    push(@cart_contents, "<TD VALIGN=top ALIGN=right>$cost</TD>\n");
    push(@cart_contents, "</TR>\n");
  }

  push(@cart_contents, "<TR>\n");
  push(@cart_contents, "<TD COLSPAN=4 ALIGN=right>Subtotal =
\$$sub</TD>\n");
```

Listing 5.10: The Display_Cart_Contents Subroutine (Continued)

```
    push(@cart_contents, "</TR>\n");

    splice(@template, 16, 0, @cart_contents);
    print "Content-type: text/html\n\n";
    print @template;
}
```

Once all of the shopping cart items are read in from the shopping cart file, you just need to format the data. The foreach loop does this. It takes each item that was added to the shopping cart file and breaks it up. Recall from the Add_Items_To_Cart subroutine that each line in the shopping cart file will be in the format item description::item price::quantity selected. First, each item is split into the individual entities—description, price and quantity—and its cost is calculated. All this information, along with the HTML tags, is then placed into the @cart_contents array. Notice that the quantity is placed in an input field so that the user can modify the amount he or she originally chose.

After each of the cart's items have been formatted for display and added to the @cart_contents array, the subtotal of all items is also added to the @cart_contents array. Then the contents of the @cart_contents array are placed within the template for the display HTML page. This is done with the splice function, in the line

```
splice(@template, 16, 0, @cart_contents);
```

which inserts the contents of the @cart_contents array into the @template array, beginning at the index 16. Because Perl arrays are indexed starting at 0, this insertion begins at the seventeenth element of the @template array. When the insertion is completed, the parsed header and the contents of the @template array are sent back to the user's Web browser.

The Modify_Cart_Contents Subroutine   The Modify_Cart_Contents subroutine is only called when the user presses the Make Changes push button on the Web page displaying the shopping cart contents. This subroutine is similar to the Add_Items_To_Cart subroutine. Because all items are sent to the CGI script in the user data, regardless of whether the quantities were changed, it is easiest to re-create the contents of the shopping cart file. Listing 5.11 contains the Perl code for the Modify_Cart_Contents subroutine.

Like the Add_Items_To_Cart subroutine, this subroutine first loops over all of the items sent in the user-supplied data and formats them in the standard format being used for the shopping cart files. The only difference between this

Listing 5.11: The Modify_Cart_Contents Subroutine

```
sub Modify_Cart_Contents {
  local (%data) = @_;
  local ($cart_item, @add_items);

  foreach $key (%data) {
    if (($key ne "cart_no") && ($key ne "submit")) {
      if ($data{$key} > 0) {
        $cart_item = join('::', $key, $data{$key});
        $cart_item .= "\n";
        push(@add_items, $cart_item);
      }
    }
  }

  # Windows users need to change the string
">$path/carts/$data{'cart_no'}"
  # to ">$path\\carts\\$data{'cart_no'}".
  open(CART, ">$path/carts/$data{'cart_no'}") || die "Content-type:
text/html\n\nCannot open cart!";
  print CART @add_items;
  close(CART);

  &Display_Cart_Contents(%data);
}
```

subroutine and the Add_Items_To_Cart subroutine is that you don't want to append the new contents to the shopping cart file. Instead, you want to over-write the current shopping cart file with the items that were just formatted. You do this simply by changing the >> operator preceding the file name in the open statement of the add subroutine to the > operator. Remember, the >> operator means append to and the > operator means output to (overwriting if necessary).

The Checkout Subroutine   The Perl code for a Checkout subroutine will vary depending on how your ordering system works, so it is not included here. You may want your Checkout subroutine to display all the items in the shopping cart; a subtotal for the items; any applicable tax, shipping, and handling; and a total. You may also need fields to accept credit card information if this is how you want to handle the transaction. If you already have a computerized ordering system, you may wish to place this order right into that system, or send the order via e-mail to one of your employees so he or she can handle it.

In any case, all the code you would write for the Checkout subroutine would go after the declaration of local variables, as in

```
sub Checkout {
  local (%data) = @_;

  # Place your code here.
}
```

Putting It All Together: The shcart.pl File   Now that you've completed all the code for Shopping Cart subroutines, you can put together your shopping cart script. Let's call the file shcart.pl. As in the guest book example, you want to remove any Server Side Includes that the user may have placed in the input fields. Also, you can determine whether the user requested a different Web page, such as the Envelopes page, or pressed a push button by checking the value for the REQUEST_METHOD environment variable. However, in this example, unlike the guest book example, the user could have pressed a variety of push buttons. To accommodate this, you can write one more subroutine that checks the value of the name/value pair of the submit button and calls the appropriate subroutine. This subroutine, the Which_Post subroutine, is included in Listing 5.12, which contains the Perl code for the entire shcart.pl example. Remember to remove the first line and make the other specified changes if you are using this script on a Windows system.

THE NETSCAPE COOKIE

From the shopping cart script, you might notice the difficulty of storing and retrieving information for the various users. As a solution to this problem, Netscape Communications Corporation (Netscape, for short) implemented a method for storing state information on the client side. *State information* is just information from previous requests that under normal circumstances is lost. The state information is placed within an object and sent from a CGI script through the Web server to the Web browser. When appropriate, the Web browser sends the object along with its standard HTTP request header. The new object that Netscape created is called a cookie, which is named that for what they say is "no compelling reason."

A cookie first comes into existence from the server side where it is created. Usually, a cookie is created within a CGI script, which sends the cookie to the Web server as a parsed header. The cookie is then sent to the Web browser as part of the standard response header. When it receives the cookie, the Web browser stores it in a file. Each cookie contains a range of URLs under which it is valid, and the Web browser sends the cookie as part of the HTTP request

Listing 5.12: The shcart.pl File

```perl
#!/usr/local/bin/perl

# For Windows systems, this line would need to look
# like $path = "c:\\robertm";
$path = "/users/robertm";
%data_received = &User_Data;
&No_SSI(*data_received);

$ENV{'REQUEST_METHOD'} eq "POST" ? &Which_Post(%data_received)  :
&Display_Store_Page(%data_received);

sub Which_Post {
  local (%data) = @_;

  &Display_Cart_Contents(%data) if $data{'submit'} eq "View Cart
Contents";
  &Add_Items_To_Cart(%data) if $data{'submit'} eq "Add Items to Cart";
  &Modify_Cart_Contents(%data) if $data{'submit'} eq "Make Changes";
  &Checkout(%data) if $data{'submit'} eq "Checkout";

}

sub Display_Store_Page {
  local (%data) = @_;

  # Windows users need to change the '/'s below to
  # '\\'s. For example '/vshome.tmpl' would be
  # '\\vshome.tmpl' for Windows machines.
  local (%products) =
      ( 'home', $path . '/vshome.tmpl',
        'paper', $path . '/paper.tmpl',
        'envelopes', $path . '/envelope.tmpl',
        'writing', $path . '/writing.tmpl', );
  local (@template);

  $data{'cart_no'} = &Assign_Cart_Number unless $data{'cart_no'};
  $data{'page'} = 'home' unless $data{'page'};

  open(TEMPLATE, "$products{$data{'page'}}") || die "Content-type:
text/html\n\nCannot open templates!";
  @template = <TEMPLATE>;
  close(TEMPLATE);

  foreach (@template) {
```

Listing 5.12: The shcart.pl File (Continued)

```perl
    s/XXXX/$data{'cart_no'}/ge;
  }

  print "Content-type: text/html\n\n";
  print @template;

}

sub Assign_Cart_Number {
  local ($cart_no);

  # Windows users need to change the "ls $path/carts |" string
  # to "dir $path\\carts |".
  open(FILES, "ls $path/carts |") || die "Content-type:
text/html\n\nCannot list existing carts!";

  while (<FILES>) {
    chop;
    unlink $_ unless -M $_ < 1;
  }
  close(FILES);

  srand(time|$$);
  $cart_no = time . "." . int(rand(999));

  # Windows users must change the string ">$path/carts/$cart_no"
  # to ">$path\\carts\\$cart_no".
  open(CART, ">$path/carts/$cart_no") || die "Content-type:
text/html\n\nCannot open new cart!";
  close(CART);
  return $cart_no;
}

sub Add_Items_To_Cart {
  local (%data) = @_;
  local ($cart_item, @add_items);

  foreach $key (%data) {
    if (($key ne "cart_no") && ($key ne "submit")) {
      if ($data{$key} > 0) {
        $cart_item = join('::', $key, $data{$key});
        $cart_item .= "\n";
        push(@add_items, $cart_item);
      }
```

Listing 5.12: The shcart.pl File (Continued)

```perl
    }
  }

  # Windows users need to change the string
">>$path/carts/$data{'cart_no'}"
  # to ">>$path\\carts\\$data{'cart_no'}".
  open(CART, ">>$path/carts/$data{'cart_no'}") || die "Content-type:
text/html\n\nCannot open cart!";
  print CART @add_items;
  close(CART);

  &Display_Cart_Contents(%data);
}

sub Modify_Cart_Contents {
  local (%data) = @_;
  local ($cart_item, @add_items);

  foreach $key (%data) {
    if (($key ne "cart_no") && ($key ne "submit")) {
      if ($data{$key} > 0) {
        $cart_item = join('::', $key, $data{$key});
        $cart_item .= "\n";
        push(@add_items, $cart_item);
      }
    }
  }

  # Windows users need to change the string
">$path/carts/$data{'cart_no'}"
  # to ">$path\\carts\\$data{'cart_no'}".
  open(CART, ">$path/carts/$data{'cart_no'}") || die "Content-type:
text/html\n\nCannot open cart!";
  print CART @add_items;
  close(CART);

  &Display_Cart_Contents(%data);
}

sub Display_Cart_Contents {
  local (%data) = @_;
  local (@template, @cart_raw, @cart_contents, $item, $price,
         $quantity, $cost, $sub);
```

Listing 5.12: The shcart.pl File (Continued)

```perl
  # Windows users need to change the string "$path/display.tmpl"
  # to "$path\\display.tmpl"
  open(TEMPLATE, "$path/display.tmpl") || die "Content-type:
text/html\n\nCannot open template!";
  @template = <TEMPLATE>;
  close(TEMPLATE);

  foreach (@template) {
    s/XXXX/$data{'cart_no'}/ge;
  }

  # Windows users need to change the string
"$path/carts/$data{'cart_no'}"
  # to $path\\carts\\$data{'cart_no'}".
  open(CART, "$path/carts/$data{'cart_no'}") || die "Content-type:
text/html\n\nCannot open cart!";
  @cart_raw = <CART>;
  close(CART);

  $sub = 0;
  foreach (@cart_raw) {
    chop;

    ($item, $price, $quantity) = split(/::/);
    $cost = $price * $quantity;
    $sub += $cost;

    push(@cart_contents, "<TR>\n");
    push(@cart_contents, "<TD VALIGN=top ALIGN=left>$item</TD>\n");
    push(@cart_contents, "<TD VALIGN=top ALIGN=right>\$$price</TD>\n");
    push(@cart_contents, "<TD VALIGN=top ALIGN=left><INPUT TYPE=text
NAME=\"$item\:\:$price\" VALUE=\"$quantity\" SIZE=4></TD>\n");
    push(@cart_contents, "<TD VALIGN=top ALIGN=right>$cost</TD>\n");
    push(@cart_contents, "</TR>\n");
  }

  push(@cart_contents, "<TR>\n");
  push(@cart_contents, "<TD COLSPAN=4 ALIGN=right>Subtotal =
\$$sub</TD>\n");
  push(@cart_contents, "</TR>\n");

  splice(@template, 16, 0, @cart_contents);
  print "Content-type: text/html\n\n";
  print @template;
```

Listing 5.12: The shcart.pl File (Continued)

```perl
}

sub Checkout {
  local (%data) = @_;

  # Place your code here.
}

sub No_SSI {
  local (*data) = @_;

  foreach $key (sort keys(%data)) {
    $data{$key} =~ s/<!--(.|\n)*-->//g;
  }

}

sub User_Data {
  local (%user_data, $user_string, $name_value_pair,
         @name_value_pairs, $name, $value);

  # If the data was sent via POST, then it is available
  # from standard input. Otherwise, the data is in the
  # QUERY_STRING environment variable.
  if ($ENV{'REQUEST_METHOD'} eq "POST") {
    read(STDIN,$user_string,$ENV{'CONTENT_LENGTH'});
  } else {
    $user_string = $ENV{'QUERY_STRING'};
  }

  # This line changes the + signs to spaces.
  $user_string =~ s/\+/ /g;

  # This line places each name/value pair as a separate
  # element in the name_value_pairs array.
  @name_value_pairs = split(/&/, $user_string);

  # This code loops over each element in the name_value_pairs
  # array, splits it on the = sign, and places the value
  # into the user_data associative array with the name as the
  # key.
  foreach $name_value_pair (@name_value_pairs) {
    ($name, $value) = split(/=/, $name_value_pair);
```

Listing 5.12: The shcart.pl File (Continued)

```perl
  # These two lines decode the values from any URL
  # hexadecimal encoding. The first section searches for a
  # hexadecimal number and the second part converts the
  # hex number to decimal and returns the character
  # equivalent.
  $name =~
    s/%([a-fA-F0-9][a-fA-F0-9])/pack("C",hex($1))/ge;
  $value =~
    s/%([a-fA-F0-9][a-fA-F0-9])/pack("C",hex($1))/ge;

  # If the name/value pair has already been given a value,
  # as in the case of multiple items being selected, then
  # separate the items with a " : ".
  if (defined($user_data{$name})) {
    $user_data{$name} .= " : " . $value;
  } else {
    $user_data{$name} = $value;
  }
}
return %user_data;
}
```

header when the cookie is within its valid domain. For example, if a user of my Web site received a cookie from one of my scripts that was valid on my entire domain, the browser would store the cookie as being valid for all URLs ending with robertm.com. When the Web browser makes a request from the robertm.com domain, the browser sends the cookie along with the standard HTTP request header.

When a CGI script creates a cookie, it sends a Set-Cookie statement as part of the parsed header. The Set-Cookie statement can take up to five attributes, which are shown in Table 5.1.

Cookies remain in effect until they expire, and they can be modified or deleted. To modify a cookie, send another Set-Cookie parsed header with the exact same [NAME] and path attributes. For example, suppose you previously set a cookie with the following Set-Cookie statement

```
Set-Cookie: login=robertm; path=/
```

To modify the cookie you would need to send another Set-Cookie statement such as

```
Set-Cookie: login=rmcdaniel; path=/
```

Table 5.1: The Set-Cookie Attributes

Attribute	Description
[NAME]	The NAME attribute is the only required attribute for the Set-Cookie statement. It is used in conjunction with an associated value, such as name=value. However, it is slightly different than the other attributes in that it does not have to be called NAME. For example, in the Set-Cookie statement Set-Cookie: login=robertm the string login=robertm is the name/value attribute for the Set-Cookie statement.
expires	This attribute specifies the date and time when the cookie will expire. Its format is expires=date, where date is in the format Weekday, DD-Mon-YY HH:MM:SS GMT. The time zone (GMT) does not have to be specified for the expires attribute because GMT is the only valid time zone. If the expires attribute is not specified, the cookie will expire when the user shuts down his or her Web browser.
domain	This attribute stores the domain name of the range of URLs for which the cookie is valid. When the browser compares the current domain with the domain value for a cookie, it does tail matching. *Tail matching* is the comparison of the last parts of the domain name to see if there is a match. For example, a domain attribute of robertm.com would tail match www.robertm.com and home.domain.robertm.com. If the domain attribute is not specified, the domain for the cookie is set to the domain name of the server generating the cookie.
path	The path attribute is used to specify a subset of URLs under which the cookie is valid. It is specified as subdirectories of the domain. For example, if the domain were set to www.robertm.com and the path were set to /shopping-cart, the cookie would only be valid for URLs starting with www.robertm.com/shopping-cart (only valid for requests of items under the shopping cart subdirectory). If the path attribute is not assigned, it is given the same path as the path contained in the URI of the response header that contains the cookie.
secure	This attribute takes no values. If it is present, the Web browser only sends the cookie if it has a secure connection with the Web server with which it is making the request. A secure connection for cookies means that the server is a SSL server (Secure Sockets Layer server). If the secure attribute is not present, the Web browser sends the cookie over any type of connection.

Deleting a cookie is similar to modifying it. You must send the exact same [NAME] attribute and include an expires time that is in the past. So, if you sent

```
Set-Cookie: login=rmcdaniel; expires Monday, 01-Jan-95 00:00:01
```

the previous cookie with login=rmcdaniel would expire (be deleted).

When a browser sends a cookie as part of the request header, it is made available to your CGI script along with the other HTTP request header environment variables. The variable would be HTTP_COOKIE. The values of the cookie are all placed in one string, separated by a semicolon and space. For example, if you set two cookies with the following statements

```
Set-Cookie: login=robertm; path=/
Set-Cookie: password=mypass; path =/
```

the browser would send the following cookie whenever it entered your domain (until the cookies expired)

```
login=robertm; password=mypass
```

Cookies were introduced by Netscape but have not yet been adopted by all software manufacturers and do not work for all Web browsers. However, the two most widely used Web browsers, Netscape Navigator and Internet Explorer, both support cookies.

ADDING THE COOKIE TO THE SHOPPING CART

Now that you know about cookies, you can change the shopping cart script to use them. Instead of storing the carts in files on your server, you can store the shopping cart contents on the user's own machine.

Revising the HTML Pages   Because you do not need to keep track of which cart number belongs to which user, you do not need to use all of the template files used in the previous version. You can change the files vshome.tmpl, paper.tmpl, envelopes.tmpl, and writing.tmpl into HTML files that the users will actually see. Listings 5.13, 5.14, 5.15, and 5.16 show these modified files. All of the HTML pages, including the display.tmpl page for the cookie shopping cart example, appear in the figures for the templates of the file-based shopping cart example.

Listing 5.13: The vshome.html File

```
<HTML>
<HEAD>
<TITLE>Virtual Stationers</TITLE>
</HEAD>
<BODY>
```

Listing 5.13: The vshome.html File (Continued)

```
<H1>Virtual Stationers</H1>
Your source for paper, envelopes, and writing instruments.
<P>
<UL>
<LI><A HREF="paper.html">Paper</A>
<LI><A HREF="envelope.html">Envelopes</A>
<LI><A HREF="writing.html">Writing Instruments</A>
</UL>
</BODY>
</HTML>
```

Listing 5.14: The paper.html File

```
<HTML>
<HEAD>
<TITLE>Virtual Stationers - Paper</TITLE>
</HEAD>
<BODY>
<H1>Virtual Stationers - Paper</H1>
<FORM METHOD=POST ACTION="/cgi-bin/ckcart.pl">
<TABLE BORDER=1>
<TR>
<TH>Item</TH>
<TH>Price</TH>
<TH>Quantity</TH>
</TR>
<TR>
<TD VALIGN=top ALIGN=left>White 20lb bond, 1 Ream (500 sheets)</TD>
<TD VALIGN=top ALIGN=right>$5</TD>
<TD VALIGN=top ALIGN=left><INPUT TYPE=text NAME="White 20lb, 1
Ream::5" SIZE=4></TD>
</TR>
<TR>
<TD VALIGN=top ALIGN=left>White 20lb bond, 1 Case (10 Reams)</TD>
<TD VALIGN=top ALIGN=right>$35</TD>
<TD VALIGN=top ALIGN=left><INPUT TYPE=text NAME="White 20lb, 1
Case::35" SIZE=4></TD>
</TR>
<TR>
<TD VALIGN=top ALIGN=left>Canary 20lb bond, 1 Ream (500 sheets)</TD>
<TD VALIGN=top ALIGN=right>$6</TD>
<TD VALIGN=top ALIGN=left><INPUT TYPE=text NAME="Canary 20lb, 1
Ream::6" SIZE=4></TD>
</TR>
```

Listing 5.14: The paper.html File (Continued)

```
<TR>
<TD VALIGN=top ALIGN=left>Canary 20lb bond, 1 Case (10 Reams)</TD>
<TD VALIGN=top ALIGN=right>$40</TD>
<TD VALIGN=top ALIGN=left><INPUT TYPE=text NAME="Canary 20lb, 1
Case::40" SIZE=4></TD>
</TR>
<TR>
<TD VALIGN=top ALIGN=left>Blue 20lb bond, 1 Ream (500 sheets)</TD>
<TD VALIGN=top ALIGN=right>$6</TD>
<TD VALIGN=top ALIGN=left><INPUT TYPE=text NAME="Blue 20lb, 1 Ream::6"
SIZE=4></TD>
</TR>
<TR>
<TD VALIGN=top ALIGN=left>Blue 20lb bond, 1 Case (10 Reams)</TD>
<TD VALIGN=top ALIGN=right>$40</TD>
<TD VALIGN=top ALIGN=left><INPUT TYPE=text NAME="Blue 20lb, 1
Case::40" SIZE=4></TD>
</TR>
</TABLE>
<P>
<INPUT TYPE=submit NAME="submit" VALUE="Add Items to Cart">
<INPUT TYPE=submit NAME="submit" VALUE="View Cart Contents">
<INPUT TYPE=submit NAME="submit" VALUE="Checkout">
<P>
[ <A HREF="envelope.html">Envelopes</A> | <A
HREF="writing.html">Writing Instruments</A> ]
</FORM>
</BODY>
</HTML>
```

Listing 5.15: The envelope.html File

```
<HTML>
<HEAD>
<TITLE>Virtual Stationers - Envelopes</TITLE>
</HEAD>
<BODY>
<H1>Virtual Stationers - Envelopes</H1>
<FORM METHOD=POST ACTION="/cgi-bin/ckcart.pl">
<TABLE BORDER=1>
<TR>
<TH>Item</TH>
<TH>Price</TH>
<TH>Quantity</TH>
```

Listing 5.15: The envelope.html File (Continued)

```
</TR>
<TR>
<TD VALIGN=top ALIGN=left>#10 White (500)</TD>
<TD VALIGN=top ALIGN=right>$5</TD>
<TD VALIGN=top ALIGN=left><INPUT TYPE=text NAME="#10 White (500)::5"
SIZE=4></TD>
</TR>
<TR>
<TD VALIGN=top ALIGN=left>#10 Window (500)</TD>
<TD VALIGN=top ALIGN=right>$6</TD>
<TD VALIGN=top ALIGN=left><INPUT TYPE=text NAME="#10 Window (500)::6"
SIZE=4></TD>
</TR>
<TR>
<TD VALIGN=top ALIGN=left>6x9 Padded Mailer (10)</TD>
<TD VALIGN=top ALIGN=right>$7</TD>
<TD VALIGN=top ALIGN=left><INPUT TYPE=text NAME="6x9 Padded Mailer
(10)::7" SIZE=4></TD>
</TR>
<TR>
<TD VALIGN=top ALIGN=left>9x12 Clasp (100)</TD>
<TD VALIGN=top ALIGN=right>$6</TD>
<TD VALIGN=top ALIGN=left><INPUT TYPE=text NAME="9x12 Clasp (100)::6"
SIZE=4></TD>
</TR>
<TR>
<TD VALIGN=top ALIGN=left>10x13 Clasp (100)</TD>
<TD VALIGN=top ALIGN=right>$8</TD>
<TD VALIGN=top ALIGN=left><INPUT TYPE=text NAME="10x13 Clasp (100)::8"
SIZE=4></TD>
</TR>
</TABLE>
<P>
<INPUT TYPE=submit NAME="submit" VALUE="Add Items to Cart">
<INPUT TYPE=submit NAME="submit" VALUE="View Cart Contents">
<INPUT TYPE=submit NAME="submit" VALUE="Checkout">
<P>
[ <A HREF="paper.html">Paper</A> | <A HREF="writing.html">Writing
Instruments</A> ]
</FORM>
</BODY>
</HTML>
```

Listing 5.16: The writing.html File

```
<HTML>
<HEAD>
<TITLE>Virtual Stationers - Writing Instruments</TITLE>
</HEAD>
<BODY>
<H1>Virtual Stationers - Writing Instruments</H1>
<FORM METHOD=POST ACTION="/cgi-bin/ckcart.pl">
<TABLE BORDER=1>
<TR>
<TH>Item</TH>
<TH>Price</TH>
<TH>Quantity</TH>
</TR>
<TR>
<TD VALIGN=top ALIGN=left>Ballpoint pen, black (12)</TD>
<TD VALIGN=top ALIGN=right>$1</TD>
<TD VALIGN=top ALIGN=left><INPUT TYPE=text NAME="Ballpoint pen, black
(12)::1" SIZE=4></TD>
</TR>
<TR>
<TD VALIGN=top ALIGN=left>Ballpoint pen, blue (12)</TD>
<TD VALIGN=top ALIGN=right>$1</TD>
<TD VALIGN=top ALIGN=left><INPUT TYPE=text NAME="Ballpoint pen, blue
(12)::1" SIZE=4></TD>
</TR>
<TR>
<TD VALIGN=top ALIGN=left>Highlighter, yellow (2)</TD>
<TD VALIGN=top ALIGN=right>$1</TD>
<TD VALIGN=top ALIGN=left><INPUT TYPE=text NAME="Highlighter, yellow
(2)::1" SIZE=4></TD>
</TR>
<TR>
<TD VALIGN=top ALIGN=left>#2 Pencil (12)</TD>
<TD VALIGN=top ALIGN=right>$2</TD>
<TD VALIGN=top ALIGN=left><INPUT TYPE=text NAME="#2 Pencil (12)::2"
SIZE=4></TD>
</TR>
</TABLE>
<P>
<INPUT TYPE=submit NAME="submit" VALUE="Add Items to Cart">
<INPUT TYPE=submit NAME="submit" VALUE="View Cart Contents">
<INPUT TYPE=submit NAME="submit" VALUE="Checkout">
<P>
```

Listing 5.16: The writing.html File (Continued)

```
[ <A HREF="paper.html">Paper</A> | <A
HREF="envelope.html">Envelopes</A> ]
</FORM>
</BODY>
</HTML>
```

Notice that all of the XXXX cart_no placeholders have been removed. You no longer need these placeholders because the shopping cart is actually on the user's machine. Without the placeholders, there is no need to generate these files from a CGI script. Therefore all of the links to the other pages (the links to the paper, envelopes, and writing instruments pages) no longer call the shcart.pl script.

The display.tmpl file, however, needs to remain a template. Even though you do not need to change any cart_no place holders, your shopping cart script still needs to generate the contents and place it in a HTML file. Listing 5.17 shows the revised display.tmpl file for the cookie version of the shopping cart.

Listing 5.17: The display.tmpl File

```
<HTML>
<HEAD>
<BASE HREF="http://www.robertm.com/display.html">
<TITLE>Virtual Stationers - Contents of Your Shopping Cart</TITLE>
</HEAD>
<BODY>
<H1>Virtual Stationers</H1>
<H2>Contents of Your Shopping Cart</H2>
<FORM METHOD=POST ACTION="/cgi-bin/ckcart.pl">
<TABLE BORDER=1>
<TR>
<TH>Item</TH>
<TH>Price</TH>
<TH>Quantity</TH>
<TH>Item Subtotal</TH>
</TR>
</TABLE>
<P>
<INPUT TYPE=submit NAME="submit" VALUE="Make Changes">
<INPUT TYPE=submit NAME="submit" VALUE="Checkout">
<P>
[ <A HREF="paper.html">Paper</A> | <A
HREF="envelope.html">Envelopes</A> | <A
HREF="writing.html">Writing</A> ]
```

Listing 5.17: The display.tmpl File (Continued)

```
</FORM>
</BODY>
</HTML>
```

The Cookie-Based Shopping Cart Script If you use the cookie, the shopping cart script becomes much easier. You no longer need the functions Display_ Store_Page or Assign_Cart_Number, and the script only gets called when the user presses one of the push buttons. For the cookie-based shopping cart, you need subroutines for adding, displaying, and modifying as well as for checkout.

The Add_Items_To_Cart Subroutine When you use cookies, the Add_Items_To_Cart subroutine becomes very easy. Because multiple Set-Cookie parsed headers can be sent back to the Web browser, you just need to send a Set-Cookie for every item the user selected from your Web page. The Perl code in Listing 5.18 loops over all of the data received when the user pressed the Add Items to Cart push button and sends a Set-Cookie parsed header for each one. The cookie that is sent contains only the [NAME] and path attributes. The [NAME] attribute in each instance is the item description and price separated by the two colons. For example, if the user selected 3 reams of white paper, the Set-Cookie statement sent to the Web browser would look like this:

```
Set-Cookie: White 20lb, 1 Ream::5=3; path=/
```

Listing 5.18: The Add_Items_To_Cart Subroutine

```
sub Add_Items_To_Cart {
  local (%data) = @_;

  foreach $key (%data) {
    if (($key ne "submit") && ($data{$key} > 0)) {
      $data{'new_item'} .= "; " if $data{'new_item'};
      $data{'new_item'} .= "$key=$data{$key}";
      print "Set-Cookie: $key=$data{$key}; path=/\n";
    }
  }

  &Display_Cart_Contents(%data);
}
```

Within the foreach loop, two lines assign elements to the array element $data{'new_item'}. You will learn the purpose of these lines in the next section, which discusses the Display_Cart_Contents subroutine.

The Display_Cart_Contents Subroutine   The cookie version of the Display_Cart_Contents subroutine is a bit more challenging because of the three different ways it can be called: It can be called by the user pressing the View Cart Contents push button, it can be called at the end of the Add_Items_To_Cart subroutine, and it can be called at the end of the Modify_Cart_Contents subroutine. In the first instance, the contents of the HTTP_COOKIE environment variable will contain all of the items to be displayed. The raw data of the cart elements will be taken from the HTTP_COOKIE variable, instead of the shopping cart file as in the file version of the shopping cart. The foreach that loops over the elements of the @cart_raw array is only slightly different than the same loop in the file-based example. Replace the single split statement in the file-based example with the two lines

```
($item_price, $quantity) = split(/=/);
($item, $price) = split(/::/, $item_price);
```

These lines first split name/value pairs of the cookie and then split the [NAME] attribute at the two colons. Listing 5.19 contains the complete Perl code for the Display_Cart_Contents subroutine.

Listing 5.19: The Display_Cart_Contents Subroutine

```
sub Display_Cart_Contents {
  local (%data) = @_;
  local (@template, @cart_raw, @cart_contents, $item, $price,
         $item_price, $quantity, $cost, $sub);

  # Windows users need to change the string "$path/display.tmpl"
  # to "$path\\display.tmpl".
  open(TEMPLATE, "$path/display.tmpl") || die "Content-type:
text/html\n\nCannot open template!";
  @template = <TEMPLATE>;
  close(TEMPLATE);

  if ($data{'new_item'}) {
    $ENV{'HTTP_COOKIE'} .= "; " if $ENV{'HTTP_COOKIE'};
    $ENV{'HTTP_COOKIE'} .= $data{'new_item'}
  }

  $ENV{'HTTP_COOKIE'} = $data{'items'} if $data{'items'};
```

Listing 5.19: The Display_Cart_Contents Subroutine (Continued)

```perl
  @cart_raw = split(/; /, $ENV{'HTTP_COOKIE'});

  $sub = 0;
  foreach (@cart_raw) {
    ($item_price, $quantity) = split(/=/);
    ($item, $price) = split(/::/, $item_price);
    $cost = $price * $quantity;
    $sub += $cost;

    push(@cart_contents, "<TR>\n");
    push(@cart_contents, "<TD VALIGN=top ALIGN=left>$item</TD>\n");
    push(@cart_contents, "<TD VALIGN=top ALIGN=right>\$$price</TD>\n");
    push(@cart_contents, "<TD VALIGN=top ALIGN=left><INPUT TYPE=text
NAME=\"$item\:\:$price\" VALUE=\"$quantity\" SIZE=4></TD>\n");
    push(@cart_contents, "<TD VALIGN=top ALIGN=right>$cost</TD>\n");
    push(@cart_contents, "</TR>\n");
  }

  push(@cart_contents, "<TR>\n");
  push(@cart_contents, "<TD COLSPAN=4 ALIGN=right>Sub-Total =
\$$sub</TD>\n");
  push(@cart_contents, "</TR>\n");

  splice(@template, 16, 0, @cart_contents);
  print "Content-type: text/html\n\n";
  print @template;

}
```

When Display_Cart_Contents is called at the end of the Add_Item_To_Cart subroutine, the HTTP_COOKIE variable contains only the items that were previously in the cart, not the new items. The HTTP_COOKIE variable only reflects these additions the next time the script is called. To accommodate this situation, any items that have been added are placed in the $data{'new_item'} variable with the lines

```perl
$data{'new_item'} .= "; " if $data{'new_item'};
$data{'new_item'} .= "$key=$data{$key}";
```

in the Add_Items_To_Cart subroutine. Then, in Display_Cart_Contents, these items are appended to the HTTP_COOKIE variable in the lines

```perl
if ($data{'new_item'}) {
    $ENV{'HTTP_COOKIE'} .= "; " if $ENV{'HTTP_COOKIE'};
```

```
    $ENV{'HTTP_COOKIE'} .= $data{'new_item'}
}
```

By checking whether $data{'new_item'} is not empty, you guarantee that the lines appending information onto the HTTP_COOKIE environment variable only take place when the Display_Cart_Contents subroutine is called from the Add_Items_To_Cart subroutine.

A similar problem occurs when Display_Cart_Contents is called from the Modify_Cart_Contents subroutine. The HTTP_COOKIE variable no longer holds the current contents of the user's shopping cart. The user has requested changes that are not yet reflected in this variable. The Modify_Cart_Contents subroutine allows for this by creating a new version of the contents of the HTTP_COOKIE variable. This new version of the contents has been placed in the variable $data{'items'}. So, if the variable is not empty, Display_Cart_Contents is being called from the Modify_Cart_Contents subroutine and the contents of the HTTP_COOKIE variable must be replaced with the contents of the $data{'items'} variable. You do this with the following Perl code:

```
$ENV{'HTTP_COOKIE'} = $data{'items'} if $data{'items'};
```

The Modify_Cart_Contents Subroutine   Like Add_Items_To_Cart, the Modify_Cart_Contents subroutine just needs to loop over all of the items returned in the %data associative array and return a Set-Cookie parsed header for each one. In the file-based example, remember that you removed any items whose quantities had been changed to a value less than 0. In this case, you need to send a Set-Cookie parsed header with an expiration date in the past to remove these items. Listing 5.20 shows the Perl code for the Modify_Cart_Contents subroutine.

Listing 5.20: The Modify_Cart_Contents Subroutine

```
sub Modify_Cart_Contents {
  local (%data) = @_;

  foreach $key (%data) {
    if ($key ne "submit") {
      if ($data{$key} > 0) {
        $data{'items'} .= "; " if $data{'items'};
        $data{'items'} .= "$key=$data{$key}";
        print "Set-Cookie: $key=$data{$key}; path=/\n";
      } else {
        print "Set-Cookie: $key=$data{$key}; path=/; expires=Monday,
01-Jan-95 00:00:01\n";
      }
```

Listing 5.20: The Modify_Cart_Contents Subroutine (Continued)

```
    }
  }

  &Display_Cart_Contents(%data);
}
```

The section about the Display_Cart_Contents subroutine mentioned that the new contents for the HTTP_COOKIE variable were placed in the $data{'items'} variable. You do this with the following two lines of code:

```
$data{'items'} .= "; " if $data{'items'};
$data{'items'} .= "$key=$data{$key}";
```

The first line checks whether the variable already contains some items. If so, it appends a semicolon and space. The next line appends the next item to the list of all current items.

The Checkout Subroutine   As in the file-based shopping cart example, it's up to you to develop the contents of the Checkout subroutine. All the code for the Checkout subroutine would go after the declaration of local variables, as in

```
sub Checkout {
  local (%data) = @_;

  # Place your code here.
}
```

Putting It All Together: The ckcart.pl File   Now that you've finished all the subroutines for the cookie-based shopping cart, you can place them all together in a file called ckcart.pl. As in the file-based shopping cart, you need the Which_Post subroutine to call the appropriate subroutine, depending on which push button the user pressed. Because the ckcart.pl script does not need to be called with the GET method, you do not need to check the REQUEST_METHOD environment variable before calling this subroutine. Listing 5.21 contains the Perl code for the ckcart.pl file. Remember to remove the first line and make all noted changes if you are using it on a Windows system.

Listing 5.21: The ckcart.pl File

```
#!/usr/local/bin/perl

# Windows users will need to change this line
# to look like $path = "c:\\robertm";
```

Listing 5.21: The ckcart.pl File (Continued)

```perl
$path = "/users/robertm";
%data_received = &User_Data;
&No_SSI(*data_received);

&Which_Post(%data_received);

sub Which_Post {
  local (%data) = @_;

  &Display_Cart_Contents(%data) if $data{'submit'} eq "View Cart
Contents";
  &Add_Items_To_Cart(%data) if $data{'submit'} eq "Add Items to Cart";
  &Modify_Cart_Contents(%data) if $data{'submit'} eq "Make Changes";
  &Checkout(%data) if $data{'submit'} eq "Checkout";

}

sub Add_Items_To_Cart {
  local (%data) = @_;

  foreach $key (%data) {
    if (($key ne "submit") && ($data{$key} > 0)) {
      $data{'new_item'} .= "; " if $data{'new_item'};
      $data{'new_item'} .= "$key=$data{$key}";
      print "Set-Cookie: $key=$data{$key}; path=/\n";
    }
  }

  &Display_Cart_Contents(%data);
}

sub Modify_Cart_Contents {
  local (%data) = @_;

  foreach $key (%data) {
    if ($key ne "submit") {
      if ($data{$key} > 0) {
        $data{'items'} .= "; " if $data{'items'};
        $data{'items'} .= "$key=$data{$key}";
        print "Set-Cookie: $key=$data{$key}; path=/\n";
      } else {
        print "Set-Cookie: $key=$data{$key}; path=/; expires=Monday,
01-Jan-95 00:00:01\n";
      }
    }
  }
```

Listing 5.21: The ckcart.pl File (Continued)

```perl
  }

  &Display_Cart_Contents(%data);
}

sub Display_Cart_Contents {
  local (%data) = @_;
  local (@template, @cart_raw, @cart_contents, $item, $price,
         $item_price, $quantity, $cost, $sub);

  # Windows users need to change the string "$path/display.tmpl"
  # to "$path\\display.tmpl".
  open(TEMPLATE, "$path/display.tmpl") || die "Content-type:
text/html\n\nCannot open template!";
  @template = <TEMPLATE>;
  close(TEMPLATE);

  if ($data{'new_item'}) {
    $ENV{'HTTP_COOKIE'} .= "; " if $ENV{'HTTP_COOKIE'};
    $ENV{'HTTP_COOKIE'} .= $data{'new_item'}
  }

  $ENV{'HTTP_COOKIE'} = $data{'items'} if $data{'items'};
  @cart_raw = split(/; /, $ENV{'HTTP_COOKIE'});

  $sub = 0;
  foreach (@cart_raw) {
    ($item_price, $quantity) = split(/=/);
    ($item, $price) = split(/::/, $item_price);
    $cost = $price * $quantity;
    $sub += $cost;

    push(@cart_contents, "<TR>\n");
    push(@cart_contents, "<TD VALIGN=top ALIGN=left>$item</TD>\n");
    push(@cart_contents, "<TD VALIGN=top ALIGN=right>\$$price</TD>\n");
    push(@cart_contents, "<TD VALIGN=top ALIGN=left><INPUT TYPE=text
NAME=\"$item\:\:$price\" VALUE=\"$quantity\" SIZE=4></TD>\n");
    push(@cart_contents, "<TD VALIGN=top ALIGN=right>$cost</TD>\n");
    push(@cart_contents, "</TR>\n");
  }

  push(@cart_contents, "<TR>\n");
  push(@cart_contents, "<TD COLSPAN=4 ALIGN=right>Sub Total =
\$$sub</TD>\n");
  push(@cart_contents, "</TR>\n");
```

Listing 5.21: The ckcart.pl File (Continued)

```perl
    splice(@template, 16, 0, @cart_contents);
    print "Content-type: text/html\n\n";
    print @template;

}

sub Checkout {
  local (%data) = @_;

  #Place your code here.
}

sub No_SSI {
  local (*data) = @_;

  foreach $key (sort keys(%data)) {
    $data{$key} =~ s/<!--(.|\n)*-->//g;
  }


}

sub User_Data {
  local (%user_data, $user_string, $name_value_pair,
         @name_value_pairs, $name, $value);

  # If the data was sent via POST, then it is available
  # from standard input. Otherwise, the data is in the
  # QUERY_STRING environment variable.
  if ($ENV{'REQUEST_METHOD'} eq "POST") {
    read(STDIN,$user_string,$ENV{'CONTENT_LENGTH'});
  } else {
    $user_string = $ENV{'QUERY_STRING'};
  }

  # This line changes the + signs to spaces.
  $user_string =~ s/\+/ /g;

  # This line places each name/value pair as a separate
  # element in the name_value_pairs array.
  @name_value_pairs = split(/&/, $user_string);

  # This code loops over each element in the name_value_pairs
  # array, splits it on the = sign, and places the value
  # into the user_data associative array with the name as the
```

Listing 5.21: The ckcart.pl File (Continued)

```perl
# key.
foreach $name_value_pair (@name_value_pairs) {
  ($name, $value) = split(/=/, $name_value_pair);

  # These two lines decode the values from any URL
  # hexadecimal encoding. The first section searches for a
  # hexadecimal number and the second part converts the
  # hex number to decimal and returns the character
  # equivalent.
  $name =~
    s/%([a-fA-F0-9][a-fA-F0-9])/pack("C",hex($1))/ge;
  $value =~
    s/%([a-fA-F0-9][a-fA-F0-9])/pack("C",hex($1))/ge;

  # If the name/value pair has already been given a value,
  # as in the case of multiple items being selected, then
  # separate the items with a " : ".
  if (defined($user_data{$name})) {
    $user_data{$name} .= " : " . $value;
  } else {
    $user_data{$name} = $value;
  }
}
return %user_data;
}
```

Adding an Access Counter

A TEXT ACCESS COUNTER

A GRAPHICAL ACCESS COUNTER

Chapter 6

As mentioned in Chapter 1, CGI programs can make your Web pages dynamic, and one popular application of CGI is the addition of an access counter. An access counter is a text or graphical representation of the number of times that your Web page has been requested. Access counters work either by including a CGI script within an HTML page with Server Side Includes or the <IMG> tag, or by generating the entire HTML page from a CGI script. When a user requests the HTML page containing an access counter, the CGI script checks the current access count, increments it by one, and displays the results in the Web page. Many Web sites have added access counters to their home pages. Figure 6.1 displays some ways that access counters can be displayed.

As shown in the figure, access counters can be displayed as text or as an image file representing the value of the counter. As you might imagine, the graphical version requires more work in the CGI script than simply displaying the value of the counter as text. To display the graphic, you must either have a graphic file for every possible number the counter can reach or you must construct the graphical image from several image files. If you use the latter method, you only need to store 10 files, one for each digit 0 through 9. Then, when necessary, your CGI script creates the image file by putting together the separate GIF graphic files into a single GIF that the browser displays. For example, when the access counter is at 986, the CGI script takes the individual GIF files of the digits 9, 8, and 6 and combines them into one GIF that is the combination of all three. GIF image files are just one of many image file formats. Two other types of image file types that you can work with are JPEG and

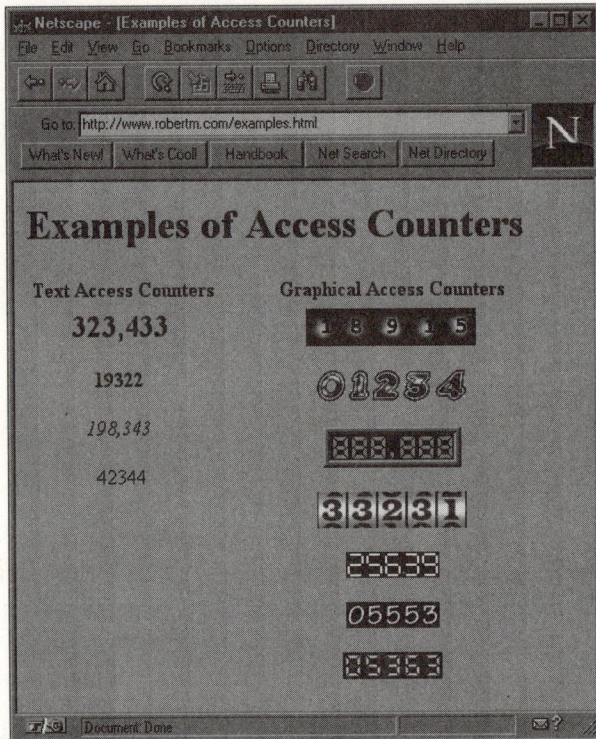

Figure 6.1: Access counters

XBM images, because many Web browsers can display them. However, this chapter uses GIF image files, as you'll see in the section "A Graphical Access Counter" later in this chapter.

This chapter starts with an example text access counter. You should read this section even if you want to create a graphical access counter, because the basic functionality of the two types of counters is the same. The second half of the chapter explains how to create a graphical access counter. In this case, the process is a bit more challenging, but the results are a lot more impressive.

A TEXT ACCESS COUNTER

The text access counter displays the count number in plain text within the HTML page. Figure 6.1 displayed several text and graphical access counters. Because the text counter uses plain text, it is much easier to implement than a graphical counter. The biggest decision is how to call the access counter script.

It's easiest to do this with Server Side Includes, but not all systems have Server Side Includes enabled. The following sections describe how to create the text access counter script and explain two different ways of adding it to your Web pages.

CREATING THE COUNTER SCRIPT

Before starting your CGI script, you should spend a moment thinking about what it must do. The script needs access to the current value of the access counter. For this information to be available, you must store it in a text file. Every time your text access counter script is called, it opens the counter file in which the current access count is stored, increments the access count, and saves the new number in the counter file. After the counter value has been incremented, the number is included in the Web page.

The Increment subroutine   Your text access counter first needs to read in the current access count, which is stored in the counter file. In this chapter, the text file containing the access count is named count.dat. You can read in the value stored in count.dat simply by opening the file and reading the first line into the variable $count,, as in the following lines of Perl code:

```
open(COUNT, "$file") || die "Content-type: text/html\n\nCannot open counter
file!";
$count = <COUNT>;
close(COUNT);
```

The first line opens the file whose name is stored in the variable $file. You set this variable when you put together the entire text access counter script shown in Listing 6.2. For now, just note that $file will contain the path and name of the file that stores the current number of accesses to your Web page. The second part of the first line of Perl code contains a die statement that will terminate the program and output the contents of the string:

```
Content-type: text/html\n\nCannot open counter file!
```

The || operator between the open and die statements is the logical OR operator. When this operator is between the two statements, the Perl interpreter first tries to execute the open statement. If the open is successful, the Perl interpreter moves on to the next line of code. However, if the file cannot be opened, the Perl interpreter executes the die statement. This is a common way to verify that a file is successfully opened and to terminate the Perl program if it is not.

The second line of code reads in the contents of the first line of the counter file from the input stream <COUNT> and places it into the variable $count. After the line has been read in from the file, you can close the input stream <COUNT> by using the close command, as in the third line of code.

Now that you have the code to get the current value of the access counter, you need to increment the value and write the new value to the counter file. You can easily increment the value by using the ++ operator. If you append this operator to a variable name, the integer value stored in the variable is increased by 1. For example, if the current value of the access counter were 2, the Perl code

```
$count++;
```

would change the value to 3.

Once the access count has been incremented, you need to store the new value in the counter file for the next time the script is called. The following three lines of Perl code open the counter file and write the new access count to the file:

```
open(COUNT, ">$file") || die "Content-type: text/html\n\nCannot open counter
file!";
print COUNT $count;
close(COUNT);
```

Again, you use the open statement to open the counter file. However, this time you output to the file instead of receiving input from the file. Notice the > operator before the $file variable in the open statement. This operator opens the file for output. If the file already exists, it is overwritten. The second line prints the contents of the $count variable into the file.

You now have all the code necessary to read in the current access count, increment it, and write it back to the file. To make your code easier to read, place it within a subroutine called Increment. Listing 6.1 shows the contents of the Increment subroutine.

Listing 6.1: The Increment Subroutine

```
sub Increment {
  local ($count);

  # Get the current value of the access counter.
  open(COUNT, "$file") || die "Content-type: text/html\n\nCannot open
counter file!";
  $count = <COUNT>;
  close(COUNT);

  # Increment the access counter

  $count++;
```

Listing 6.1: The Increment Subroutine (Continued)

```
# Store the value of the counter in the counter file.
open(COUNT, ">$file") || die "Content-type: text/html\n\nCannot open
counter file!";
print COUNT $count;
close(COUNT);

return $count;
}
```

Besides the sub Increment line, which declares the subroutine, the only lines of code that have been added are the local statement at the beginning and the return statement at the end. The local statement,

```
local ($count);
```

declares that the $count variable is local only to the Increment subroutine. A local variable is a variable that exists only within a portion of your Perl code, usually within a subroutine. If a variable with the same name existed outside the subroutine, Perl would consider it a different variable than the one that is declared local within the subroutine. Declaring your subroutine's variables as local helps to keep your subroutines from overwriting values of global variables. A global variable is one that is accessible throughout the entire Perl program, including any subroutines in the same Perl file. In Listing 6.1, the variable $file is a global variable. Listing 6.2 in the next section will show where this variable is set.

The other line of Perl code added to your Increment subroutine is the return statement

```
return $count;
```

This statement causes the subroutine to return the current value of the count as its return value. In Perl, every subroutine returns a value. You can set this return value explicitly by using the return statement. The next section demonstrates how this return value is used.

The complete text access counter script Now that it can increment the counter, your script just needs to return the value of the counter for display in the Web page. You can do this by using the following three lines of Perl:

```
$access_number = &Increment;
print "Content-type: text/html\n\n";
print $access_number;
```

The first line calls the Increment subroutine and assigns the return value to the variable $access_number. The next line prints the required parsed header. The last line prints the value of the access counter.

You can place the preceding lines of Perl code, along with the code for the Increment subroutine, in a file called access.pl. Listing 6.2 shows the complete access.pl file. Notice that the global variable $file is set at the beginning of the file and is used within the Increment subroutine. Also, if you use this counter on a machine running a version of Windows, remove the first line and change the path for the count.dat file.

Listing 6.2: The access.pl file

```perl
#!/usr/local/bin/perl

# All users need to change the value of this
# variable to the path for their machine. Windows
# users need to use a format similar to
# "c:\\robertm\\count.dat"
$file = "/users/robertm/count.dat";

$access_number = &Increment;
print "Content-type: text/html\n\n";
print $access_number;

sub Increment {
  local ($count);

  # Get the current value of the access counter.
  open(COUNT, "$file") || die "Content-type: text/html\n\nCannot open
  counter file!";
  $count = <COUNT>;
  close(COUNT);

  # Increment the access counter
;
  $count++;

  # Store the value of the counter in the counter file.
  open(COUNT, ">$file") || die "Content-type: text/html\n\nCannot open
  counter file!";
  print COUNT $count;
  close(COUNT);

  return $count;
}
```

SEEDING THE COUNTER

Before you can use your access counter, you need to supply the file count.dat with the initial count value. This is called seeding the counter. Normally, you can simply create a text file with the number 0 on the first line. This will start your counter at zero. The first person visiting your Web page with the counter would see the access number 1. (For the graphical counter script, you need to seed the count.dat file with the number 1 for the first person visiting your Web page to see the access number 1. You'll learn why in the section "A Graphical Access Counter" later in this chapter.) If you want to start your counter at a higher number, just change the first line of the count.dat file to that number. For example, if your Web page has already been accessed 342 times, create a text file named count.dat with the number 342 on the first line (use 343 for the graphical counter).

ADDING THE COUNTER TO YOUR HTML PAGE

With the access.pl and count.dat files completed, you are now ready to add the counter to your Web page. The easiest way to do so is to use a Server Side Include. However, after reading about security issues in Chapter 3 you may have disabled Server Side Includes on your system. Or you may be using a Web server on which the administrator has turned off Server Side Includes and does not wish to re-enable them. For these reasons, this section also describes an alternative way of adding your text access counter that doesn't require a Server Side Include. This technique takes more work to implement, however, because you have to make changes to the access.pl script.

With Server Side Includes   As mentioned, it's easiest to implement your text access counter using Server Side Includes. Simply choose which Web page you want to display your counter and add some surrounding text and the following Server Side Include:

```
<!--#exec cgi="/cgi-bin/access.pl" -->
```

If Server Side Includes are enabled on your Web server, the Web server will parse this line before sending it to the user's Web browser. The CGI script access.pl is executed and the output from the script is substituted for the preceding line in the HTML.

For example, the following HTML code demonstrates how to add the Server Side Include statement to your existing HTML page:

```
<HTML>
<HEAD>
<TITLE>Example of Text Access Counter</TITLE>
</HEAD>
```

```
<BODY>
<H1>Text Access Counter</H1>
This is my Home page. Thank you for visiting. Please come again.
<P>This page has been accessed
<!--#exec cgi="/cgi-bin/access.pl" -->
 times.
</BODY>
</HTML>
```

As you can see, the Server Side Include was added along with some surrounding text to explain what the number represents. The surrounding text is "This page has been accessed *x* times." The *x* represents where the Web server would insert the value returned by your access.pl script. Figure 6.2 shows how the HTML page will appear when the access count is 13.

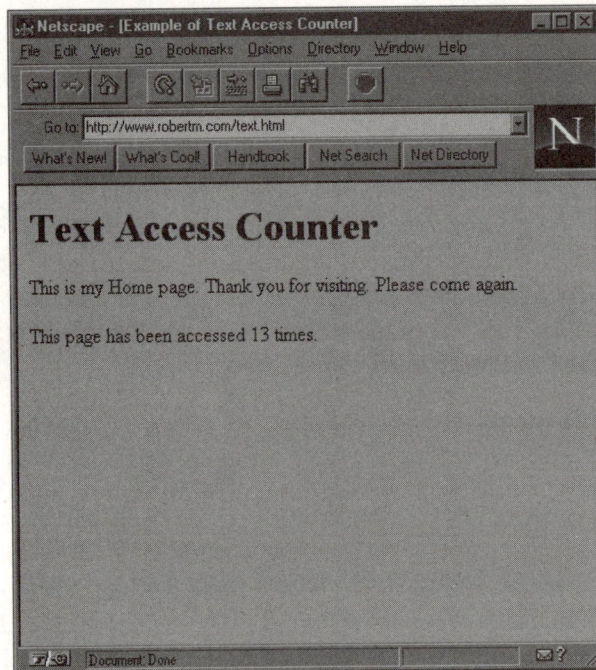

Figure 6.2: The text access counter

Without Server Side Includes Suppose you want to use the text access counter without using a Server Side Include. It is still possible, but you have to generate the entire page from your CGI script. You can change your HTML page to a template and have your CGI script read in the template, place the current value of the counter within the template, and output the entire page to the user's Web browser.

Creating the Template File   The first thing to do is to change the HTML file, which you want to contain the counter, into a template file. Do this by changing the file's extension to .tmpl (.tmp if you want to use a three-character extension). Then edit the file, inserting the text that will surround the counter value. Use the value XXXX as a placeholder for where you will insert the access count. For example, using the HTML from the preceding example, you would place the HTML code in a file called text.tmpl, whose contents are shown here:

```
<HTML>
<HEAD>
<TITLE>Example of Text Access Counter</TITLE>
</HEAD>
<BODY>
<H1>Text Access Counter</H1>
This is my Home page. Thank you for visiting. Please come again.
<P>This page has been accessed XXXX times.
</BODY>
</HTML>
```

Modifying the access.pl Script   After you have created the template file, you must modify your access.pl script to open the template file, read in the contents, change the XXXX placeholder into the current access count, and output the HTML code to the Web browser. It is easiest to add this code in a subroutine called Display_Page and simply call the subroutine after the counter has been incremented. Listing 6.3 contains the Perl code for this subroutine.

Listing 6.3: The Display_Page Subroutine

```
sub Display_Page {
  local ($count) = @_;

  # All users need to change the following path
  # to be correct for their system. Windows users
  # need it in the form "c:\\robertm\\text.tmpl".
  local ($html) = "/users/robertm/text.tmpl";
  local (@template);

  open(TEMPLATE, "$html") || die "Content-type: text/html \n\nCannot
  open template!";
  @template = <TEMPLATE>;
  close(TEMPLATE);
```

Listing 6.3: The Display_Page Subroutine (Continued)

```perl
# Be sure to change the index number to the correct one
# for your HTML template. Count down from the first line
# being at 0 to the line containing the XXXX placeholder.
$template[7] =~ s/XXXX/$count/e;

print "Content-type: text/html\n\n";
print @template;

}
```

The Display_Page subroutine begins by declaring the two variables and one array that will be local to this subroutine. The variable $html stores the name and path to the template file that the access counter will be added to. Then the template file is opened and all of its contents are read into the @template array. In this example, the placeholder for the access number XXXX is on the eighth line of text.tmpl file. When the file is read into the array, the eighth line is placed in the eighth element of the @template array. Because the index of Perl arrays begins with 0, the eighth element is at index 7. So, the statement

```perl
$template[7] =~ s/XXXX/$count/e;
```

takes the eighth element of the @template array and replaces the access number placeholder with the current count. If you use this subroutine for your HTML template, you need to change the index of the @template array element to the correct index for your template file.

After the placeholder for the access count is changed to the actual count number, the required parsed header and the contents of the @template array are returned to the user's Web browser. Because this entire page is being generated from the CGI script, you need to change all the links to this page to call your CGI script, access.pl, which should now be modified to contain the new Display_Page subroutine. Listing 6.4 is the Perl code for the new access.pl script. Notice how the two lines that previously output the parsed header and the access count have been replaced with a call to the Display_Page subroutine. Don't forget to modify the paths for the $file and $html variables to contain the correct paths for your system. Also, Windows users must remember to remove the first line of the script file. Figure 6.3 shows how Netscape displays a call to the modified access.pl script when the counter value is 13. Notice that the page looks the same as the one in Figure 6.2, which is called with a Server Side Include.

Listing 6.4: The modified access.pl script

```
#!/usr/local/bin/perl

# All users need to change the value of this
# variable to the path for their machine. Windows
# users need to use a format similar to
# "c:\\robertm\\count.dat"
$file = "/users/robertm/count.dat";

$access_number = &Increment;
&Display_Page($access_number);

sub Increment {
  local ($count);

  # Get the current value of the access counter.
  open(COUNT, "$file") || die "Content-type: text/html\n\nCannot open
  counter file!";
  $count = <COUNT>;
  close(COUNT);

  # Increment the access counter

  $count++;

  # Store the value of the counter in the counter file.
  open(COUNT, ">$file") || die "Content-type: text/html\n\nCannot open
  counter file!";
  print COUNT $count;
  close(COUNT);

  return $count;
}

sub Display_Page {
  local ($count) = @_;

  # All users need to change the following path
  # to be correct for their system. Windows users
  # need it in the form "c:\\robertm\\text.tmpl".
  local ($html) = "/users/robertm/text.tmpl";
  local (@template);

  open(TEMPLATE, "$html") || die "Content-type: text/html\n\nCannot
  open template!";
```

Listing 6.4: The modified access.pl script (Continued)

```perl
@template = <TEMPLATE>;
close(TEMPLATE);

# Be sure to change the index number to the correct one
# for your HTML template. Count down from the first line
# being at Ø to the line containing the XXXX placeholder.
$template[7] =~ s/XXXX/$count/e;

print "Content-type: text/html\n\n";
print @template;

}
```

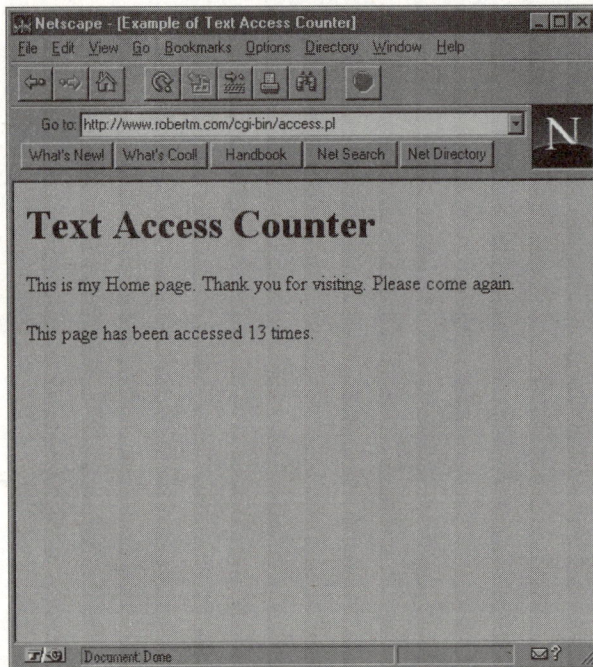

Figure 6.3: The results of the modified access.pl

A GRAPHICAL ACCESS COUNTER

The graphical access counter presents more challenges than the text counter. The graphical counter has the same basic functionality as the text access counter, such as reading in the counter value from the counter file, incrementing the counter value, and saving the value in the counter file. However, it must also create a graphical image that is a representation of the access count. For example, if the access count were 293, the graphical access counter would return an image containing the number 293.

The easiest way to accomplish this is to have a GIF file for every possible number the access counter can reach. For example, if the counter value were 769, your graphical counter script would only have to return the GIF file containing the number 769. However, doing the counter this way wastes a great deal of disk space. If your access counter only goes up to 1,000, you have to create and save 1,000 different GIF files on your Web server. Even if these files are 1K or less apiece, this still amounts to nearly 1 megabyte in disk storage. Maybe 1 megabyte doesn't seem like that big of a deal to you, but keep in mind that 1,000 accesses on the World Wide Web is a very small number. Realistically, if you have a moderately popular site, you want your counter to reach at least 100,000. It would take a tremendous amount of disk space and a lot of time to create files for this many numbers.

The more difficult method for returning a graphical image for the counter value is to create the graphical image dynamically from ten existing GIF files for the digits 0 through 9. Your CGI script would construct the graphical counter image from these digits by combining the GIF files in a new image. For example, if the counter value were 769, your CGI script would take the digit file for the 7, append the digit file for the 6, and then append the digit file for the 9, creating a GIF image representing the number 769.

As you can imagine, this approach is much more difficult than the text access counter example. To write the code for this GIF creation, you need to know quite a bit about the GIF file format and must be able to write routines that create a single GIF image from multiple existing GIF files. Although you could probably learn how to do this, there is a easier way.

Recall from Chapter 3 that one of the reasons to use a common language for CGI scripting is to be able to use library routines written by other people. Well, now is a perfect time to take advantage of one such library. Thomas Boutell has written a graphics library of functions in C that handle GIF creation and manipulation. This library, called gd, is available from http://www.boutell.com/gd/. His only restriction on the use of the gd library is that the credit and copyright given to the Quest Protein Database Center, Cold Spring Harbor Labs remain intact in all derived works. In other words, if you distribute the gd graphics library files with your code you cannot remove the copyright lines in the gd files. Although Lincoln Stein has written a Perl interface to the gd graphics library called GD.pm, the following graphical access counter does not use GD.pm. To use GD.pm, you must still download and install the gd graphics library, and GD.pm may not be easily installed on all systems. For this reason, the C programming language is used to create the graphical counter script for this graphical access counter example.

Before you start creating the graphical counter script, you should download and install the gd graphics library. You can download the source files from Thomas Boutell's Web site, http://www.boutell.com/gd/. Once you have downloaded and uncompressed the source files for gd, you should find a README file that contains directions for installing the graphics library.

Most of the code for the graphical access counter script is logically similar to the code for the text access counter. There is one major difference, however. In the text access counter example, the counter file contained the current count. When the text access counter script is called, it increments the counter value before displaying it in the Web page. The graphical counter, in contrast, stores the next counter value in the counter file instead of the current counter value. When the graphical counter script is called, it displays the value read from the file as the current count, not the incremented value. This makes it easier to create the GIF image, as explained in more detail in the section "Creating the GIF Image."

INCREMENTING THE COUNTER

Incrementing the graphical access counter is similar to incrementing the text access counter. However, the C code for the graphical counter looks dramatically different than the Perl code for the text access counter. Listing 6.5 contains the C code that reads in the counter value from the counter file, increments the value, and writes the new counter value to the counter file.

Listing 6.5: The C code for incrementing the counter

```
/* Counter file handle */
FILE *counter;

/* string version of counter file value */
  char s_count[20];

/* Counter file
    All users need to change the path to the actual
    path for their machines. Windows users need to
```

Listing 6.5: The C code for incrementing the counter (Continued)

```c
    use a path in the form "c:\\robertm\\count.dat" */
char *cnt_file = "/users/robertm/count.dat";

  /* integer version of count */
int count;

/* open the counter file */
counter = fopen(cnt_file, "r");

/* check whether the file was opened successfully */
if (!counter) {
  printf("Content-type: text/html\n\nCannot open counter file!\n");
  return(0);
} else {
  /* if the file was opened, read in the string containing the count */
  fgets(s_count, 20, counter);
  fclose(counter);

  /* extract the integer value of the count from the string */
  sscanf(s_count, "%d", &count);

  /* increment the count */
  count++;

  /* open the count file for output */
  counter = fopen(cnt_file, "w");

  /* check whether the file was opened successfully */
  if (!counter) {
    printf("Content-type: text/html\n\nCannot open counter file!\n");
    return(0);
  } else {
    /* if the file was opened, write the count value to it */
    fprintf(counter, "%d", count);
    fclose(counter);
  }
}
```

The first several lines define the variables that will be used in this code. After the variable declarations, the counter file is opened with the line

```c
counter = fopen(cnt_file, "r");
```

This line opens an input stream, named counter, to the file whose name and path are in the cnt_file variable. The "r" string designates that the file will be opened for input only. It is always a good idea to verify whether the file has been successfully opened. The line

```
if (!counter) {
```

does this by making sure that the counter holds a nonzero value. If the file cannot be opened, the counter variable is set to 0. If counter is equal to 0, the first part of the if...else statement executes. In this section, you output an error message that the file could not be opened.

Under the else portion of the if...else, the access counter value is read in from the file with the line

```
fgets(s_count, 20, counter);
```

This statement reads up to 20 characters from the file pointed to by the counter variable and places the characters in the s_count string. (Actually, s_count is an array of characters, which is the C equivalent of a string.)

After the access counter value is read from the file, the stream to the file is closed. The next line

```
sscanf(s_count, "%d", &count);
```

converts the counter value from a string to an integer and stores the integer value in the count variable, which can then be incremented with the

```
count++;
```

statement.

Finally, the counter file is once more opened, and the incremented value of the access count is written to the file. Notice how the open statement

```
counter = fopen(cnt_file, "w");
```

has the string "w" rather than the string "r". The "w" means to open the file for output. The value of the access counter is written to the file with the line

```
fprintf(counter, "%d", count);
```

which prints the decimal value of the count variable into the file pointed to by the counter variable, which is the access counter file.

CREATING THE GIF IMAGE

Once the counter value has been read in from the count.dat file, the GIF image can be created. Recall that you create the GIF image from the counter value you read in from the file, not from the incremented value. This is because the incremented version is stored in an integer, and it is easier to create the GIF based on a value stored in a string. Remember, a string in C is actually an array of characters. So, if the counter value is 769, the s_count variable contains the string 769. Each individual digit can easily be accessed by addressing the specific array element. For example, the first digit, 7, can be accessed by using the variable s_count[0], which is the first element in the s_count array. In this way, you can loop over each digit in the counter value and append the corresponding GIF image file to the GIF image you are creating. With the 769 example, you would first add the contents of the 7 GIF image file, next the contents of the 6 GIF image file, and then the contents of the 9 GIF image file.

Before looping over the s_count array and creating the new GIF image, you must either create or download the ten GIF images representing each digit. For this example, the ten GIF images have been downloaded from the Digit Mania Web site, http://cervantes.learningco.com/kevin/digits/index.html. This Web site contains many digit styles for use in graphical access counter programs. The style used here is the tiny style, which was created by Muhammad A. Muquit. Each one of these GIF digits is a 9-pixel wide by 13-pixel high image. To implement this example exactly as shown, you need to download these images and place them in a directory that your graphical counter CGI script can access.

Now that you have the ten GIF images, one for each digit, you can write the C code for creating the graphical counter image that will be displayed within your Web page. First you must create a blank version of the graphical counter image that is the same width and height as your final image. By doing this, you allocate the memory necessary to store the final graphical counter image and you create the image to which the individual digit images can be copied. Because the digit images will each be 13 pixels high, your final image will also be 13 pixels high. However, the width must be calculated based on the number of digits the number contains. Remember that the length of the s_count array is also the number of digits your graphical counter image will contain. Therefore, you can calculate the width of your final image by multiplying the length of the s_count array by the width of each individual digit image, which in this case is 9 pixels. You can do this with the code

```
width = strlen(s_count) * real_width;
```

where real_width is an integer that is set to 9 earlier in the program. Listings 6.6 and 6.7 later in this chapter show where the real_width variable is set.

After you have calculated the dimensions of the graphical counter image, you can use the gdImageCreate function from the gd library to create the new graphical counter image. This function takes two parameters, a width and height, and creates a blank GIF image with the specified dimensions. The C statement

```
im_final = gdImageCreate(width, real_height);
```

calls the gdImageCreate function, passing it the width value that was just calculated and the height of the individual digit images, which is stored in the variable real_height. Listings 6.7 and 6.8 will show the code that sets the real_height variable to 13, which is the height for the tiny style digit images. Notice that the return value of the function gdImageCreate is assigned to the variable im_final. This variable is a pointer to the image that was just created, and it is through this variable that you will reference the image later on in the code.

Next you need to loop over the array s_count and append the digit image files to the im_final image you just created. The loop you use will be similar to the for loops used in Perl. The line

```
for (i=0; i < strlen(s_count); i++) {
```

starts the for loop. The loop executes once for every element in the s_count array and the variable i represents the index of the current s_count array element. For example, if s_count holds the string 769, the for loop executes three times. The first time, the i variable is 0, so the first digit of the s_count array can be accessed by using the variable s_count[i]. As i is incremented, the variable s_count[i] moves to the next elements in the array. For each iteration of the loop, you should check the value of the s_count[i] array element, open the digit image file that corresponds to that value, and append the contents of that digit's GIF image file to the graphical counter image you are creating. Listing 6.6 shows the C code for the entire for loop.

Listing 6.6: The graphical counter for loop

```
for (i=0; i < strlen(s_count); i++) {
  switch (s_count[i]) {
    case '0':
      image = fopen(zero_gif, "rb");
      break;
    case '1':
      image = fopen(one_gif, "rb");
      break;
    case '2':
      image = fopen(two_gif, "rb");
      break;
    case '3':
```

Listing 6.6: The graphical counter for loop (Continued)

```
      image = fopen(three_gif, "rb");
      break;
    case '4':
      image = fopen(four_gif, "rb");
      break;
    case '5':
      image = fopen(five_gif, "rb");
      break;
    case '6':
      image = fopen(six_gif, "rb");
      break;
    case '7':
      image = fopen(seven_gif, "rb");
      break;
    case '8':
      image = fopen(eight_gif, "rb");
      break;
    case '9':
      image = fopen(nine_gif, "rb");
      break;
    default :
      break;
  }

  if (!image) {
    printf("Content-type: text/html\n\nCannot open image file!\n");
    return(0);
  } else {
    im_file = gdImageCreateFromGif(image);
    fclose(image);
    gdImageCopy(im_final, im_file,
                destx, 0, 0, 0, real_width, real_height);
    destx += real_width;
    gdImageDestroy(im_file);
  }
}
```

The first section of the for loop uses the switch conditional, which compares the value of the s_count[i] array element with each case until a match is found. When a matching case is found, the code under the case is executed. If no match is found, the code under the default is executed. For example, if the s_count array contains 769, the first iteration of the loop would have the s_count[i] element equal to 7. The switch would·execute the code under the case '7': line, which is

```
image = fopen(seven_gif, "rb");
break;
```

The first line opens the 7 digit's GIF image file, whose path and file name are stored in the seven_gif variable. The code setting this variable is shown in Listings 6.6 and 6.7. The difference between this fopen statement, and the ones in the previous section is the "rb" string. This string specifies to open the file for binary input.

At the end of the switch statement, an if...else conditional verifies that the image file has been successfully opened. In the else portion of the conditional, the digit image is appended to the graphical counter image being created. This is done with the following lines of code:

```
im_file = gdImageCreateFromGif(image);
fclose(image);
gdImageCopy(im_final, im_file,
                  destx, 0, 0, 0, real_width, real_height);
destx += real_width;
gdImageDestroy(im_file);
```

The first line creates a new gd graphical image from the digit's GIF image file. The pointer im_file points to this image. After the im_file image has been created, you can close the stream to the file with the fclose statement. The statement

```
gdImageCopy(im_final, im_file,
                  destx, 0, 0, 0, real_width, real_height);
```

appends the digit's image just read in from the image file to the graphical counter image that is being constructed. The parameters for gdImageCopy are the following: a pointer to the destination image, a pointer to the source image, the x coordinate in the destination image to start placing the copy, the y coordinate in the destination image to start placing the copy, the x coordinate in the source image to begin the copy, the y coordinate in the source image to begin the copy, the number of pixels to copy in the x direction, the number of pixels to copy in the y direction. In this statement, the destination image is the graphical counter image you are creating, which is pointed to with the im_final variable. The source image is the image that was just read in from the digit's GIF file, and is pointed to with the im_file. The x coordinate for the destination of the copy is a variable, destx. This variable is increased after each iteration of the loop, in the line

```
destx += real_width;
```

For example, with the s_count array containing 769, the first iteration copies the 7 digit's GIF image file to the im_final image. Because this is the first image being copied, the x coordinate in the destination image is 0. However, on the next iteration of the loop, the im_final image already contains the 7 digit. So, the x coordinate has to be moved over 9 pixels. Why 9 pixels? Because that is the width of each individual digit's GIF image. After the 6 digit's image file is added to the im_final image, the destx variable is increased by another 9 pixels. So, when the 9 digit is added to the im_final image, the destx variable is 18, which is the sum of the widths of the previous two digits 7 and 6. Finally, after the im_file image is appended to the im_final image, the im_file image is destroyed with the gdImageDestroy command. Listing 6.7 shows the all of the C code for creating the graphical counter image.

Listing 6.7: The C code for creating the graphical counter image

```
/* Image file handle */
FILE *image;

/* Input and output images */
gdImagePtr im_file, im_final;

/* Image files
     All users need to change the paths to the actual
     paths for their machines. Windows users need to
     use paths in the form "c:\\robertm\\0tiny.gif" */
char *zero_gif = "/users/robertm/0tiny.gif";
char *one_gif = "/users/robertm/1tiny.gif";
char *two_gif = "/users/robertm/2tiny.gif";
char *three_gif = "/users/robertm/3tiny.gif";
char *four_gif = "/users/robertm/4tiny.gif";
char *five_gif = "/users/robertm/5tiny.gif";
char *six_gif = "/users/robertm/6tiny.gif";
char *seven_gif = "/users/robertm/7tiny.gif";
char *eight_gif = "/users/robertm/8tiny.gif";
char *nine_gif = "/users/robertm/9tiny.gif";

/* string version of counter file value */
char s_count[20];

/* width of image created image,
   x position for new image, and loop variable */
int width;
int destx = 0;
int i;

/* the real_height is the height (in pixels) for all of the image files.
   the real_width is the width (in pixels) for all of the image files. */
```

Listing 6.7: The C code for creating the graphical counter image (Continued)

```
int real_height = 13;
int real_width = 9;

width = strlen(s_count) * real_width;
im_final = gdImageCreate(width, real_height);

for (i=0; i < strlen(s_count); i++) {
  switch (s_count[i]) {
    case '0':
      image = fopen(zero_gif, "rb");
      break;
    case '1':
      image = fopen(one_gif, "rb");
      break;
    case '2':
      image = fopen(two_gif, "rb");
      break;
    case '3':
      image = fopen(three_gif, "rb");
      break;
    case '4':
      image = fopen(four_gif, "rb");
      break;
    case '5':
      image = fopen(five_gif, "rb");
      break;
    case '6':
      image = fopen(six_gif, "rb");
      break;
    case '7':
      image = fopen(seven_gif, "rb");
      break;
    case '8':
      image = fopen(eight_gif, "rb");
      break;
    case '9':
      image = fopen(nine_gif, "rb");
      break;
    default :
      break;
  }

  if (!image) {
    printf("Content-type: text/html\n\nCannot open image file!\n");
    return(0);
  } else {
    im_file = gdImageCreateFromGif(image);
    fclose(image);
    gdImageCopy(im_final, im_file,
```

Listing 6.7: The C code for creating the graphical counter image (Continued)

```
                    destx, 0, 0, 0, real_width, real_height);
        destx += real_width;
        gdImageDestroy(im_file);
    }
}
```

RETURNING THE GRAPHICAL COUNTER IMAGE

Now that the counter value is incremented and saved to the file and the graphical counter image is created, you are ready to return the graphical counter image from your CGI script. Just before returning the image, you can call the gd library function

```
gdImageInterlace(im_final, 1);
```

which interlaces the im_final image. Interlacing displays the GIF image incrementally as it is downloaded in certain Web browsers that support interlaced GIFs. An interlaced GIF first appears somewhat distorted and then gradually become more clear as the remainder of the file is downloaded across the Internet. When you use interlaced GIF images, the users viewing your Web pages see an image more quickly, even if it's a little distorted. This makes it appear as though the whole image is downloading more quickly. Because the graphical counter image is not very large, interlacing is not imperative. However, if you used one of the larger digit styles available from the Digit Mania Web page, you would probably want to interlace your image.

Before outputting the graphical counter image, you must return a parsed header, as you did for the text access counter. However, the parsed header for the graphical image counter needs to specify that the data being returned is a GIF image. The following lines output the parsed header and the graphical counter image.

```
printf("Content-type: image/gif\n\n");
gdImageGif(im_final, stdout);
```

With the graphical counter image returned for inclusion in your Web page, you can now destroy the im_final image with the statement

```
gdImageDestroy(im_final);
```

You should always call the gdImageDestroy function when you are finished with a gd Image because it frees up any memory that was allocated for that image.

THE GRAPHICAL COUNTER SCRIPT

 In the previous two sections, you developed all of the code for the graphical counter script. Listing 6.8 puts all of the code together and places the necessary #include statements at the beginning. You need to make the specified changes to the variable assignments that assign the path and file names of the counter and digit image files. Because the graphical counter script is written in C, you also need to compile the code before you run it. The procedure for doing so varies depending on what system you are on and which C compiler you have. Using your C compiler, compile the graphical-counter.c file and create the graphical-counter executable file. (If your system restricts you to an eight-character file name, call the file gph-cnt.c and the executable gph-cnt.)

Listing 6.8: The graphical-counter.c File

```c
#include <stdio.h>
#include <string.h>
#include "gd.h"

int main(void)
{
  /* Counter file handle and image file handle */
  FILE *counter;
  FILE *image;

  /* Input and output images */
  gdImagePtr im_file, im_final;

  /* Counter file and image files
     All users need to change the paths to the actual
     paths for their machines. Windows users need to
     use paths in the form "c:\\robertm\\count.dat" */
  char *cnt_file = "/users/robertm/count.dat";
  char *zero_gif = "/users/robertm/0tiny.gif";
  char *one_gif = "/users/robertm/1tiny.gif";
  char *two_gif = "/users/robertm/2tiny.gif";
  char *three_gif = "/users/robertm/3tiny.gif";
  char *four_gif = "/users/robertm/4tiny.gif";
  char *five_gif = "/users/robertm/5tiny.gif";
  char *six_gif = "/users/robertm/6tiny.gif";
  char *seven_gif = "/users/robertm/7tiny.gif";
  char *eight_gif = "/users/robertm/8tiny.gif";
  char *nine_gif = "/users/robertm/9tiny.gif";

  /* string version of counter file value */
  char s_count[20];

  /* integer version of count, width of image,
     x position for new image, and loop variable */
```

Listing 6.8: The graphical-counter.c File (Continued)

```c
int count;
int width;
int destx = 0;
int i;

/* the real_height is the height (in pixels) for all of the image files.
   the real_width is the width (in pixels) for all of the image files.
   Note: If you want to use different digit image files, replace these
   numbers with the width and height (in pixels) of the digit image
   files you will be using. */
int real_height = 13;
int real_width = 9;

/* open the counter file */
counter = fopen(cnt_file, "r");

/* check whether the file was opened successfully */
if (!counter) {
  printf("Content-type: text/html\n\nCannot open counter file!\n");
  return(0);
} else {
  /* if the file was opened, read in the string containing the count */
  fgets(s_count, 20, counter);
  fclose(counter);

  /* extract the integer value of the count from the string */
  sscanf(s_count, "%d", &count);

  /* increment the count */
  count++;

  /* open the count file for output */
  counter = fopen(cnt_file, "w");

  /* check whether the file was opened successfully */
  if (!counter) {
    printf("Content-type: text/html\n\nCannot open counter file!\n");
    return(0);
  } else {
    /* if the file was opened, write the count value to it */
    fprintf(counter, "%d", count);
    fclose(counter);
  }
}

width = strlen(s_count) * real_width;
im_final = gdImageCreate(width, real_height);

for (i=0; i < strlen(s_count); i++) {
```

Listing 6.8: The graphical-counter.c File (Continued)

```c
switch (s_count[i]) {
  case '0':
    image = fopen(zero_gif, "rb");
    break;
  case '1':
    image = fopen(one_gif, "rb");
    break;
  case '2':
    image = fopen(two_gif, "rb");
    break;
  case '3':
    image = fopen(three_gif, "rb");
    break;
  case '4':
    image = fopen(four_gif, "rb");
    break;
  case '5':
    image = fopen(five_gif, "rb");
    break;
  case '6':
    image = fopen(six_gif, "rb");
    break;
  case '7':
    image = fopen(seven_gif, "rb");
    break;
  case '8':
    image = fopen(eight_gif, "rb");
    break;
  case '9':
    image = fopen(nine_gif, "rb");
    break;
  default :
    break;
}

if (!image) {
  printf("Content-type: text/html\n\nCannot open image file!\n");
  return(0);
} else {
  im_file = gdImageCreateFromGif(image);
  fclose(image);
  gdImageCopy(im_final, im_file,
              destx, 0, 0, 0, real_width, real_height);
  destx += real_width;
  gdImageDestroy(im_file);
}
}

gdImageInterlace(im_final, 1);
```

Listing 6.8: The graphical-counter.c File (Continued)

```
  printf("Content-type: image/gif\n\n");
  gdImageGif(im_final, stdout);
  gdImageDestroy(im_final);
}
```

CALLING THE COUNTER WITH THE <IMG> TAG

With the graphical counter script completed, you are ready to add the graphical access counter to your Web page. As with the text access counter, you need to create and seed the count.dat file. If you didn't follow the text access counter example, read the section "Seeding the Counter" earlier in this chapter. The graphical access counter is called from the <IMG> HTML tag. The line

```
<IMG SRC="/cgi-bin/graphical-counter">
```

calls the graphical-counter file and displays the results returned from the script. Listing 6.9 contains the HTML code for an example using the graphical counter script, and Figure 6.4 shows how the page would appear in the Netscape browser.

Listing 6.9: HTML Example Using the Graphical Counter

```
<HTML>
<HEAD>
<TITLE>Example of the Graphical Access Counter</TITLE>
</HEAD>
<BODY>
<H1>Graphical Access Counter</H1>
This is my Home page. Thank you for visiting. Please come again.
<P>This page has been accessed <IMG SRC="/cgi-bin/graphical-counter">
times.
</BODY>
</HTML>
```

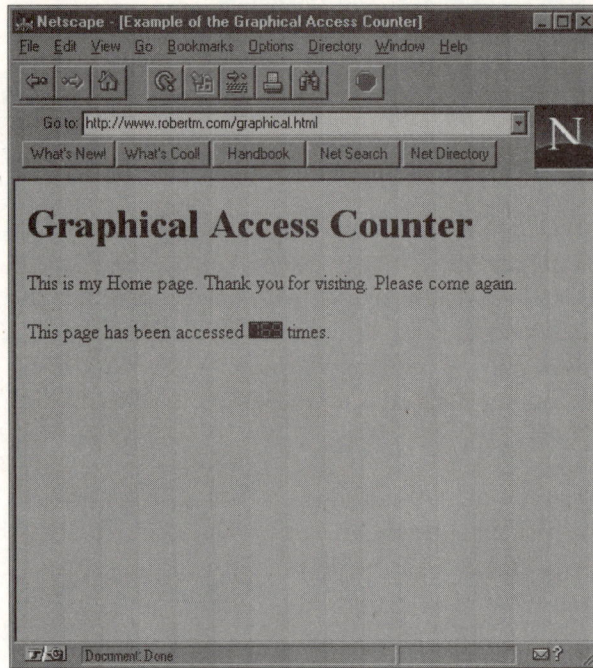

Figure 6.4: The graphical access counter

Interacting with Databases

A SIMPLE DATABASE EXAMPLE

INTERACTING WITH COMPLEX
DBMS PROGRAMS

database is an organized collection of related data. For example, a phone book is a database of names, addresses, and phone numbers. A phone book contains all the names and addresses of individuals and companies who have phones and want their number to be listed, and is usually organized alphabetically. For users, the phone book is a database. For the phone company, it is only a hard copy of the database they have in electronic form.

Many companies and individuals now use computerized, or electronic, databases to store information. Such databases enable you to retrieve data very rapidly. Computers can quickly sort through thousands of records, returning only those that match specified criteria. It's also easy to update the data in an electronic database. Finally, electronic databases can store large amounts of data in a small amount of space.

Databases can bring the same benefits to your Web site. You can store large amounts of data for publishing on the World Wide Web in databases that Web users can access easily. You just need to build the interface to the database once, and your Web pages can be dynamically generated from your database. If you take this approach, your HTML pages will always be current, with no outdated links or information. You can store your data in a database, where you can easily manipulate and change it. You can even use CGI scripts to build in search capabilities that wouldn't be possible in plain HTML pages. For example, a database of information about restaurants in your city could contain data such as food type, average meal price, and restaurant phone number. You could interface this database to the Web by building a search interface, one part of which is an HTML form that lets users enter parameters to search for, such as Mexican food. The rest of the search interface lies in the CGI script, which takes the user's input and searches through all the records in the database, returning only the records of restaurants serving Mexican food.

In this chapter, you develop a database that uses a simple text file to store data. If you read the file-based shopping cart example in Chapter 5, you might recognize that the shopping cart files were small databases, a separate one for each user. Text file databases are relatively easy to use and require no special software to implement.

After the text file database example is a brief discussion about interfacing with more complex database programs. (Database programs are sometimes called DBMSs, for database management systems.) DBMSs control input to and output from a database. The CGI script you write to interact with the text file database is a very simple database management program. Most commercially available database management programs—such as Oracle, Sybase, or Paradox—are highly specialized and more difficult to interact with than a text file database. For the sake of simplicity, the upcoming example contains only a text file database.

A SIMPLE DATABASE EXAMPLE

For the database example in this chapter, you develop a Web site listing advertisements of cars for sale. The database consists of a single file, car.dat. This data file will contain fields for several types of information. A *field* is a single category of data within a database record—such as car make or car model. A *record* is a collection of field values that make up an entry in the database—for example, all the fields that make up a single car advertisement. Typically, each record's fields are separated by some delimiter, such as spaces, colons, commas, or quotes. In the phone book, the listing

```
Robert McDaniel 732 Sunset Blvd 432-3232
```

is a single record composed of the three fields name, address, and phone number.

In the car database, only certain authorized users, referred to as administrators, can manipulate records within the database—adding, modifying, and deleting entries. All other users interact with the database by searching through the records for certain criteria, such as the make or model of a car. Because the car database is used very differently by administrators and general users, it has two scripts, one for administering and one for searching.

ADMINISTERING THE DATABASE

Instead of editing the database file with a text editor every time you want to make a change, you will develop some Web pages and a CGI script that you or the administrator can use to add, delete, and modify records. For this example, you will password protect access to these administration pages so that only authorized users can make the changes. Entering the correct password displays the contents of the database. You can add new records by pressing an Add push button. You can modify or delete existing records by selecting the record and pressing the appropriate push button. You can perform all database administration from these pages.

Because access to the database is restricted and because almost all of the Web pages for administering the database will contain dynamic information, you must generate the administration Web pages from a CGI script. Your administration script must be able to display the current contents of the database, add new records, modify and delete existing records, and restrict access by checking a password.

Password Protecting Access to the Database   To password protect the pages, you need an HTML page that requires the administrator to enter a password. This HTML page will contain a form with a password input element in which the administrator types the password. Listing 7.1 contains the HTML code for the admin.html file. When displayed in a Web browser, this file allows the administrator to enter the password for accessing the database. Figure 7.1 shows how Netscape displays this HTML.

Listing 7.1: The admin.html File

```
<HTML>
<HEAD>
<TITLE>On-line Car Ads Administration Home Page</TITLE>
</HEAD>
<BODY>
<H1>On-line Car Ads Administration Page</H1>
This page is for administrators to add, delete and modify records in
the On-line Car Ads Database.
<P>You must be authorized to make changes to the database. Please
enter your password to access the database.
<FORM METHOD=POST ACTION="/cgi-bin/admin.pl">
<P>Password: <INPUT TYPE=password NAME="password" SIZE=10>
<P><INPUT TYPE=submit NAME="submit" VALUE="Enter">
</FORM>
</BODY>
</HTML>
```

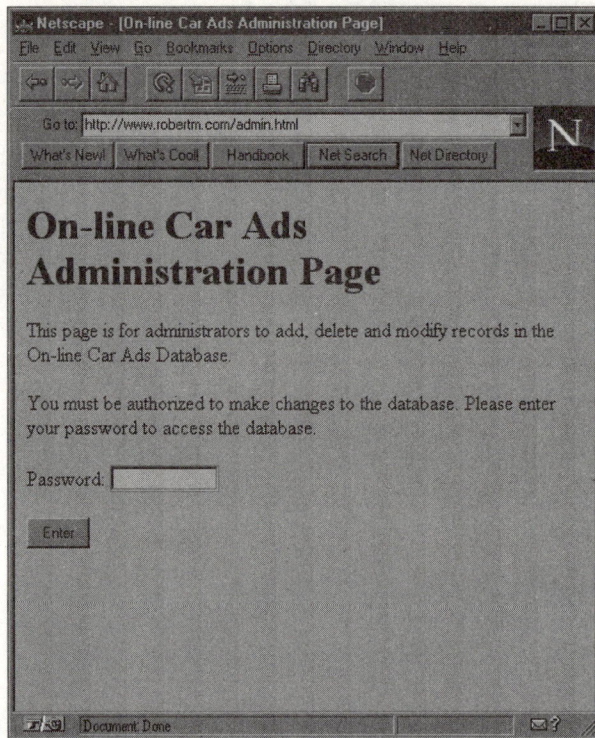

Figure 7.1: The administration home page

When the administrator enters the password into the password input field and presses the Enter push button (or simply presses the Return or Enter key on the keyboard), the administration script is sent the password value for verification. If the password matches, the script allows access to the database. This password verification is accomplished with the Perl code shown in Listing 7.2, which contains the Authorize subroutine.

Listing 7.2: The Authorize Subroutine

```
sub Authorize {
  local (%data) = @_;

  if ($data{'password'} ne $password) {
    print "Content-type: text/html\n\n";
    print "<H1>Invalid Password</H1>";
    print "You must enter a valid password to enter the Database";
  } else {
```

Listing 7.2: The Authorize Subroutine (Continued)

```
   &Display_Database(%data);
  }
}
```

The Authorize subroutine checks the value of the password that the administrator entered, which has been placed in the %data associative array, and compares it to the value stored in the $password variable. The code showing where the %data associative array and the $password variable are assigned values is in Listing 7.13 later in this chapter. For now, just note that the variable $password is assigned a value outside the Authorize subroutine, and that the user-supplied data will be sent to the Authorize subroutine as a parameter. The Authorize subroutine uses the if...else conditional to check the value the administrator typed as the password. If this password is not equal to the contents of the $password variable, the Invalid Password error is sent to the user's Web browser. If the password matches the contents of the $password variable, the current contents of the database are displayed by calling the Display_Database subroutine, which is developed in the next section.

Viewing the Contents of the Database   Once the administrator has entered the correct administration password for the database, the administration script displays the current contents of the database. Because the administrator must select records that need to be modified and deleted, the administration script displays all of the database records in a scrollable list. From this list, the user administering the database can select records to delete or modify. There is also a push button for going to the add page to add a record to the database.

As with the other examples in this book, you will place most of the HTML tags for the display database page in a template file. When the administration script needs to display the contents of the database, this template file will be read into an array, the contents of the database will be added in the appropriate location, and the results will be sent to the user's Web browser. To display the database, you need a template file that has the scrollable list where the database records will be placed. Listing 7.3 contains the HTML code for the database.tmpl file. (If your system limits you to a three-character extension, name the file database.tml.)

Listing 7.3: The database.tmpl File

```
<HTML>
<HEAD>
<TITLE>On-line Car Ads - Database Page</TITLE>
</HEAD>
```

Listing 7.3: The database.tmpl File (Continued)

```
<BODY>
<H1>On-line Car Ads - Database Page</H1>
Select a record and press the Delete or Modify push button, or press
the Add New Entry push button to add a new entry.
<FORM METHOD=POST ACTION="/cgi-bin/admin.pl">
<SELECT NAME="entry" SIZE=10>
YYYY
</SELECT>
<P><INPUT TYPE=submit NAME="submit" VALUE="Delete"> <INPUT TYPE=submit
NAME="submit" VALUE="Modify"> <INPUT TYPE=submit NAME="submit"
VALUE="Add New Entry">
</FORM>
</BODY>
</HTML>
```

This template file contains a form with a scrollable list and three push buttons: Delete, Modify, and Add New Entry. Notice that the contents of the scrollable list is just the letters YYYY. This is a placeholder where the administration script will substitute the actual records from the database. This substitution is done with the Display_Database subroutine in the administration script.

The Display_Database subroutine first needs to open the database and read in all of the records. This is done with the following three lines of Perl code:

```
open(DATABASE, "$database") || die "Content-type: text/html\n\nCannot open
database!";
@database = <DATABASE>;
close(DATABASE);
```

The first line opens the database file for input. The path and file name of the database file are stored in the $database variable, which is set outside of the Display_Database subroutine. The die statement in the first line of Perl code causes the program to terminate and output the contents of the string

```
Content-type: text/html\n\nCannot open database!
```

The || operator between the open and die statements is the logical or operator. When you place this operator between the two statements, the Perl interpreter first tries to execute the open statement. If the open is successful, the Perl interpreter moves on to the next line of code. However, if the file cannot be opened, the Perl interpreter executes the die statement. This is a common way to verify whether a file is successfully opened and to terminate the Perl program if it is not.

The second line of code reads in the contents of the database file from the input stream <DATABASE> and places each line in an element of the array @database. After the records have been read in from the database file, you can close the input stream <DATABASE> by using the close command, as in the third line.

Besides reading in the records from the database, you need to read in the contents of the database.tmpl file. You do this with similar lines of Perl code:

```
open(TEMPLATE, "$tmpl_files{'database'}") || die "Content-type:
text/html\n\nCannot open template!";
@template = <TEMPLATE>;
close(TEMPLATE);
```

The only changes from the previous open statement are the name of the file, $tmpl_files{'database'}, the name of the input stream, <TEMPLATE>, and the name of the array to hold the contents of the file, @template. Again, the code to assign the path and file name to the $tmpl_files{'database'} array element is outside of the Display_Database subroutine and will be shown in Listing 7.13, which contains the entire code for the administration script.

With the contents of both files read in, all you need to do is to format the records from the database for display within the scrollable list. You can do this with the following lines of Perl code:

```
foreach (@database) {
  chop;
  ($id, $year, $make, $model, $description, $price, $contact) =
      split(/::/);
  $data_string .= "<OPTION>$year | $make | $model | $contact | $id";
}
```

This foreach loop takes each element in the @database array and executes the body of the loop for that element. Because each record in the database will be in a separate element in the @database array, this code executes the body of the loop for each record in the database. The first statement in the body of the foreach loop is chop;. This statement removes the last character from the current element of the @database array. Because the records are stored in a text file database with each record on a separate line, each line contains a new line character, \n. The chop; statement just removes this new line character from the end of the record. For more information on the format of records in the database, see the section "Adding Records to the Database."

The next line in the foreach loop is

```
($id, $year, $make, $model, $description, $price, $contact) =   split(/::/);
```

This line splits the current record into separate variables for each field of the record. When records are added to the database, each record is one long string with two colons separating the individual fields. For example, the record

```
831153195::1987::Toyota::Camry::White, Automatic, AM-FM/Cassette, moon roof,
Power Windows and Doors, Excellent Condition::5000::Sam Matlend 805-324-5343
```

has seven fields, a unique ID (as explained under "Adding Records to the Database"), the year of the car, the make, the model, the description, the asking price, and the contact information. Each field is separated by two colons. The preceding line of Perl separates the fields into separate variables.

Once the record has been divided into separate fields, some of the fields are inserted into a new string, the $data_string variable, which contains the HTML formatting necessary to include the string in the HTML page. The line of Perl code

```
$data_string .= "<OPTION>$year | $make | $model | $contact | $id";
```

does this formatting by placing the <OPTION> HTML tag before some of the fields of the database record. Because this same line of code is executed for each iteration of the foreach loop, the .= operator is used instead of the = operator. This .= operator appends the values on the right side to the variable on the left side, formatting all of the records from the database into one long string. For example, suppose the database contained these two records:

```
831153195::1987::Toyota::Camry::White, Automatic, AM-FM/Cassette, moon roof,
Power Windows and Doors, Excellent Condition::5000::Sam Matlend 805-324-5343
831153288::1985::Honda::Accord::2dr Hatchback, Power Windows and Locks, new
paint, tires.::3500::Debbie Welch 212-323-3223
```

After the first iteration of the loop, the $data_string variable would be

```
<OPTION>1987 | Toyota | Camry | Sam Matlend 805-324-5343 | 831153195
```

and after the second iteration of the loop, the $data_string variable would be

```
<OPTION>1987 | Toyota | Camry | Sam Matlend 805-324-5343 | 831153195<OPTION>1985
| Honda | Accord | Debbie Welch 212-323-3223 | 831153288
```

After the records from the database have been formatted and placed in the $data_string variable, simply substitute the placeholder YYYY in the @template array with the contents of the $data_string variable, and send the modified contents of the @template array back to the Web browser. You can do this with the following lines of Perl code:

```
$template[9] =~ s/YYYY/$data_string/e;
```

```
print "Content-type: text/html\n\n";
print @template;
```

In this example, the placeholder for the contents of the database, YYYY, is on the tenth line of database.tmpl file. When the file is read into the @template array, the tenth line is placed in the tenth element of the @template array. Because the index of Perl arrays begins with 0, the tenth element is at index 9. So, the statement

```
$template[9] =~ s/YYYY/$data_string/e;
```

takes the tenth element of the @template array and replaces the placeholder with the actual records from the database. Then the next two lines of Perl code print the required parsed header and the contents of the @template array, which sends the contents of the @template array back to the Web browser.

Listing 7.4 contains all the Perl code for the Display_Database subroutine. Besides the sub Display_Database line, which declares the subroutine, the only lines of code that have been added are the local statements at the beginning and if...else conditional toward the end. The local statements

```
local (%data) = @_;
local (@database, @template, $data_string, $year, $make, $model,
        $description, $price, $contact, $id);
local (@template);
```

declare the arrays and variables as local to the Display_Database subroutine. A *local variable* exists only within a portion of your Perl code, usually within a subroutine. If a variable with the same name exists outside the subroutine, Perl considers it a different variable than the one within the subroutine. Declaring your subroutine's variables as local helps to keep your subroutines from overwriting values of global variables. A *global variable* is one that is accessible throughout the entire Perl program, including any subroutines in the same Perl file. In Listing 7.4, the variable $database is a global variable.

Listing 7.4: The Display_Database Subroutine

```
sub Display_Database {
  local (%data) = @_;
  local (@database, @template, $data_string, $year, $make, $model,
          $description, $price, $contact, $id);
  local (@template);

  open(DATABASE, "$database") || die "Content-type:
text/html\n\nCannot open database!";
  @database = <DATABASE>;
```

Listing 7.4: The Display_Database Subroutine (Continued)

```
close(DATABASE);

open(TEMPLATE, "$tmpl_files{'database'}") || die "Content-type:
text/html\n\nCannot open template!";
@template = <TEMPLATE>;
close(TEMPLATE);

if (@database == 0) {
  $template[9] =~ s/YYYY//;
} else {
  foreach (@database) {
    chop;
    ($id, $year, $make, $model, $description, $price, $contact) =
        split(/::/);
    $data_string .= "<OPTION>$year | $make | $model | $contact |
$id";
  }

  $template[9] =~ s/YYYY/$data_string/e;
}

print "Content-type: text/html\n\n";
print @template;

}
```

The if...else conditional added toward the end of Listing 7.4 places the foreach loop and the placeholder substitution you developed earlier within the else portion. The if statement

```
if (@database == 0) {
```

checks whether the length of the @database array is 0, which means there are no records in the database. If so, the placeholder for the database records in the @template array can simply be deleted. The following line deletes the YYYY string from the tenth element of the @template array:

```
$template[9] =~ s/YYYY//;
```

Figure 7.2 shows how Netscape displays the contents of the database with some example records.

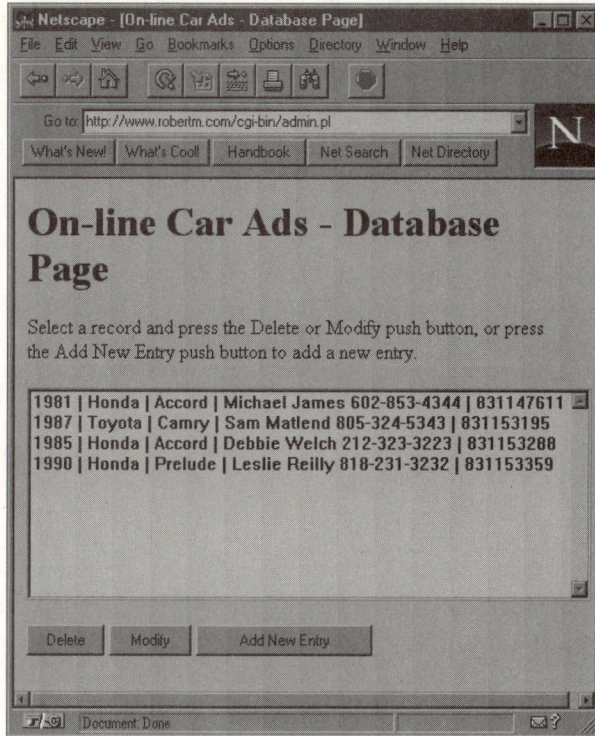

Figure 7.2: Example contents of the database

Adding Records to the Database   One of the tasks of administering the car database is to add new entries to the database. To do so, the administrator needs a form in which he or she can enter values for the various fields. For the car database, you want fields for the year, make, and model of the car, a description, the asking price, and the contact information of the seller. These pieces of information can all be captured with text input fields. Listing 7.5 contains the HTML code for add.tmpl, the template file the administration script uses to create the form for adding records to the database.

Listing 7.5: The add.tmpl File

```
<HTML>
<HEAD>
<TITLE>On-line Car Ads - Adding Records Page</TITLE>
</HEAD>
```

Listing 7.5: The add.tmpl File (Continued)

```
<BODY>
<H1>On-line Car Ads - Adding Records Page</H1>
<FORM METHOD=POST ACTION="/cgi-bin/admin.pl">
Year: <INPUT NAME="year" SIZE=4> Make: <INPUT NAME="make" SIZE=10>
Model: <INPUT NAME="model" SIZE=20>
<P>
Description: <INPUT NAME="description" SIZE=43>
<P>
Price: <INPUT NAME="price" SIZE=10> Contact: <INPUT NAME="contact"
SIZE=30>
<P><INPUT TYPE=submit NAME="submit" VALUE="Submit"> <INPUT TYPE=reset
VALUE="Reset"> <INPUT TYPE=submit NAME="submit" VALUE="Back to
Database">
</FORM>
</BODY>
</HTML>
```

Like database.tmpl, add.tmpl is a template file. (If your system limits you to a three-character extension, call the file add.tml.) When displayed in a Web browser, this page has text input fields to capture all of the necessary information as well as three push buttons, Submit, Reset, and Back to Database. add.tmpl is a template file instead of a regular HTML file because of the password protection. You must generate this page from the administration script so the administrator only has to enter the password once. Otherwise, you would need to add a password field to the page to keep other people from adding records to the database.

To display the page for adding records, the administration script needs a subroutine to open the add.tmpl template and output the contents to the user's Web browser. This subroutine, shown in Listing 7.6, is called when the administrator presses the Add New Entry push button on the page developed in the previous section. The Display_Add subroutine should look familiar to you because each line of code is similar to a line of code in the Display_Database subroutine. Figure 7.3 shows how Netscape displays the Adding Records page.

Listing 7.6: The Display_Add Subroutine

```
sub Display_Add {
  local (%data) = @_;
  local (@template);
```

Listing 7.6: The Display_Add Subroutine (Continued)

```
open(TEMPLATE, "$tmpl_files{'add'}") || die "Content-type:
text/html\n\nCannot open template!";
  @template = <TEMPLATE>;
  close(TEMPLATE);

  print "Content-type: text/html\n\n";
  print @template;

}
```

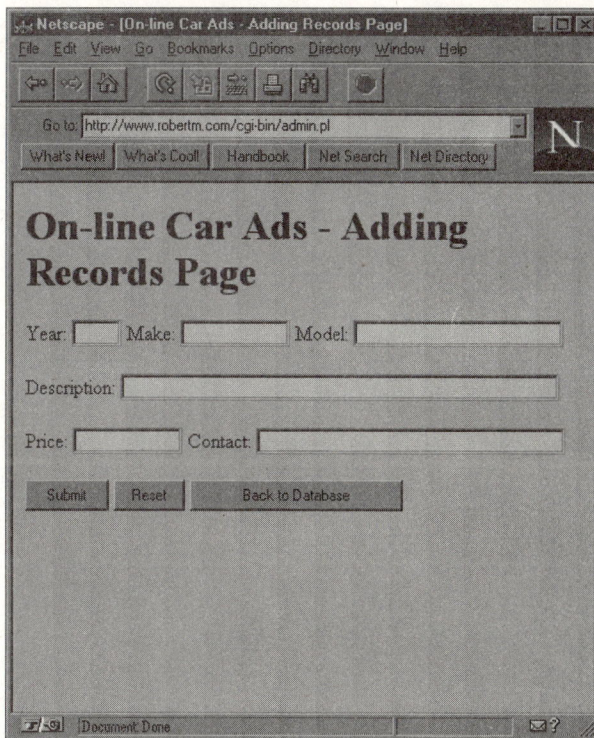

Figure 7.3: The Adding Records page

You also need a subroutine to add a new entry to the database when the administrator presses the Submit push button on the Adding Records page. Because new entries are added by an authorized administrator, the Add_Entry subroutine does not need to check for values in every field. For simplicity, the

Add_Entry subroutine only checks for a value in the year field. It does this with the if statement

```
if ($data{'year'} ne "") {
```

If you want to place checks for values in the other fields, you can check whether the other fields are blank as well. To do so, add lines such as

```
$data{'make'} ne ""
```

If the year field is not blank, a unique identifier is assigned to the new record. A unique identifier is used to prevent identical records from being placed in the database. For this example, the current time is used as the unique identifier. The line

```
$data{'time'} = time;
```

assigns the current value of time to the time element of the %data associative array.

After the unique identifier is assigned, you only need to open the database file and append the new record. You can do this with these three lines of Perl code:

```
open(DATABASE, ">>$database") || die "Content-type: text/html\n\nCannot open
database!";
print DATABASE
"$data{'time'}::$data{'year'}::$data{'make'}::$data{'model'}::$data{'description'}
::$data{'price'}::$data{'contact'}\n";
close(DATABASE);
```

The first line opens the database file. The $database variable is preceded with the >> operator, which opens the file for output and appends the output to the current contents of the file. The next statement outputs the new record to the database. The string

```
"$data{'time'}::$data{'year'}::$data{'make'}::$data{'model'}::$data{'description'}
::$data{'price'}::$data{'contact'}\n";
```

formats the record by separating all of the fields with two colons. This formats records as in the two examples in the previous section. Finally, the stream to the database file is closed with the close statement in the third line.

Listing 7.7 contains the entire Perl code for the Add_Entry subroutine. Notice that the line

```
&Display_Database(%data);
```

is added to the end of the subroutine. This line displays the contents of the database after every addition.

Listing 7.7: The Add_Entry Subroutine

```
sub Add_Entry {
  local (%data) = @_;

  if ($data{'year'} ne "") {
    $data{'time'} = time;
    open(DATABASE, ">>$database") || die "Content-type:
text/html\n\nCannot open database!";
    print DATABASE
"$data{'time'}::$data{'year'}::$data{'make'}::$data{'model'}::$data{'de
scription'}::$data{'price'}::$data{'contact'}\n";
    close(DATABASE);
  }

  &Display_Database(%data);
}
```

Modifying Records in the Database   Car database administrators also have
the task of modifying records in the database. If you enter a record incorrectly,
it is usually easier to modify what you already entered than to delete the old
record and type in a new one. To allow administrators to modify existing database records, you will create a Modify Entry page. This page will look very similar to the Adding Records page. Like the Adding Records page, it is generated
from the administration script. However, unlike the Adding Records page, the
Modify Entry page will contain dynamic data that must be entered by the administration script. Listing 7.8 contains the HTML code for the modify.tmpl
(or modify.tml) file.

Listing 7.8: The modify.tmpl File

```
<HTML>
<HEAD>
<TITLE>On-line Car Ads - Modify Entry Page</TITLE>
</HEAD>
<BODY>
<H1>On-line Car Ads - Modify Entry Page</H1>
<FORM METHOD=POST ACTION="/cgi-bin/admin.pl">
Year: <INPUT NAME="year" VALUE="AAAA" SIZE=4>
Make: <INPUT NAME="make" VALUE="BBBB" SIZE=10>
Model: <INPUT NAME="model" VALUE="CCCC" SIZE=20>
<P>
Description: <INPUT NAME="description" VALUE="DDDD" SIZE=43>
<P>
Price: <INPUT NAME="price" VALUE="EEEE" SIZE=10>
```

Listing 7.8: The modify.tmpl File (Continued)

```
Contact: <INPUT NAME="contact" VALUE="FFFF" SIZE=30>
<INPUT TYPE=hidden NAME="id" VALUE="GGGG">
<P><INPUT TYPE=submit NAME="submit" VALUE="Make Changes"> <INPUT
TYPE=submit NAME="submit" VALUE="Cancel">
</FORM>
</BODY>
</HTML>
```

Recall from Chapter 4 that the VALUE attribute is used to contain a default value when used in the text input element. In Listing 7.8, the values assigned to the VALUE attributes are to be used as placeholders for actual data from the database. The database administrator accesses the Modify Entry page by selecting an entry from the scrollable list on the Database page constructed in the section "Viewing the Contents of the Database." The Display_Modify subroutine, shown in Listing 7.9, changes these placeholders in the modify.tmpl file to the values of the record that is currently selected from the Database page.

Listing 7.9: The Display_Modify Subroutine

```
sub Display_Modify {
  local(%data) = @_;
  local (@database, @template, $data_string, $year, $make, $model,
         $description, $price, $contact, $id, $year2, $make2, $model2,
         $contact2, $id2);
  local (@template);

  if ($data{'entry'} eq "") {
    &Display_Database(%data);
  } else {
    open(DATABASE, "$database") || die "Content-type:
text/html\n\nCannot open database!";
    @database = <DATABASE>;
    close(DATABASE);

    open(TEMPLATE, "$tmpl_files{'modify'}") || die "Content-type:
text/html\n\nCannot open template!";
    @template = <TEMPLATE>;
    close(TEMPLATE);

    ($year2, $make2, $model2, $contact2, $id2) = split(/ \| /,
$data{'entry'});
    foreach (@database) {
      ($id, $year, $make, $model, $description, $price, $contact) =
```

Listing 7.9: The Display_Modify Subroutine (Continued)

```
            split(/::/);
      last if $id eq $id2;
   }


   $template[7]  =~ s/AAAA/$year/e;
   $template[8]  =~ s/BBBB/$make/e;
   $template[9]  =~ s/CCCC/$model/e;
   $template[11] =~ s/DDDD/$description/e;
   $template[13] =~ s/EEEE/$price/e;
   $template[14] =~ s/FFFF/$contact/e;
   $template[15] =~ s/GGGG/$id/e;

   print "Content-type: text/html\n\n";
   print @template;
 }

}
```

The body of the Display_Modify subroutine is one large if...else conditional that begins with the if statement

```
if ($data{'entry'} eq "") {
```

This statement checks whether a value has been selected in the scrollable list. If it has, the $data{'entry'} array element contains the selection. Otherwise, the $data{'entry'} element is blank. If no entry was selected when the administrator pressed the Modify push button, the Database page is reloaded by calling the Display_Database subroutine

```
&Display_Database(%data);
```

In the else portion of the if...else conditional, both the database file and the modify.tmpl file are opened and the contents read into the @database and @template arrays. Then the selected entry, which is in the $data{'entry'} array element, is split up into the individual field elements. Remember, each record in the database was put in a specific format for viewing in the scrollable list. Each field of the record that was placed in the scrollable list was separated by a space, vertical bar, and space. So, the line

```
($year2, $make2, $model2, $contact2, $id2) = split(/ \| /, $data{'entry'});
```

splits up this string and places the values in the respective variables.

Now that the selected entry is split up, you can use the unique identifier to locate the record in the database. You do this by looping over each record in the database and comparing the value of the unique identifier with the value of the identifier taken from the selected entry. The following foreach loop performs this search:

```
foreach (@database) {
  ($id, $year, $make, $model, $description, $price, $contact) =
      split(/::/);
  last if $id eq $id2;
}
```

The line

```
last if $id eq $id2;
```

causes the loop to exit when the matching record is found.

Once the matching record has been found, you can display the Modify Entry page by changing the values of the placeholders and outputting the results to the Web browser. The lines

```
$template[7]  =~ s/AAAA/$year/e;
$template[8]  =~ s/BBBB/$make/e;
$template[9]  =~ s/CCCC/$model/e;
$template[11] =~ s/DDDD/$description/e;
$template[13] =~ s/EEEE/$price/e;
$template[14] =~ s/FFFF/$contact/e;
$template[15] =~ s/GGGG/$id/e;

print "Content-type: text/html\n\n";
print @template;
```

perform the substitutions and output the results. Each substitution line is similar to the line used in the Display_Database subroutine. Remember, Perl arrays are indexed starting at 0. So, each index number for the elements of the @template array that are going to be changed is one less that the line number containing the placeholder in Listing 7.8. Figure 7.4 shows how the Modify Entry page appears with an example database record.

When the database administrator presses the Make Changes push button on the Modify Entry page, the administration script needs to modify that record in the database. Up to this point, only the Modify Entry page has been displayed. The record in the database has not yet been changed. Listing 7.10 contains the Modify_Entry subroutine, which is called when the administrator presses the Make Changes push button. In this subroutine, the database is opened with a typical open statement and the contents of the database are read into the @database array. Then comes the following for loop:

```
for ($i=0; $i<@database; $i++) {
  ($id, $year, $make, $model, $description, $price, $contact) =
```

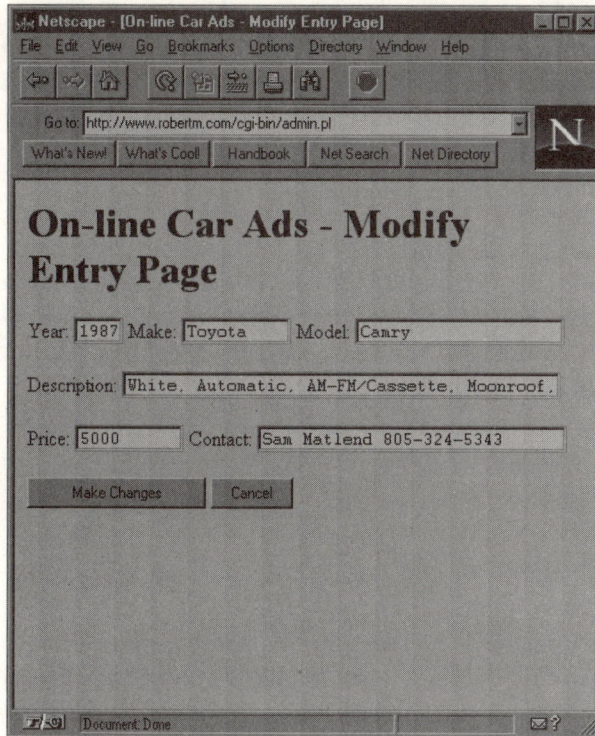

Figure 7.4: The Modify Entry page

```
      split(/::/, $database[$i]);
  if ($id eq $data{'id'}) {
    $data_string =
"$data{'id'}::$data{'year'}::$data{'make'}::$data{'model'}::$data{'description'}::
$data{'price'}::$data{'contact'}\n";
    splice(@database, $i, 1, $data_string);
    last;
  }
}
```

This code loops over each element of the @database array until the matching record is found. A for loop is used instead of a foreach loop, as in the Display_Modify subroutine, because the loop needs to keep track of the index of the current element so the new data can be placed at the correct array index of the @database array. The first line of the for loop divides the current database record into its respective fields. Then the unique identifier of the current database record is compared with the unique identifier of the record being modified. If the identifiers do not match, the index variable $i is incremented and the next record in the database is checked. If there is a match, the new data sent from the Modify Entry page is formatted into the $data_string variable, which is then substituted into the @database array for the old record with the statement

```
splice(@database, $i, 1, $data_string);
```

This statement inserts the contents of the $data_string variable into the @database array at index $i, which is the index where the unique identifiers matched. The digit 1 means replace the current value in the @database array at index $i with the contents of the $data_string. After this substitution is made, the last command causes the loop to exit.

With the substitution into the @database array complete, the new array can be written to the database file with these lines of Perl code:

```
open(DATABASE, ">$database") || die "Content-type: text/html\n\nCannot open
database!";
print DATABASE @database;
close(DATABASE);
```

Notice how the operator > precedes the $database variable in the open statement. This operator specifies to open the file for output, overwriting the file if it already exists. Because the @database array contains all of the current contents of the database, including the modified record, you can just overwrite the file with the contents of the @database array. Finally, the Display_Database subroutine is called, displaying the modified contents of the database.

Listing 7.10: The Modify_Entry Subroutine

```
sub Modify_Entry {
  local(%data) = @_;
  local (@database, @template, $data_string, $year, $make, $model,
        $description, $price, $contact, $id, $year2, $make2, $model2,
        $contact2, $id2);
  local (@template);

  open(DATABASE, "$database") || die "Content-type:
text/html\n\nCannot open database!";
  @database = <DATABASE>;
  close(DATABASE);

  for ($i=0; $i<@database; $i++) {
    ($id, $year, $make, $model, $description, $price, $contact) =
        split(/::/, $database[$i]);
```

Listing 7.10: The Modify_Entry Subroutine (Continued)

```
    if ($id eq $data{'id'}) {
      $data_string =
"$data{'id'}::$data{'year'}::$data{'make'}::$data{'model'}::$data{'desc
ription'}::$data{'price'}::$data{'contact'}\n";
      splice(@database, $i, 1, $data_string);
      last;
    }
  }

  open(DATABASE, ">$database") || die "Content-type:
text/html\n\nCannot open database!";
  print DATABASE @database;
  close(DATABASE);

  &Display_Database(%data);

}
```

Deleting Records in the Database   The final task for the administration
script is to allow the administrator to delete records. You can easily do this
with a Delete_Entry subroutine, which is shown in Listing 7.11. This subroutine is very similar to the Modify_Entry subroutine. First, you only delete a
record from the database if the administrator selects a record and presses the
Delete push button. As in the Modify_Entry subroutine, if the user presses the
Delete push button without selecting a record, the Display_Database subroutine is called. No records are deleted. If the administrator did select an entry
and press the Delete push button, the record is deleted from the database file.

Listing 7.11: The Delete_Entry Subroutine

```
sub Delete_Entry {
  local(%data) = @_;
  local (@database, @template, $year, $make, $model,
         $description, $price, $contact, $id, $year2, $make2, $model2,
         $contact2, $id2);
  local (@template);

  if ($data{'entry'} eq "") {
    &Display_Database(%data);
  } else {
    open(DATABASE, "$database") || die "Content-type:
text/html\n\nCannot open database!";
    @database = <DATABASE>;
```

Listing 7.11: The Delete_Entry Subroutine (Continued)

```
    close(DATABASE);

    ($year2, $make2, $model2, $contact2, $id2) = split(/ \| /,
$data{'entry'});
    for ($i=0; $i<@database; $i++) {
      ($id, $year, $make, $model, $description, $price, $contact) =
          split(/::/, $database[$i]);
      if ($id eq $id2) {
        splice(@database, $i, 1);
        last;
      }
    }

    open(DATABASE, ">$database") || die "Content-type:
text/html\n\nCannot open database!";
    print DATABASE @database;
    close(DATABASE);

    &Display_Database(%data);
  }

}
```

First the database file must be opened and the contents placed in the @database array with the following lines of Perl code.

```
open(DATABASE, "$database") || die "Content-type: text/html\n\nCannot open
database!";
@database = <DATABASE>;
close(DATABASE);
```

Next, the unique identifier is extracted from the entry the administrator selected in the statement

```
($year2, $make2, $model2, $contact2, $id2) = split(/ \| /,
$data{'entry'});
```

which is identical to the split statement in the Display_Modify subroutine. Then a for loop—similar to the for loop in the Modify_Entry subroutine—loops over the @database array until the matching record is found for the entry the administrator selected.

```
for ($i=0; $i<@database; $i++) {
  ($id, $year, $make, $model, $description, $price, $contact) =
      split(/::/, $database[$i]);
```

```
  if ($id eq $id2) {
    splice(@database, $i, 1);
    last;
  }
}
```

Once the matching record is found in the @database array, that element is removed from the array. The preceding splice statement removes the element at index $i from the @database array.

With the element removed from the @database array, the array once more contains the current contents of the database. So, as in the Modify_Entry subroutine, the database file is opened for output and the contents of the @database array overwrites the previous contents of the file. This is done with the three lines

```
open(DATABASE, ">$database") || die "Content-type: text/html\n\nCannot open
database!";
print DATABASE @database;
close(DATABASE);
```

Finally, the Display_Database subroutine that displays the contents of the database file is called; it will no longer have the entry the administrator selected for deletion. Listing 7.11 contains all the Perl code for the Delete_Entry subroutine.

Putting Together the Administration Script   In the previous sections, you developed all of the subroutines for displaying the Web pages for the database and adding, modifying, and deleting database records. To finish the administration script, you need to set the values of your global variables, create a subroutine that calls the appropriate subroutine you developed previously, and place all of the code in a file called admin.pl.

Setting the values of the global variables is relatively easy. The code for doing so is shown is Listing 7.13. Developing the subroutine to call the appropriate subroutine you have already developed should be relatively easy as well. All of your subroutines perform tasks that are the result of forms being submitted by the administrator. Each of the forms is submitted with the POST method. So you just need a subroutine that identifies which form is being submitted. The following lines of Perl check the REQUEST_METHOD environment variable:

```
if ($ENV{'REQUEST_METHOD'} eq "POST") {
  &Which_Post(%data_received);
} else {
  print "Content-type: text/html\n\nYou are not using this script correctly!";
}
```

If the variable equals POST, the Which_Post subroutine is called. Otherwise, the string

```
You are not using this script correctly!
```

is displayed in the user's Web browser.

In the HTML for the Administration, Database, Adding Records, and Modify Entry pages, every push button has a different value for the VALUE attribute. When a form is submitted, the name/value pair submit=X is sent to your administration script, where X is the string assigned to the VALUE attribute of the push button that was pressed. For example, if the Delete push button is pressed, the name/value pair is submit=Delete. So, the Which_Post subroutine only needs to check the values of the $data{'submit'} array element, which is where the user's data is placed, and then call the related subroutine. Listing 7.12 contains the Perl code for the Which_Post subroutine.

Listing 7.12: The Which_Post Subroutine

```perl
sub Which_Post {
  local (%data) = @ ;

  &Authorize(%data) if ($data{'submit'} eq "" || $data{'submit'} eq
"Enter");
  &Display_Add(%data) if $data{'submit'} eq "Add New Entry";
  &Display_Database(%data) if ($data{'submit'} eq "Back to Database"
|| $data{'submit'} eq "Cancel");
  &Add_Entry(%data) if $data{'submit'} eq "Submit";
  &Display_Modify(%data) if $data{'submit'} eq "Modify";
  &Modify_Entry(%data) if $data{'submit'} eq "Make Changes";
  &Delete_Entry(%data) if $data{'submit'} eq "Delete";

}
```

Notice that the Authorize subroutine can be called if the value for $data{'submit'} is blank or Enter. Recall that the Authorize subroutine verifies the password being entered on the Administration Home page. Because this page has only a single text input field and the Enter push button, the user can simply enter a value in the text field and press the Return or Enter key on the keyboard to submit the form. When the form is submitted in this fashion—which only works when there is just a single text input field and at most a single submit push button, no other input fields, scrollable or drop-down lists, or text areas—the $data{'submit'} array element will be empty.

Listing 7.13 contains the complete Perl code for the admin.pl script. Be sure to change the value for the path global variable to the correct path for your machine. Also notice that the current password is set to the string mypassword. You can change this string to whatever you want the current password to be. If you will be using the script on a Windows machine, you should remove the first line.

Listing 7.13: The admin.pl File

```perl
#!/usr/local/bin/perl

# All users should change the value of the $path
# variable to the correct value for their machine.
# Windows users need a value in the form
# $path = "c:\\robertm\\";
$path = "/users/robertm/";
%tmpl_files =
   ( 'add' , $path . 'add.tmpl',
     'database', $path . 'database.tmpl',
     'modify', $path. 'modify.tmpl', );
$database = $path . "car.dat";

# Change this string if you want to change the password.
$password = "mypassword";
%data_received = &User_Data;
&No_SSI(*data_received);

if ($ENV{'REQUEST_METHOD'} eq "POST") {
  &Which_Post(%data_received);
} else {
  print "Content-type: text/html\n\nYou are not using this script correctly!";
}

sub Which_Post {
  local (%data) = @_;

  &Authorize(%data) if ($data{'submit'} eq "" || $data{'submit'} eq "Enter");
  &Display_Add(%data) if $data{'submit'} eq "Add New Entry";
  &Display_Database(%data) if ($data{'submit'} eq "Back to Database" ||
$data{'submit'} eq "Cancel");
  &Add_Entry(%data) if $data{'submit'} eq "Submit";
  &Display_Modify(%data) if $data{'submit'} eq "Modify";
  &Modify_Entry(%data) if $data{'submit'} eq "Make Changes";
  &Delete_Entry(%data) if $data{'submit'} eq "Delete";

}

sub Authorize {
  local (%data) = @_;
```

Listing 7.13: The admin.pl File (Continued)

```perl
  if ($data{'password'} ne $password) {
    print "Content-type: text/html\n\n";
    print "<H1>Invalid Password</H1>";
    print "You must enter a valid password to enter the Database";
  } else {
    &Display_Database(%data);
  }
}

sub Display_Add {
  local (%data) = @_;
  local (@template);

  open(TEMPLATE, "$tmpl_files{'add'}") || die "Content-type: text/html\n\nCannot
open template!";
  @template = <TEMPLATE>;
  close(TEMPLATE);

  print "Content-type: text/html\n\n";
  print @template;

}

sub Add_Entry {
  local (%data) = @_;

  if ($data{'year'} ne "") {
    $data{'time'} = time;
    open(DATABASE, ">>$database") || die "Content-type: text/html\n\nCannot open
database!";
    print DATABASE
"$data{'time'}::$data{'year'}::$data{'make'}::$data{'model'}::$data{'description'}
::$data{'price'}::$data{'contact'}\n";
    close(DATABASE);
  }

  &Display_Database(%data);
}

sub Display_Database {
  local (%data) = @_;
  local (@database, @template, $data_string, $year, $make, $model,
         $description, $price, $contact, $id);
  local (@template);

  open(DATABASE, "$database") || die "Content-type: text/html\n\nCannot open
database!";
  @database = <DATABASE>;
```

Listing 7.13: The admin.pl File (Continued)

```perl
  close(DATABASE);

  open(TEMPLATE, "$tmpl_files{'database'}") || die "Content-type:
text/html\n\nCannot open template!";
  @template = <TEMPLATE>;
  close(TEMPLATE);

  if (@database == 0) {
    $template[9] =~ s/YYYY//;
  } else {
    foreach (@database) {
      chop;
      ($id, $year, $make, $model, $description, $price, $contact) =
          split(/::/);
      $data_string .= "<OPTION>$year | $make | $model | $contact | $id";
    }

    $template[9] =~ s/YYYY/$data_string/e;
  }

  print "Content-type: text/html\n\n";
  print @template;

}

sub Display_Modify {
  local(%data) = @_;
  local (@database, @template, $data_string, $year, $make, $model,
         $description, $price, $contact, $id, $year2, $make2, $model2,
         $contact2, $id2);
  local (@template);

  if ($data{'entry'} eq "") {
    &Display_Database(%data);
  } else {
    open(DATABASE, "$database") || die "Content-type: text/html\n\nCannot open
database!";
    @database = <DATABASE>;
    close(DATABASE);

    open(TEMPLATE, "$tmpl_files{'modify'}") || die "Content-type:
text/html\n\nCannot open template!";
    @template = <TEMPLATE>;
    close(TEMPLATE);

    ($year2, $make2, $model2, $contact2, $id2) = split(/ \| /, $data{'entry'});
    foreach (@database) {
      ($id, $year, $make, $model, $description, $price, $contact) =
          split(/::/);
```

Listing 7.13: The admin.pl File (Continued)

```perl
        last if $id eq $id2;
    }

    $template[7] =~ s/AAAA/$year/e;
    $template[8] =~ s/BBBB/$make/e;
    $template[9] =~ s/CCCC/$model/e;
    $template[11] =~ s/DDDD/$description/e;
    $template[13] =~ s/EEEE/$price/e;
    $template[14] =~ s/FFFF/$contact/e;
    $template[15] =~ s/GGGG/$id/e;

    print "Content-type: text/html\n\n";
    print @template;
  }

}

sub Modify_Entry {
  local(%data) = @_;
  local (@database, @template, $data_string, $year, $make, $model,
         $description, $price, $contact, $id, $year2, $make2, $model2,
         $contact2, $id2);
  local (@template);

  open(DATABASE, "$database") || die "Content-type: text/html\n\nCannot open
database!";
  @database = <DATABASE>;
  close(DATABASE);

  for ($i=0; $i<@database; $i++) {
    ($id, $year, $make, $model, $description, $price, $contact) =
        split(/::/, $database[$i]);
    if ($id eq $data{'id'}) {
      $data_string =
"$data{'id'}::$data{'year'}::$data{'make'}::$data{'model'}::$data{'description'}::
$data{'price'}::$data{'contact'}\n";
      splice(@database, $i, 1, $data_string);
      last;
    }
  }

  open(DATABASE, ">$database") || die "Content-type: text/html\n\nCannot open
database!";
  print DATABASE @database;
  close(DATABASE);

  &Display_Database(%data);

}
```

Listing 7.13: The admin.pl File (Continued)

```perl
sub Delete_Entry {
  local(%data) = @_;
  local (@database, @template, $year, $make, $model,
         $description, $price, $contact, $id, $year2, $make2, $model2,
         $contact2, $id2);
  local (@template);

  if ($data{'entry'} eq "") {
    &Display_Database(%data);
  } else {
    open(DATABASE, "$database") || die "Content-type: text/html\n\nCannot open
database!";
    @database = <DATABASE>;
    close(DATABASE);

    ($year2, $make2, $model2, $contact2, $id2) = split(/ \| /, $data{'entry'});
    for ($i=0; $i<@database; $i++) {
      ($id, $year, $make, $model, $description, $price, $contact) =
          split(/::/, $database[$i]);
      if ($id eq $id2) {
        splice(@database, $i, 1);
        last;
      }
    }

    open(DATABASE, ">$database") || die "Content-type: text/html\n\nCannot open
database!";
    print DATABASE @database;
    close(DATABASE);

    &Display_Database(%data);
  }

}

sub No_SSI {
  local (*data) = @_;

  foreach $key (sort keys(%data)) {
    $data{$key} =~ s/<!--(.|\n)*-->//g;
  }

}

sub User_Data {
  local (%user_data, $user_string, $name_value_pair,
         @name_value_pairs, $name, $value);
```

Listing 7.13: The admin.pl File (Continued)

```perl
# If the data was sent via POST, then it is available
# from standard input. Otherwise, the data is in the
# QUERY_STRING environment variable.
if ($ENV{'REQUEST_METHOD'} eq "POST") {
  read(STDIN,$user_string,$ENV{'CONTENT_LENGTH'});
} else {
  $user_string = $ENV{'QUERY_STRING'};
}

# This line changes the + signs to spaces.
$user_string =~ s/\+/ /g;

# This line places each name/value pair as a separate
# element in the name_value_pairs array.
@name_value_pairs = split(/&/, $user_string);

# This code loops over each element in the name_value_pairs
# array, splits it on the = sign, and places the value
# into the user_data associative array with the name as the
# key.
foreach $name_value_pair (@name_value_pairs) {
  ($name, $value) = split(/=/, $name_value_pair);

  # These two lines decode the values from any URL
  # hexadecimal encoding. The first section searches for a
  # hexadecimal number and the second part converts the
  # hex number to decimal and returns the character
  # equivalent.
  $name =~
    s/%([a-fA-F0-9][a-fA-F0-9])/pack("C",hex($1))/ge;
  $value =~
    s/%([a-fA-F0-9][a-fA-F0-9])/pack("C",hex($1))/ge;

  # If the name/value pair has already been given a value,
  # as in the case of multiple items being selected, then
  # separate the items with a " : ".
  if (defined($user_data{$name})) {
    $user_data{$name} .= " : " . $value;
  } else {
    $user_data{$name} = $value;
  }
}
return %user_data;
}
```

SEARCHING THROUGH THE DATABASE

In the previous sections, you developed the administration script that allows users with the password to make changes to the database file. In this section, you will develop the interface that lets any user view the records in your database. Because this example deals with a database of car advertisements, the best interface for other users is a search form. In this form, users enter parameters they want in a car, and the search script searches the database and displays any records that match the specified criteria.

The Search Form   Because all users have access to the Search feature, you can create the search form in a regular HTML file. You don't need to create a template file and have the script display the page. Listing 7.14 contains the HTML code for the Search page, and Figure 7.5 shows how Netscape displays the form.

Listing 7.14: The search.html File

```
<HTML>
<HEAD>
<TITLE>On-line Car Ads - Search Page</TITLE>
</HEAD>
<BODY>
<H1>On-line Car Ads - Search Page</H1>
To search for a car, enter what you are looking for below. You do not
need to enter values for all fields, but you must enter a value for
the Make field. If you enter years, please use a four digit number,
such as 1989.
<FORM METHOD=POST ACTION="/cgi-bin/search.pl">
<P><B>Make:</B> <INPUT NAME="make" SIZE=10> <B>Model:</B> <INPUT
NAME="model" SIZE=20>
<P><B>Years</B> <INPUT NAME="lowyear" SIZE=4> <B>to</B> <INPUT
NAME="highyear" SIZE=4>
<P><B>Priced from</B> <INPUT NAME="lowprice" SIZE=7> <B>to</B> <INPUT
NAME="highprice" SIZE=7>
<P><INPUT TYPE=submit VALUE="Search"> <INPUT TYPE=reset VALUE="Reset">
</FORM>
</BODY>
</HTML>
```

The search form contains text input fields for the make and model of car the user is looking for. There are two text input fields for both the year and price so that the user can specify a range to search for. Notice that the user must enter a value for the make field, and that year values must be specified as four-digit numbers. When the user enters data into the form and presses the Search push button, the form is submitted and the search.pl script is called.

The search script loops over every record in the database, returning any records that match the search parameters. So, the search script first needs to

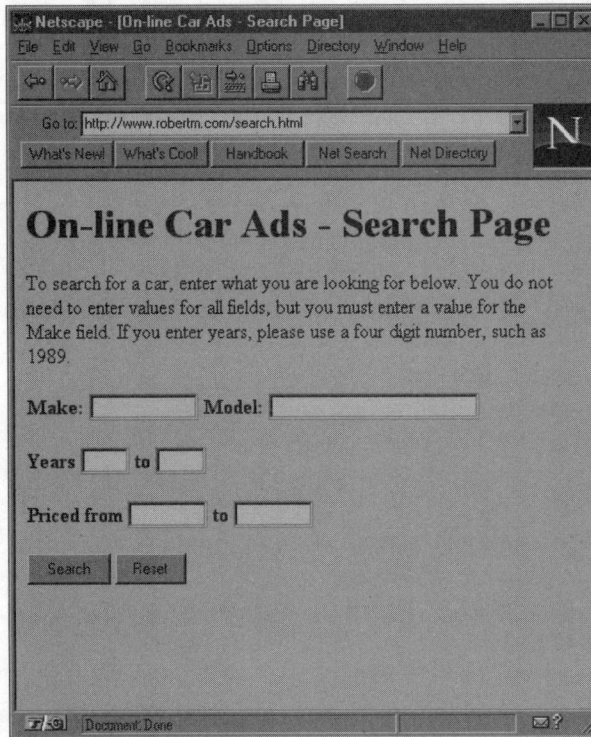

Figure 7.5: The Search page

open the database file and read the contents into the @database array. It does this with the following lines of Perl code:

```
open(DATABASE, "$database") || die "Content-type: text/html\n\nCannot open
database!";
@database = <DATABASE>;
close(DATABASE);
```

With the contents of the database file in the @database array, the search script can loop over all the elements of the @database array and compare the values of the current record with the values entered by the user in the search form. To loop over the array, you can use a foreach loop such as

```
foreach (@database) {
```

Inside the body of the foreach loop, the current record from the @database array can be split using the statement

```
($id, $year, $make, $model, $description, $price, $contact) = split(/::/);
```

which is similar to split statements used in the Modify_Entry subroutine of the administration script.

Now that the record is divided into separate fields, each field can be compared to the values entered by the user in the search form. Because the make field is the only value the user must enter, check this value first. Using the if statement,

```
if (($make =~ /\b$data{'make'}/i) || ($data{'make'} =~ /\b$make/i))
```

compare the value from the database, $make, with the value the user entered for the make of the car, $data{'make'}. The Perl expression

```
$make =~ /\b$data{'make'}/i
```

evaluates to true if the beginning of the $make variable contains the contents of the $data{'make'} variable, ignoring case. For example, if $make were equal to Honda, the expression would be true if $data{'make'} were Honda, Hon, Hond, or honda, but would be false if $data{'make'} were Hondas. To make the search more flexible—so it will find the make Honda if the user types Hondas—the preceding if statement contains the or operator || and the expression

```
$data{'make'} =~ /\b$make/i
```

This is a Perl regular expression that evaluates to true if the beginning of the $data{'make'} variable contains the contents of the $make variable, ignoring case. This way, the user can enter a wide variety of strings resembling Honda and get all Hondas in the database. The expressions also ensure that the strings will match only if the user's entry and the field from the current record head match and do not tail match. *Head matching* is matching up the first part of the word; in contrast, *tail matching* matches up the last parts of the word. For example, both Ford and Clifford tail match (ignoring case), but do not head match, whereas toy and Toyota head match.

The model value the user enters for a search parameter can be compared against the model field of the current record with similar statements. To check to see if the model the user entered matches the model in the record, use

```
if (($model =~ /\b$data{'model'}/i) || ($data{'model'} =~ /\b$model/i)
          || $data{'model'} eq "")
```

This line adds one more or operator (||) and another conditional expression than was in the make example. The expression

```
$data{'model'} eq ""
```

evaluates to true if the user left the model field blank, which is allowed. So, the model will match if either of the regular expressions returns true, or if the $data{'model'} element is blank.

The year and price matching are different than the matching used for the make and model. Because the values for these fields should be numbers, the comparison is whether the user's value is greater than or less than the value from the current record. For example, with the year value, the if statement would be

```
if ( (($data{'lowyear'} <= $year) && ($data{'highyear'} >= $year)) ||
        (($data{'lowyear'} eq "") && ($data{'highyear'} eq "")) )
```

which checks whether the price of the current record is greater than or equal to the user's low price value and less than or equal to the user's high price value. The statement is also true if both the low price field and the high price field are blank. The price comparison is identical to the earlier statement for the year comparisons.

```
if ( (($data{'lowprice'} <= $price) && ($data{'highprice'} >= $price))
        || (($data{'lowprice'} eq "") && ($data{'highprice'} eq "")) )
```

The current record in the database matches the user's search criteria if all of these if statements are true. So, the if statements will be nested one inside the other with the if statement for the $make being on top, as in

```
if (($make =~ /\b$data{'make'}/i) || ($data{'make'} =~ /\b$make/i)) {

  # make matched, check model
  if (($model =~ /\b$data{'model'}/i) || ($data{'model'} =~ /\b$model/i)
      || $data{'model'} eq "") {

    # model matched, check year
    if ( (($data{'lowyear'} <= $year) && ($data{'highyear'} >= $year)) ||
          (($data{'lowyear'} eq "") && ($data{'highyear'} eq "")) ) {

      # year is in range, check price
      if ( (($data{'lowprice'} <= $price) && ($data{'highprice'} >= $price))
          || (($data{'lowprice'} eq "") && ($data{'highprice'} eq "")) ) {

        # price matched, add entry to user's list of matches
        $matched .= "<HR>$year $make $model<BR>$description<BR>Asking
\$$price<BR>Contact: $contact\n";
        $count++;
      }
    }
  }
}
```

The two lines

```
$matched .= "<HR>$year $make $model<BR>$description<BR>Asking
```

```
\$$price<BR>Contact: $contact\n";
$count++;
```

are only executed if all the search parameters match the current record. When the parameters do match the current record, the values from the current record are appended to the $matched variable. Appending them to the variable enables you to output the contents of the variable as the search results, as described in the next section, "Displaying the Results." The second line increments the $count variable, which is used to store the total number of matching records from the database. Listing 7.15 contains the code you have so far for the Search subroutine.

Listing 7.15: The First Part of the Search Subroutine

```
sub Search {
  local (%data) = @_;
  local ($count) = 0;
  local (@database, $id, $year, $make, $model, $description, $price, $contact,
       @template, $matches, $search);

  open(DATABASE, "$database") || die "Content-type: text/html\n\nCannot open
database!";
  @database = <DATABASE>;
  close(DATABASE);

  foreach (@database) {
    ($id, $year, $make, $model, $description, $price, $contact) = split(/::/);
    if (($make =~ /\b$data{'make'}/i) || ($data{'make'} =~ /\b$make/i)) {

      # make matched, check model
      if (($model =~ /\b$data{'model'}/i) || ($data{'model'} =~ /\b$model/i)
         || $data{'model'} eq "") {

        # model matched, check year
        if ( (($data{'lowyear'} <= $year) && ($data{'highyear'} >= $year)) ||
           (($data{'lowyear'} eq "") && ($data{'highyear'} eq "")) ) {

          # year is in range, check price
          if ( (($data{'lowprice'} <= $price) && ($data{'highprice'} >= $price))
             || (($data{'lowprice'} eq "") && ($data{'highprice'} eq "")) ) {

            # price matched, add entry to user's list of matches
            $matched .= "<HR>$year $make $model<BR>$description<BR>Asking
\$$price<BR>Contact: $contact\n";
            $count++;
          }
        }
      }
    }
  }
```

Listing 7.15: The First Part of the Search Subroutine (Continued)

```
  }

}
```

Displaying the Results   With the searching done, your search script just needs to output the results of the search to the user's Web browser. The basic format for the Results page will be stored in a template file results.tmpl (or results.tml). Listing 7.16 contains the HTML code for the results.tmpl file.

Listing 7.16: The results.tmpl File

```
<HTML>
<HEAD>
<TITLE>On-line Car Ads - Results Page</TITLE>
</HEAD>
<BODY>
<H1>On-line Car Ads - Results Page</H1>
XXXX
YYYY
<HR>
</BODY>
</HTML>
```

Notice the two placeholders in Listing 7.16, XXXX and YYYY. The first placeholder will be changed to a string indicating how many records in the database matched the search and the second placeholder will be replaced with the actual results from the search.

In the previous section, you developed the code for comparing the user's parameters with all of the records in the database. Whenever a match occurred, the code in Listing 7.15 appended the fields from the record to the $matched variable and incremented the number of matches stored in the $count variable. To output the results, your Search subroutine just needs some lines of code to read in the template, replace the placeholders with the number of results and the actual results, and output the @template array.

Instead of just outputting the value of the count variable, create another variable that specifies how many entries matched the search, such as

```
$search = "$count entries matched your search for <B>$data{'year'} $data{'make'}
$data{'model'}</B>.\n";
```

This line creates a heading that tells the user how many records matched their search parameters. Then, open the template file and read in the contents to the @template array with

```
open(TEMPLATE, "$tmpl_file") || die "Content-type: text/html\n\nCannot
 open template!";
@template = <TEMPLATE>;
close(TEMPLATE);
```

   With the contents of the template file in the @template array, substitute the real data for the placeholders and output the results to the user's Web browser. The lines

```
$template[6] =~ s/XXXX/$search/e;
$template[7] =~ s/YYYY/$matched/e;
```

perform the substitutions. Keep in mind that the seventh line in Listing 7.15 will correspond to the sixth element in the @template array because the indexing begins at 0. Also, if no records matched the search, the $matched variable will be blank and the second substitution will just remove the YYYY placeholder from the @template array. Finally, with the @template array containing the correct information, the array can be returned to the user's Web browser with the following two lines

```
print "Content-type: text/html\n\n";
print @template;
```

   Listing 7.17 contains the complete Search subroutine.

Listing 7.17: The Complete Search Subroutine

```
sub Search {
  local (%data) = @_;
  local ($count) = 0;
  local (@database, $id, $year, $make, $model, $description, $price, $contact,
         @template, $matches, $search);

  open(DATABASE, "$database") || die "Content-type: text/html\n\nCannot open
database!";
  @database = <DATABASE>;
  close(DATABASE);

  foreach (@database) {
    ($id, $year, $make, $model, $description, $price, $contact) = split(/::/);
    if (($make =~ /\b$data{'make'}/i) || ($data{'make'} =~ /\b$make/i)) {

      # make matched, check model
      if (($model =~ /\b$data{'model'}/i) || ($data{'model'} =~ /\b$model/i)
```

Listing 7.17: The Complete Search Subroutine (Continued)

```
        || $data{'model'} eq "") {

      # model matched, check year
      if ( (($data{'lowyear'} <= $year) && ($data{'highyear'} >= $year)) ||
          (($data{'lowyear'} eq "") && ($data{'highyear'} eq "")) ) {

        # year is in range, check price
        if ( (($data{'lowprice'} <= $price) && ($data{'highprice'} >= $price))
            || (($data{'lowprice'} eq "") && ($data{'highprice'} eq "")) ) {

          # price matched, add entry to user's list of matches
          $matched .= "<HR>$year $make $model<BR>$description<BR>Asking
\$$price<BR>Contact: $contact\n";
          $count++;
        }
      }
    }
  }
}

$search = "$count entries matched your search for <B>$data{'year'}
$data{'make'} $data{'model'}</B>.\n";
open(TEMPLATE, "$tmpl_file") || die "Content-type: text/html\n\nCannot
open template!";
@template = <TEMPLATE>;
close(TEMPLATE);

$template[6] =~ s/XXXX/$search/e;
$template[7] =~ s/YYYY/$matched/e;

print "Content-type: text/html\n\n";
print @template;

}
```

Putting Together the Search Script   Now that you have completed the
Search subroutine, you have all the pieces for your search script. You just need
to combine the Search subroutine with the No_SSI and User_Data subroutines in a file called search.pl. Listing 7.18 contains all the Perl code for the
search script. You need to change the value for the $path variable to the path
to the database and template files on your machine. Also, if you will be using
this script on a Windows machine, you should remove the first line of code.
Figure 7.6 shows the results of a sample search, where the user entered the
string Honda for the make to search for.

Listing 7.18: The search.pl File

```perl
#!/usr/local/bin/perl

# All users need to change the $path
# variable to the path to the database
# and template files on their machine.
# Windows users need a path in the form
# $path = "c:\\robertm\\";
$path = "/users/robertm/";
$database = $path . "car.dat";
$tmpl_file = $path . "results.tmpl";
%data_received = &User_Data;
&No_SSI(*data_received);

if ($ENV{'REQUEST_METHOD'} eq "POST") {
  &Search(%data_received);
} else {
  print "Content-type: text/html\n\nYou are not using this script correctly!";
}

sub Search {
  local (%data) = @_;
  local ($count) = 0;
  local (@database, $id, $year, $make, $model, $description, $price, $contact,
         @template, $matches, $search);

  open(DATABASE, "$database") || die "Content-type: text/html\n\nCannot open
database!";
  @database = <DATABASE>;
  close(DATABASE);

  foreach (@database) {
    ($id, $year, $make, $model, $description, $price, $contact) = split(/::/);
    if (($make =~ /\b$data{'make'}/i) || ($data{'make'} =~ /\b$make/i)) {

      # make matched, check model
      if (($model =~ /\b$data{'model'}/i) || ($data{'model'} =~ /\b$model/i)
          || $data{'model'} eq "") {

        # model matched, check year
        if ( (($data{'lowyear'} <= $year) && ($data{'highyear'} >= $year)) ||
            (($data{'lowyear'} eq "") && ($data{'highyear'} eq "")) ) {

          # year is in range, check price
          if ( (($data{'lowprice'} <= $price) && ($data{'highprice'} >= $price))
              || (($data{'lowprice'} eq "") && ($data{'highprice'} eq "")) ) {

            # price matched, add entry to user's list of matches
            $matched .= "<HR>$year $make $model<BR>$description<BR>Asking
\$$price<BR>Contact: $contact\n";
```

Listing 7.18: The search.pl File (Continued)

```perl
            $count++;
          }
        }
      }
    }
  }

  $search = "$count entries matched your search for <B>$data{'year'}
$data{'make'} $data{'model'}</B>.\n";
  open(TEMPLATE, "$tmpl_file") || die "Content-type: text/html\n\nCannot
 open template!";
  @template = <TEMPLATE>;
  close(TEMPLATE);

  $template[6] =~ s/XXXX/$search/e;
  $template[7] =~ s/YYYY/$matched/e;

  print "Content-type: text/html\n\n";
  print @template;

}

sub No_SSI {
  local (*data) = @_;

  foreach $key (sort keys(%data)) {
    $data{$key} =~ s/<!--(.|\n)*-->//g;
  }

}

sub User_Data {
  local (%user_data, $user_string, $name_value_pair,
        @name_value_pairs, $name, $value);

  # If the data was sent via POST, then it is available
  # from standard input. Otherwise, the data is in the
  # QUERY_STRING environment variable.
  if ($ENV{'REQUEST_METHOD'} eq "POST") {
    read(STDIN,$user_string,$ENV{'CONTENT_LENGTH'});
  } else {
    $user_string = $ENV{'QUERY_STRING'};
  }

  # This line changes the + signs to spaces.
  $user_string =~ s/\+/ /g;

  # This line places each name/value pair as a separate
  # element in the name_value_pairs array.
```

Listing 7.18: The search.pl File (Continued)

```
@name_value_pairs = split(/&/, $user_string);

# This code loops over each element in the name_value_pairs
# array, splits it on the = sign, and places the value
# into the user_data associative array with the name as the
# key.
foreach $name_value_pair (@name_value_pairs) {
  ($name, $value) = split(/=/, $name_value_pair);

  # These two lines decode the values from any URL
  # hexadecimal encoding. The first section searches for a
  # hexadecimal number and the second part converts the
  # hex number to decimal and returns the character
  # equivalent.
  $name =~
    s/%([a-fA-F0-9][a-fA-F0-9])/pack("C",hex($1))/ge;
  $value =~
    s/%([a-fA-F0-9][a-fA-F0-9])/pack("C",hex($1))/ge;

  # If the name/value pair has already been given a value,
  # as in the case of multiple items being selected, then
  # separate the items with a " : ".
  if (defined($user_data{$name})) {
    $user_data{$name} .= " : " . $value;
  } else {
    $user_data{$name} = $value;
  }
}
return %user_data;
}
```

INTERACTING WITH COMPLEX DBMS PROGRAMS

So far in this chapter, you have been interacting with a text file database. Although this example is useful to illustrate the interaction of the Web with a database through CGI, it's unlikely that you have text file based databases. If you have any databases, they are probably in a highly specialized, complex DBMS program such as Oracle, Sybase, Access, or FileMaker Pro. However, even though these programs are more complicated than a simple text file database, you still interface them to the Web with a CGI script.

Recall from Chapter 2 that CGI defines how data passes back and forth between your Web pages and your CGI scripts. When interacting with a DBMS program, you want to take the information obtained from your Web page and get it to your DBMS. You may also have data coming out of your database that you want to display in a Web browser. Once your CGI script obtains data from

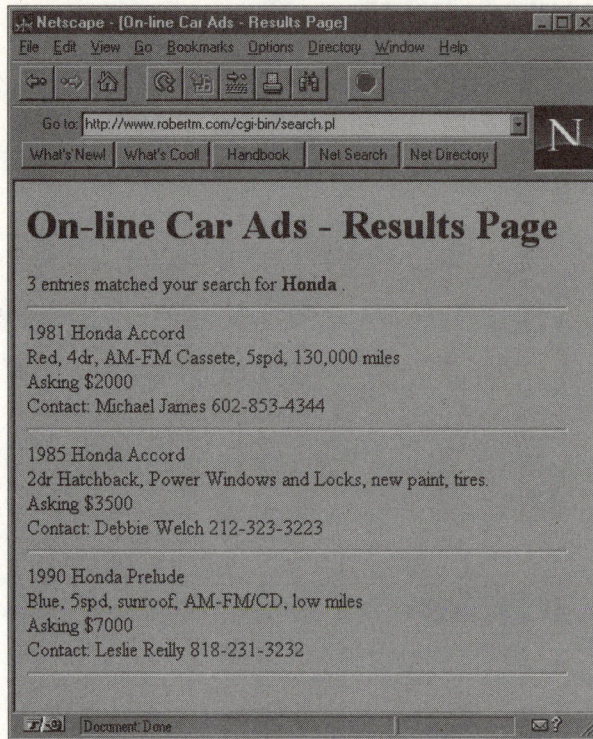

Figure 7.6: Results of a search for the make Honda

the DBMS program, you display it the same way you have displayed other data in this book: by formatting it with HTML and sending it via standard output to the user's Web browser. But you may not know how to write code to interact with the DBMS. This code would be highly specific to each type of database. For example, the code you would write to interface with Sybase would be very different than the code to interface with FileMaker Pro. Many of the more popular databases, such as Oracle and Sybase, already have interfacing routines that you can purchase or download.

Before pouring lots of time and energy into writing an interface to your database, you should look either for some library routines or for existing interfaces that you can download or purchase. First check with the company that sells your DBMS program. They may distribute an interface themselves or may know where to get one. Next explore the search directories listed in the "Search Engines and Directories" section of the Appendix. Unless you know the name of an existing interface product, search for the name of your DBMS.

There are also several resources in the "Script Archives, Gateways, and Libraries" section that contain links to existing DBMs gateways. Other good resources are newsgroups and mailing lists, which are listed in the "Usenet Newsgroups and Mailing Lists" section of the Appendix. If you are using a common database package, chances are good that someone has already interfaced with it. Hopefully, by searching and asking around, you will find an existing interface for your database. Even if you end up paying for a solution, it may be cheaper than spending the time to write your own.

Pushing and Pulling Dynamic Documents

CLIENT PULL

SERVER PUSH

Communication between a user's Web browser and your Web server always begins from the browser side. The user either enters the URL or clicks on a link containing a URL to a document on your Web server. The Web browser contacts your Web server and opens an HTTP communications channel between the two. The Web server takes the request received from the Web browser, processes it, and returns the results (usually the document requested) through the open communications channel. Having sent the results of the request, the Web server shuts down the HTTP communications channel, severing the connection between itself and the user's Web browser.

This method of communication requires you to wait for the user to request information on your Web server before sending that information. However, under some circumstances you may want to send the data before the user requests it. For example, if you wanted to display your company's current stock price on your Web page, you could easily generate the page from a CGI script that has access to the current stock price. But once the page is sent to the user's Web browser, you can no longer update the stock price until the user reloads the Web page. So, even though you generated the HTML page with a CGI script, the page will contain outdated data within minutes. Netscape has devised a solution to this problem by developing two methods of updating information in the user's Web browser without any action by the user. These methods, known as client pull and server push, are the topic of this chapter.

Note: Client pull and server push are implemented by Netscape through changes to their Navigator browser software, and are supported by all versions of Netscape Navigator starting with 1.1. However, most other browsers do not yet support either of these methods.

CLIENT PULL

Client pull is the Web browser requesting, or pulling, a Web document from a Web server without the user entering a URL, clicking on a link, or pressing the reload button. From this definition, you might imagine that your Web browser can wildly start loading any document it chooses. But this is not the case. Client pull only occurs when there is a special directive in a document you told your Web browser to request from a Web server. This special directive is a simple HTML 3.0 tag, <META>, that is used to simulate HTTP response headers. In other words, directives in the <META> tag are included with the HTTP response headers sent from the Web server. For example, when the tag

```
<META HTTP-EQUIV="Refresh" CONTENT=5>
```

is included in an HTML document, a Web browser that supports the <META> tag will include the header

```
Refresh: 5
```

with the HTTP response headers that were sent from the Web server.

You can use the <META> tag and Refresh HTTP response header together to cause a user's Web browser to reload the current page or load a different Web document after a specified amount of time. So, a document containing the preceding <META> tag would reload itself after 5 seconds had elapsed. This reload will continue to occur as long as the Web browser is displaying an HTML page with the preceding <META> tag.

As you can see, client pull does not require any CGI scripting to implement. It is defined through the use of the <META> tag and the Refresh HTTP response header. However, you can use CGI scripting along with client pull to extend what you can do with client pull alone. For example, with a static HTML page containing a <META> tag that reloads the page every five seconds—as shown in Listing 8.1 and Figure 8.1—the user would just see the same page being reloaded endlessly, without seeing any new information. If the same page contained a Server Side Include that called a CGI script that output the current date and time from the server, the user would see new information every time the page reloaded. Listing 8.2 shows the HTML code with a Server Side Include and Figure 8.2 shows what the page would look like during one of the reloads.

Listing 8.1: HTML Code for a Static HTML Client Pull

```
<HTML>
<HEAD>
<META HTTP-EQUIV="Refresh" CONTENT=5>
<TITLE>Static HTML Client Pull</TITLE>
</HEAD>
<BODY>
<H1>This Page Reloads Itself</H1>
This page will automatically reload every 5 seconds. Every time it
reloads, it will look exactly the same.
</BODY>
</HTML>
```

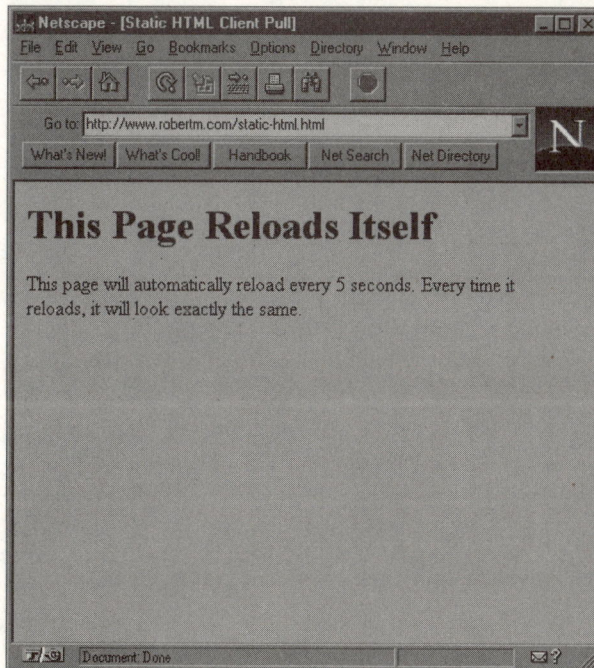

Figure 8.1: The static HTML client pull

Listing 8.2: HTML Code for a More Dynamic Client Pull

```
<HTML>
<HEAD>
<META HTTP-EQUIV="Refresh" CONTENT=5>
<TITLE>More Dynamic Client Pull</TITLE>
</HEAD>
<BODY>
<H1>This Page Reloads Itself</H1>
This page will automatically reload every 5 seconds. Every time it
reloads, the current date and time are displayed below.
<P>
<!--#exec cgi="/cgi-bin/date.pl" -->
</BODY>
</HTML>
```

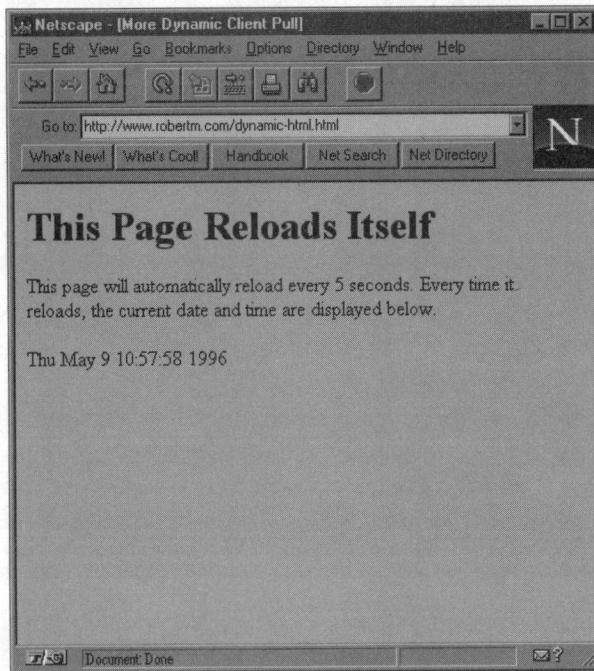

Figure 8.2: The more dynamic client pull

The following sections include some examples of client pull. The first example demonstrates how to use a splash screen and uses no CGI script. Because the splash screen requires no CGI scripting, you do it entirely in HTML. However, this example contains graphic images that you will not have on your own Web-server. For this reason, you're supplied with the URL so you can see for yourself how the HTML code works. Even though client pull is implemented to HTML, which limits you to static HTML pages, you'll see that there are still some applications for client pull alone. The second example creates a guided tour of the Educational Software Web site and demonstrates how a CGI script can further enhance the client pull feature.

A SPLASH SCREEN

Creating a splash screen for the first page of your Web site is a creative way to use client pull without any CGI scripting. A *splash screen* is an identifying image that appears when you start a program. Most commercial programs feature splash screens. For example, Netscape Navigator 2.0 for Windows displays the image shown in Figure 8.3 every time you start the program. Using Client pull, you can create a splash screen for your Web site.

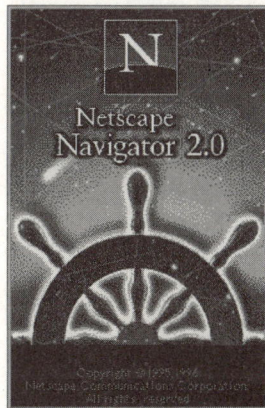

Figure 8.3: The Netscape Navigator splash screen

For this example, you will create the HTML code for a splash screen for the Actors Album Web site. Because you implement this example by adding a single line of HTML code to a normal HTML page, you'll see how to create a splash screen for your own Web site. Start by seeing how the Actors Album splash screen works. You can do this by visiting the URL http://www. castingguild.com/actors-album/splash.html using the Netscape Navigator

Web browser (a version newer than 1.1). (If you don't have Netscape, you can download it and try it for free from Netscape's Web site, http://www. netscape.com.) Looking at the Actors Album splash screen will give you a better idea of how the splash screen works. Figures 8.4 and 8.5 show the two screens you will see. First the splash screen shown in Figure 8.4 loads into your Netscape browser. Five seconds later, the Netscape browser automatically sends a request for the home page shown in Figure 8.5. Even though the browser sends the request after five seconds, how soon the page is displayed depends on the speed of your Internet connection. Listing 8.3 includes the HTML code for the Actors Album splash screen.

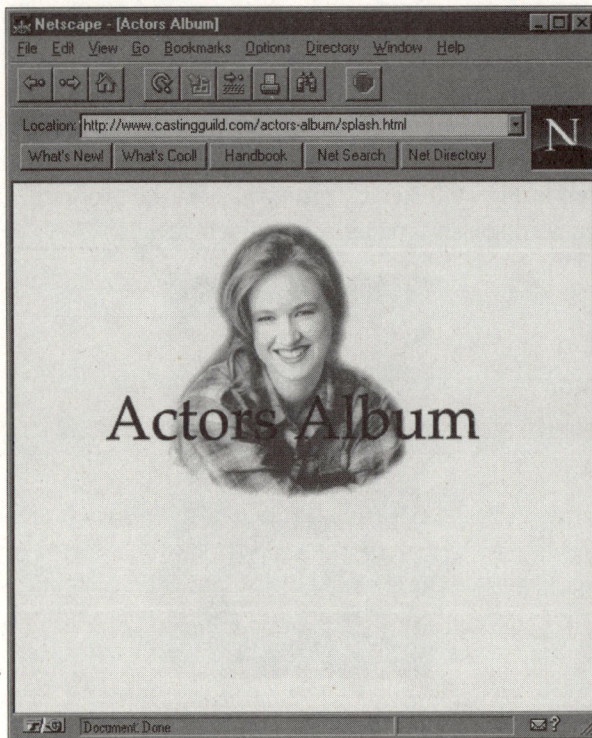

Figure 8.4: Actors Album splash screen

Apart from the <META> tag, this HTML code is similar to the code at numerous other Web sites. As you learned earlier in this chapter, the <META> tag drives the client pull action. This version of the <META> tag is slightly different from the ones you saw earlier. In the attribute CONTENT is the URL for another

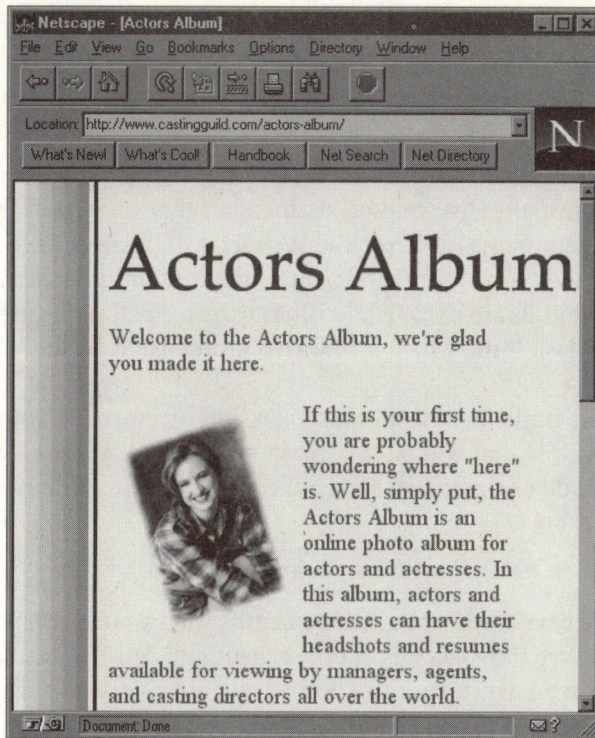

Figure 8.5: Actors Album home page

Listing 8.3: The HTML for the Actors Album Splash Screen

```
<HTML>
<HEAD>
<META HTTP-EQUIV="Refresh" CONTENT="5;
URL=http://www.castingguild.com/actors-album/">
<TITLE>Actors Album</TITLE>
</HEAD>
<BODY BGCOLOR="#FFFFFF">
<CENTER>
<IMG HEIGHT=233 WIDTH=305 VSPACE=10 HSPACE=10
SRC="graphics/splash.gif">
</CENTER>
</BODY>
</HTML>
```

document. By specifying the URL in this manner, you can instruct the Web browser to load a different document instead of reloading the same one. The line

```
<META HTTP-EQUIV="Refresh" CONTENT="5;
URL=http://www.castingguild.com/actors-album/">
```

tells a client pull enabled Web browser to load the URL http://www.castingguild.com/actors-album/ after five seconds. Remember that when the URL does not specify a document name (as here), the Web server returns the index.html file if one exists. The Actors Album's index.html file contains no <META> tag, so no further client pulls are initiated. In other words, client pull briefly displays the first page, splash.html, which is followed immediately by the Web site's home page.

You can easily implement a splash screen for your own Web site. Simply create an HTML file that will be the splash screen, and add the <META> tag to the HTML code of the splash screen file. The code for your <META> tag would look like

```
<META HTTP-EQUIV="Refresh" CONTENT="5; URL=Your home page URL">
```

with your home page's URL specified. Remember that your splash screen will only work with Web browsers that support client pull. So, if your splash screen doesn't contain any links to your real home page, as is the case in the Actors Album splash screen, don't make it the default page for your Web site. Doing so would strand users on your splash screen page if their Web browser did not support client pull. They would have no alternate way to get to your home page.

A GUIDED TOUR

Now let's take the client pull feature and extend it by using a CGI script. For this example you will create a guided tour of the Educational Software Web site. This Web site has only three pages—the home page, the Software Downloads page, and the Technical Support page. The guided tour feature will take the user through each page of the Educational Software Web site, explaining what information is on each Web page and what the user can do on the page. Although you can implement a guided tour without client pull, you will use client pull so the user does not have to click on links to go to the next page in the tour. In the next sections you will create the Web pages for the Educational Software Web site and write a CGI script that takes the user through each Web page.

The Educational Software Web Pages To set up the guided tour for the Educational Software Web site, you first need to create the home page, Software Downloads page, and Technical Support page of the Web site. The home page will contain some information about Educational Software and some announcements about software that is coming soon or is newly available. Listing 8.4 contains the HTML code for the Educational Software home page and Figure 8.6 shows the page in the Netscape browser. Notice there is already a link for the guided tour that calls the CGI script guided.pl. This is the guided tour CGI script you will be developing later in this section.

Listing 8.4: HTML Code for the Educational Software Home Page

```
<HTML>
<HEAD>
<TITLE>Educational Software</TITLE>
</HEAD>
<BODY>
<H1>Educational Software</H1>
Educational Software provides freeware software with an educational
purpose. Currently, Educational Software only has two software titles,
Algebra Primer and Vocabulary Builder, which are both available from
the <A HREF="downloads.html">software downloads page</A>. We are now
working on a third title, Elementary Physics, which should be
available in August.
<P>
If you have Netscape Navigator 1.1 or greater, you can select the <A
HREF="/cgi-bin/guided.pl">Guided Tour</A>, which will acquaint you
with our Web site.
<P>
[ <A HREF="downloads.html">Software Downloads</A> | <A HREF="tech-
support.html">Technical Support</A> | <A HREF="/cgi-
bin/guided.pl">Guided Tour</A> ]
</BODY>
</HTML>
```

Educational Software's Software Downloads page will contain links to all the software programs that are available for downloading. The software is listed as freeware—that is, it doesn't cost anything. For this example, the Software Downloads page contains two programs, Algebra Primer and Vocabulary Builder. There are Macintosh and Windows versions of the programs, which the user can download simply by clicking on the appropriate link. Listing 8.5 contains the HTML code for the Software Downloads page and Figure 8.7 shows how the page will appear in the Netscape browser.

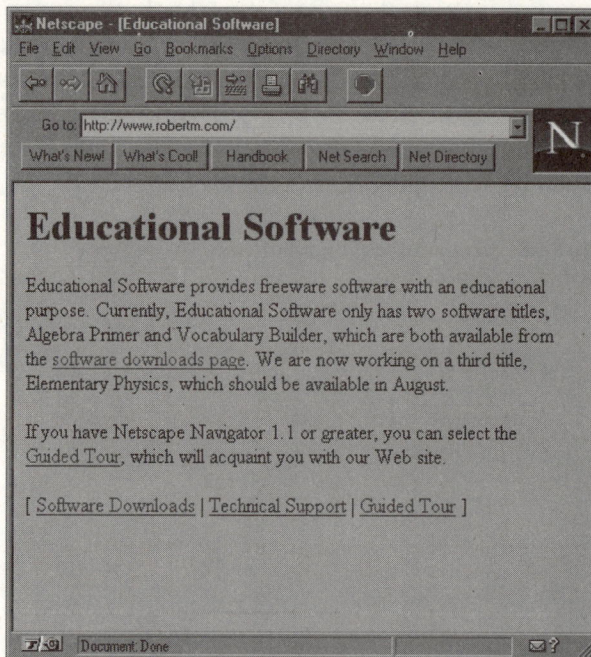

Figure 8.6: Educational Software's home page

Listing 8.5: HTML Code for the Software Downloads Page

```
<HTML>
<HEAD>
<TITLE>Educational Software - Software Downloads</TITLE>
</HEAD>
<BODY>
<H1>Educational Software - Software Downloads</H1>
<TABLE>
<TR>
<TH ALIGN=left>Macintosh</TH>
<TH WIDTH=50></TH>
<TH ALIGN=left>Windows</TH>
</TR>
<TR>
<TD ALIGN=left><A HREF="algebra.hqx">Algebra Primer</A></TD>
<TD WIDTH=50></TD>
<TD ALIGN=left><A HREF="algebra.zip">Algebra Primer</A></TD>
</TR>
```

Listing 8.5: HTML Code for the Software Downloads Page (Continued)

```
<TR>
<TD ALIGN=left><A HREF="vocab.hqx">Vocabulary Builder</A></TD>
<TD WIDTH=5Ø></TD>
<TD ALIGN=left><A HREF="vocab.zip">Vocabulary Builder</A></TD>
</TR>
</TABLE>
<P>
[ <A HREF="home.html">Home</A> | <A HREF="tech-support.html">Technical
Support</A> ]
</BODY>
</HTML>
```

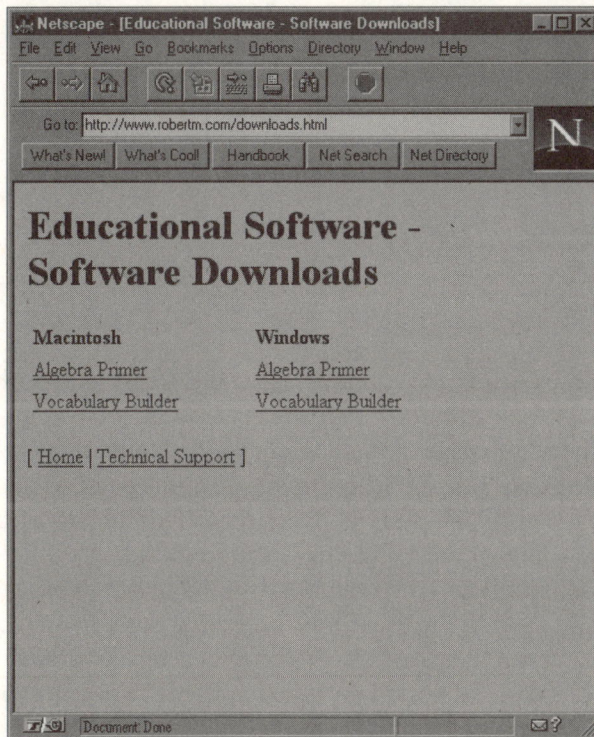

Figure 8.7: The Software Downloads page

The Technical Support page lets users of Educational Software programs send messages to Educational Software when they have technical problems with the software. The Technical Support page contains the same elements as the feedback form in Chapter 4. Listing 8.6 contains the HTML code for the Technical Support Web page, which is displayed in Figure 8.8.

Listing 8.6: HTML Code for the Technical Support Page

```
<HTML>
<HEAD>
<TITLE>Educational Software - Technical Support Form</TITLE>
</HEAD>
<BODY>
<H1>Educational Software - Technical Support Form</H1>
<FORM METHOD=POST ACTION="/cgi-bin/feedback.pl">
<B>Name</B><BR><INPUT NAME="name" SIZE=42>
<P><B>E-mail Address</B><BR><INPUT NAME="email" SIZE=42>
<P><B>Comments</B><BR><TEXTAREA NAME="comments" ROWS=10
COLS=38></TEXTAREA>
<P><INPUT TYPE="submit" VALUE="Send"></FORM>
<P>
[ <A HREF="home.html">Home</A> | <A HREF="downloads.html">Software
Downloads</A> ]
</BODY>
</HTML>
```

The Guided Tour Script   Now that you have the Web pages for the Educational Software Web site, you can write the guided tour CGI script that takes users through each Web page of the site. The guided tour begins when the user selects the guided tour link at the bottom of the home page, which calls the guided.pl script. The guided.pl script opens the HTML file for each Web page, adding some new lines at the beginning (including a line with the <META> tag to do the client pull) and then returns the modified Web page to the user's browser. After 30 seconds, the user's Web browser sends a new request to the guided.pl script, which then sends back a modified version of the next Web page. This process continues until the guided.pl script has sent modified versions of all the Web pages from the Web site. The guided tour ends by returning the user to the Educational Software home page.

When the user selects the guided tour link on the home page, the guided tour script starts. The script reads in the HTML code for the home page from the home.html file and modifies it to contain a brief explanation of the Web page. Also, the script adds the <META> tag in the header portion of the modified

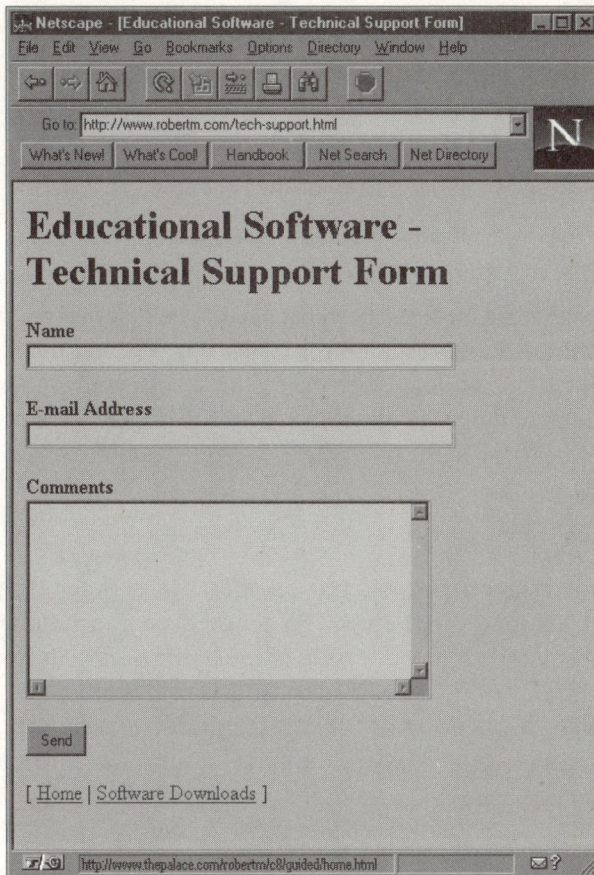

Figure 8.8: The Technical Support page

home page. Because you are using client pull for the guided tour, you need to add this line so the next page loads automatically. Because the guided tour script needs to modify the Web page before displaying it to the user, the <META> tag must request the guided.pl script file. The basic form of this <META> tag is

```
<META HTTP-EQUIV="Refresh" CONTENT="30; URL=http://www.robertm.com/cgi-
bin/guided.pl?page=pagename.html">
```

Notice that the guided tour script receives the parameter page=page-name.html when it is called. This lets the guided tour script know which Web page to return to the user's Web browser.

The guided tour script adds the preceding <META> tag to the modified versions of the Web pages. For the script to work properly, it needs to know which Web page is to be displayed next, so that it can insert the page name in the <META> tag. For example, if the current page to be displayed were the Software Downloads page, the guided tour script would need to insert the following <META> tag at the beginning of the downloads.html file:

```
<META HTTP-EQUIV="Refresh" CONTENT="30; URL=http://www.robertm.com/cgi-
bin/guided.pl?page=tech-support.html">
```

Notice that pagename.html has been changed to tech-support.html. This is because the Technical Support page is the page displayed after the Software Downloads page. To know which Web page is next, your guided tour script needs to keep track of the order in which the Web pages are to be displayed. You can do this by storing the name of all the Web pages from the site in an array, like this:

```
@pages = ("home.html", "downloads.html", "tech-support.html");
```

The script will display a modified version of each page in the array, in the order in which they appear in the array. So, for the @pages array, the guided tour script will first display a modified version of the home page, followed by modified versions of the Software Downloads page and the Technical Support page.

Now that you have the order of the Web pages stored in the @pages array, you can write the Perl code to have your guided tour script formulate the <META> tag for the page being modified:

```
shift(@pages) until $pages[0] eq $data{'page'};

if (@pages > 1) {
  $url_prefix .= $pages[1];
} else {
  $url_prefix = $homepage;
}

$add_tag = "<META HTTP-EQUIV=\"Refresh\" CONTENT=\"30; URL=$url_prefix\">\n";
```

The first line contains two parts, the shift expression, shift(@pages), and the until loop. The shift expression removes the first item from the @pages array. The until loop causes the shift statement to repeatedly execute until the first element in the @pages array is equal to the value in the $data{'page'} element. As before, the %data array is the associative array that stores the data your CGI script receives when called. For this example, the only data being passed to the CGI script is the name of the Web page to be displayed. Because you move the name of the current page to the first element of the @pages array, your script can always access the next element by referencing the second element in the @pages array. For example, if $data{'page'} were downloads.html, the first element of the @pages array, home.html, would be removed. The array would then contain only two elements, downloads.html and tech-support.html. The first element, $pages[0], would be the current page to display, downloads.html. The second element, $pages[1], would be the next page to display, tech-support. html, and would be the value to insert into the <META> tag of the downloads. html page.

The name of the next Web page to be displayed is appended to the URL prefix in the preceding if...else statement. Notice that the if statement compares the array @pages to the number 1. When the @pages array is used in this context, it is referencing the length of the array, not any individual array element. So, the if statement checks whether the array contains more than one element. If it does—as in the previous example with the downloads.html page—the next page, or $pages[1], is appended to the $url_prefix variable, which is set earlier in the code with the line

```
$url_prefix = "http://www.thepalace.com/cgi-bin/guided.pl?page=";
```

Listing 8.8, which appears later, shows exactly where the previous line is placed. If the @pages array only has one element, which would be the case when $data{'page'} is set to tech-support.html, the guided tour script is generating the last page to be displayed in the tour. When the guided tour is finished, the user is returned to the Educational Software home page. When the @pages array only contains the one element, the <META> tag needs to look like

```
<META HTTP-EQUIV="Refresh" CONTENT="30; URL=http://www.robertm.com/home.html">
```

So, the value of the $url_prefix variable is changed to the value of the $homepage variable, which is also set elsewhere in the guided tour script with the line

```
$homepage = "http://www.robertm.com/home.html";
```

After the if...else statement block, the $url_prefix variable will contain the correct path to be added in the <META> tag for the current page. The line

```
$add_tag = "<META HTTP-EQUIV=\"Refresh\" CONTENT=\"30; URL=$url_prefix\">\n";
```

creates the string for the <META> tag and stores it in the $add_tag variable for later inclusion in the HTML code that the guided tour script will send back to the user's Web browser.

With the <META> tag properly formatted for the current Web page to be displayed in the tour, the script is ready to modify the contents of the existing

Web page. First you will create a variable $guide, which stores the HTML code for the text to be included at the top of the page. This text is a simple explanation of the Web page the user is currently viewing in the tour. For example, with the home page, the text could be

```
This is the Educational Software home page. It includes announcements about new
and upcoming software releases.
```

An easy way to include the correct explanatory text for the page to be displayed is to store the explanations in an associative array keyed by the names of the Web pages. The following lines do this:

```
%guide_text =
    ( "home.html", "This is the Educational Software home page. " .
                   "It includes announcements about new and upcoming " .
                   "software releases.",
     "downloads.html", "From this page, you can download the freeware " .
                   "software. There are versions available for both " .
                   "Macintosh and Windows machines. To download, just " .
                   "click on the software title under your machine's type.",
     "tech-support.html", "Use this feedback form to send us messages when " .
                   "you have technical problems with our software.", );
```

Then, to format the explanatory text with HTML tags for inclusion in the modified version of the Web page, you would write

```
$guide = "<CENTER><HR>$guide_text{$data{\"page\"}}<HR></CENTER>";
```

Because the $data{'page'} element holds the name of the current page, using this for the key of the %guide_text array accesses the correct explanation for the current page.

Next you need to open the HTML file of the current page to be modified and displayed in the tour. You do this with the following three lines, which open the HTML file, read all of the contents into the @template array (one line per element in the array), and close the HTML file.

```
open(TEMPLATE, "$path/$data{\"page\"}") || die "Content-type: text/html\n\nCannot
open HTML files!";
@template = <TEMPLATE>;
close(TEMPLATE);
```

The first line opens the HTML file for input. The path and file name of the HTML file are stored in the $path and $data{'page'} variables, which are set at the beginning of the guided tour script. The die statement terminates the program and outputs the contents of the string.

The || operator between the open and die statements is the logical or operator. If you place this operator between the two statements, the Perl interpreter first tries to execute the open statement. If the open is successful, the Perl interpreter moves on to the next line of code. However, if the file cannot be opened, the Perl interpreter executes the die statement. This is a common way to verify whether a file has opened successfully and to terminate the Perl program if it has not.

The second line in the preceding Perl code reads in the contents of the HTML file from the input stream <TEMPLATE> and places each line in an element of the array @template. After the contents of the HTML file have been read into the @template array, you can close the input stream <TEMPLATE> with the close command, as in the third line of code.

Finally, you need to modify the lines of the @template array that will be different for the guided tour. First you will modify the line containing the <TITLE> tags. In Listings 8.4, 8.5, and 8.6, the <TITLE> tags are all on the third line of the HTML file. Because the indexing of Perl arrays begins with 0, you can change the third element by using the following line:

```
$template[2] = "<TITLE>Guided Tour - $page_names{$data{\"page\"}}</TITLE>\n";
```

This line changes the title to Guided Tour - *pagename*, where *pagename* is the name of the page currently being displayed. Because you want to display the name of the page and not the name of the HTML file, you can store the names of the pages in the %page_names associative array, which is keyed by the names of the HTML files. This is done in the following lines:

```
%page_names =
  ( "home.html", "Home Page",
    "downloads.html", "Software Downloads Page",
    "tech-support.html", "Technical Support Page", );
```

When the $data{'page'} variable is set to downloads.html, the title line is changed to

```
<TITLE>Guided Tour - Software Downloads Page</TITLE>
```

After modifying the title line, you need to add the lines containing the <META> tag and the explanation text. You do this with the following two lines of code:

```
splice(@template, 5, 0, $guide);
splice(@template, 2, 0, $add_tag);
```

Both lines use the splice operator, which inserts the contents of the variables $guide and $add_tag into the @template array. In the first line, the contents of the $guide variable are inserted into the @template array after the fifth element in the array. This places the explanatory text right after the <BODY> tag for all the Web pages, as shown in Listings 8.4, 8.5, and 8.6. The second line inserts the contents of the $add_tag variable into the @template array after the second element in the array. For all the Web pages, this would place the <META> tag immediately after the <HEAD> tag, as shown in Listings 8.4, 8.5, and 8.6. The 0 used in both lines of code indicates to Perl to insert the contents of the variables without removing any of the current elements of the array.

Finally, with the @template array containing the modified version of the HTML page to display to the user, you need to output the parsed header and the contents of the @template array. You do this with the following two lines of Perl:

```
print "Content-type: text/html\n\n";
print @template;
```

Listing 8.7 contains the Perl code that you just finished developing. For readability, it has been placed into a subroutine called Display. The only additions are the sub Display line, which declares the name of the subroutine, and the local variable declarations in the first two lines to the subroutine. The local statements

```
local (%data) = @_;
local (@template, $guide, $add_tag);
```

declare the arrays and variables as local to the Display subroutine. As you may remember, a local variable is a variable that exists only within a portion of your Perl code, usually within a subroutine. If a variable with the same name existed outside the subroutine, Perl would consider it a different variable than the one that is declared local within the subroutine. Declaring your subroutine's variables as local helps to keep your subroutines from overwriting values of global variables. A global variable is one that is accessible throughout the entire Perl program, including any subroutines in the same Perl file. In Listing 8.7, the variables $url_prefix and $path and the arrays @pages, %guide_text, and %page_names are global variables.

Listing 8.7: The Display Subroutine

```
sub Display {
  local (%data) = @_;
  local (@template, $guide, $add_tag);

  $data{'page'} = "home.html" unless $data{'page'};
  shift(@pages) until $pages[0] eq $data{'page'};

  if (@pages > 1) {
    $url_prefix .= $pages[1];
  } else {
```

Listing 8.7: The Display Subroutine (Continued)

```perl
    $url_prefix = $homepage;
  }

  $add_tag = "<META HTTP-EQUIV=\"Refresh\" CONTENT=\"30;
URL=$url_prefix\">\n";
  $guide = "<CENTER><HR>$guide_text{$data{\"page\"}}<HR></CENTER>";


  open(TEMPLATE, "$path/$data{\"page\"}") || die "Content-type:
text/html\n\nCannot open HTML files!";
  @template = <TEMPLATE>;
  close(TEMPLATE);

  $template[2] = "<TITLE>Guided Tour -
$page_names{$data{\"page\"}}</TITLE>\n";
  splice(@template, 5, 0, $guide);
  splice(@template, 2, 0, $add_tag);

  print "Content-type: text/html\n\n";
  print @template;

}
```

To finish the guided tour script, you just need to place the code for the Display subroutine, listed in Listing 8.7, into the guided.pl file along with the declarations of global variables and the code for the No_SSI and User_Data subroutines you have been using throughout this book. Listing 8.8 contains the entire code for the guided tour script. Be sure to change the $path, $url_prefix, and $homepage variables to contain the correct paths and URLs for your machine. Also, Windows users should remove the first line of the script, which is specific to UNIX systems. Figures 8.9, 8.10, and 8.11 display how the modified home page, Software Downloads page, and Technical Support pages look in the guided tour.

Listing 8.8: The guided.pl File

```perl
#!/usr/local/bin/perl

# All users need to change the paths and URLs to be correct for
# their machines. Windows users need to have the $path variable
# in the form $path = "c:\\robertm\\guided"
$path = "/users/robertm/guided";
$url_prefix = "http://www.robertm.com/cgi-bin/guided.pl?page=";
$homepage = "http://www.robertm.com/home.html";
```

Listing 8.8: The guided.pl File (Continued)

```perl
@pages = ("home.html", "downloads.html", "tech-support.html");
%page_names =
  ( "home.html", "Home Page",
    "downloads.html", "Software Downloads Page",
    "tech-support.html", "Technical Support Page", );
%guide_text =
  ( "home.html", "This is the Educational Software home page. " .
                 "It includes announcements about new and upcoming " .
                 "software releases.",
    "downloads.html", "From this page, you can download the freeware " .
                      "software. There are versions available for both " .
                      "Macintosh and Windows machines. To download, just " .
                      "click on the software title under your machine's type.",
    "tech-support.html", "Use this feedback form to send us messages when " .
                         "you have technical problems with our software.", );


if ($ENV{'REQUEST_METHOD'} eq "GET") {
  %data_received = &User_Data;
  &No_SSI(*data_received);
  &Display(%data_received);
} else {
  print "Content-type: text/html\n\nYou are not using this script correctly!";
}

sub Display {
  local (%data) = @_;
  local (@template, $guide);

  $data{'page'} = "home.html" unless $data{'page'};
  shift(@pages) until $pages[0] eq $data{'page'};

  if (@pages > 1) {
    $url_prefix .= $pages[1];
  } else {
    $url_prefix = $homepage;
  }

  $add_tag = "<META HTTP-EQUIV=\"Refresh\" CONTENT=\"30; URL=$url_prefix\">\n";
  $guide = "<CENTER><HR>$guide_text{$data{\"page\"}}<HR></CENTER>";


  # Windows users need to change the string "$path/$data{\"page\"}" to
  # "$path\\$data{\"page\"}"
  open(TEMPLATE, "$path/$data{\"page\"}") || die "Content-type:
text/html\n\nCannot open HTML files!";
  @template = <TEMPLATE>;
  close(TEMPLATE);
```

Listing 8.8: The guided.pl File (Continued)

```perl
  $template[2] = "<TITLE>Guided Tour - $page_names{$data{\"page\"}}</TITLE>\n";
  splice(@template, 5, 0, $guide);
  splice(@template, 2, 0, $add_tag);

  print "Content-type: text/html\n\n";
  print @template;

}

sub No_SSI {
  local (*data) = @_;

  foreach $key (sort keys(%data)) {
    $data{$key} =~ s/<!--(.|\n)*-->//g;
  }

}

sub User_Data {
  local (%user_data, $user_string, $name_value_pair,
         @name_value_pairs, $name, $value);

  # If the data was sent via POST, then it is available
  # from standard input. Otherwise, the data is in the
  # QUERY_STRING environment variable.
  if ($ENV{'REQUEST_METHOD'} eq "POST") {
    read(STDIN,$user_string,$ENV{'CONTENT_LENGTH'});
  } else {
    $user_string = $ENV{'QUERY_STRING'};
  }

  # This line changes the + signs to spaces.
  $user_string =~ s/\+/ /g;

  # This line places each name/value pair as a separate
  # element in the name_value_pairs array.
  @name_value_pairs = split(/&/, $user_string);

  # This code loops over each element in the name_value_pairs
  # array, splits it on the = sign, and places the value
  # into the user_data associative array with the name as the
  # key.
  foreach $name_value_pair (@name_value_pairs) {
    ($name, $value) = split(/=/, $name_value_pair);

    # These two lines decode the values from any URL
    # hexadecimal encoding. The first section searches for a
    # hexadecimal number and the second part converts the
```

Listing 8.8: The guided.pl File (Continued)

```
  # hex number to decimal and returns the character
  # equivalent.
  $name =~
    s/%([a-fA-F0-9][a-fA-F0-9])/pack("C",hex($1))/ge;
  $value =~
    s/%([a-fA-F0-9][a-fA-F0-9])/pack("C",hex($1))/ge;

  # If the name/value pair has already been given a value,
  # as in the case of multiple items being selected, then
  # separate the items with a " : ".
  if (defined($user_data{$name})) {
    $user_data{$name} .= " : " . $value;
  } else {
    $user_data{$name} = $value;
  }
}
return %user_data;
}
```

SERVER PUSH

When you use client pull, every refresh action taken by the Web browser opens a new HTTP communication channel. Recall that client pull starts when the Web browser requests a document containing the <META> tag, which instructs the Web browser to refresh the document after a specified amount of time. The Web server always shuts down the HTTP communication channel after the document has been sent. When the Web browser performs the refresh, it sends a new HTTP request to the Web server for the same document (or for the new document specified by the inclusion of a redirect URL, as demonstrated in the splash screen example earlier in this chapter). Once again, the Web browser opens communication with the Web server, which returns the document and closes the communication channel.

Unlike client pull, server push keeps the HTTP communication channel open between the Web browser and the Web server. Then, when instructed to, the Web server sends data to the Web browser through this open communications channel. By keeping the channel open, the Web server has complete control of when data is sent to the Web browser. The Web server does not have to wait for the Web browser to initiate the communication.

Server push is initiated through a CGI script that holds the communication channel between the Web browser and the Web server open until the script finishes executing. You do this by using a variation on the multipart/mixed MIME

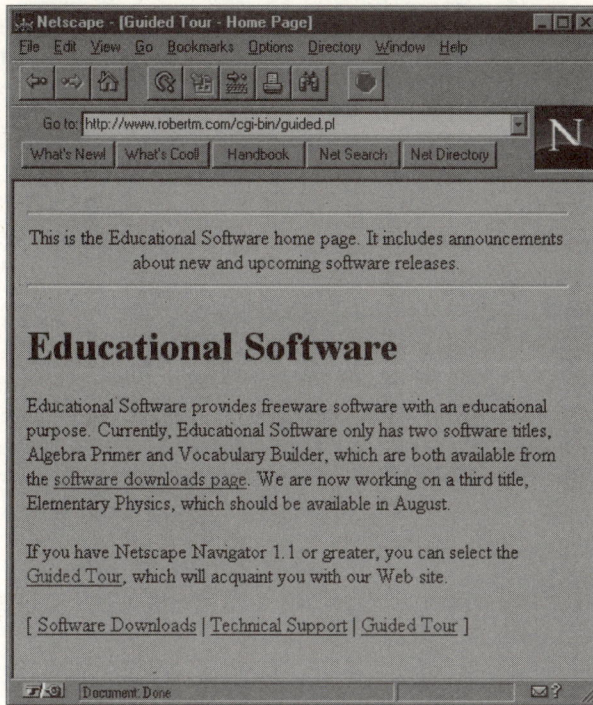

Figure 8.9: The Educational Software Home page in the guided tour

type. Recall from Chapter 2 that the parsed header Content-type takes MIME types for its values. In previous examples, you have used the text/html and image/gif MIME types. For most HTTP responses, there is only one block of data sent to the Web browser, which only needs one MIME type for the data being returned to the Web browser. However, the multipart/mixed MIME type allows for multiple blocks of data to be sent in the same HTTP response.

The multipart/mixed MIME type uses a boundary string to separate the blocks of data being returned to the Web browser. Each data block has its own MIME type specified at the beginning of the block. You can use any string for the boundary separator. However, it's important to use a string that does not occur in the data being returned. A typical multipart/mixed parsed header looks like

```
Content-type: multipart/mixed;boundary=ThisRandomString
```

where ThisRandomString is the string boundary. As with other parsed headers, the multipart/mixed must be followed immediately by a blank line. Then

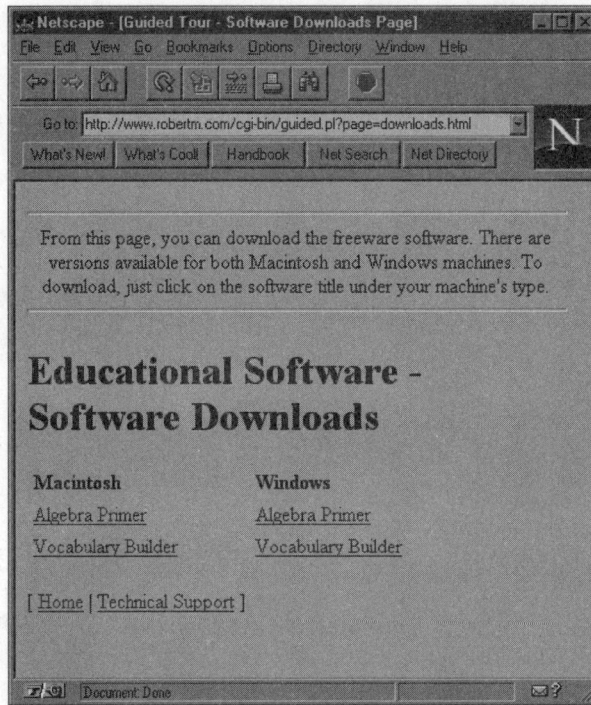

Figure 8.10: The Software Downloads page in the guided tour

at the beginning of each data block, you place the boundary string preceded by two dashes, followed on the next line by the MIME type for that block of data. You must have a blank line between the MIME type and the data being returned. You must also have a blank line immediately after the data object. So, the header and data for each block would look like

```
--ThisRandomString
Content-type: text/html

Data for the first object.
```

After you have included all the blocks of data you want returned to the user's Web browser, simply output the end of boundary string, which is the boundary string preceded and followed by two dashes, as in

```
--ThisRandomString--
```

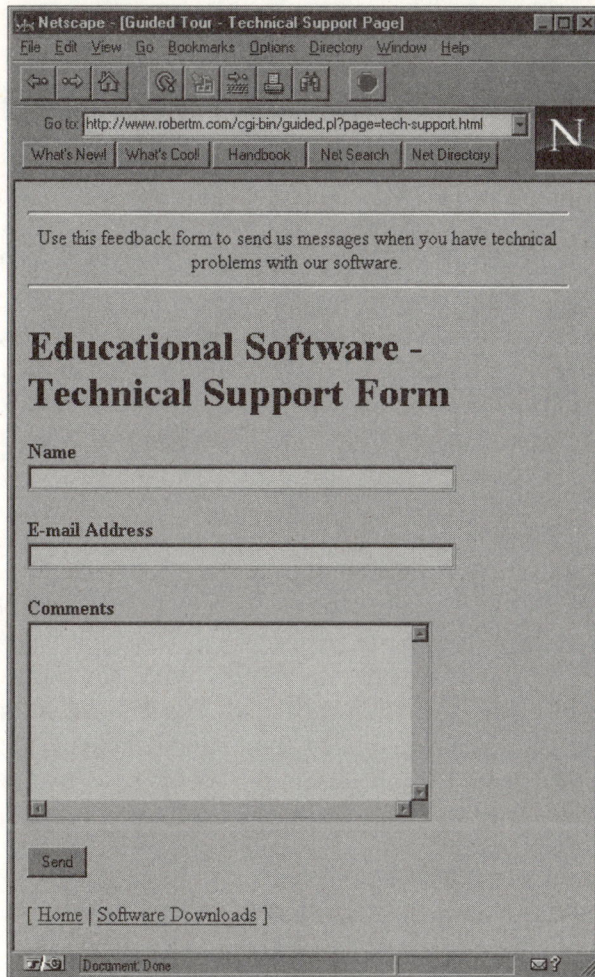

Figure 8.11: The Technical Support page in the guided tour

Here is an example of an HTTP response using the multipart/mixed MIME type:

```
Content-type: multipart/mixed;boundary=ThisRandomString

--ThisRandomString
Content-type: text/html

Data for the first object.
```

```
--ThisRandomString
Content-type: text/html

Data for the second and last object.

--ThisRandomString--
```

This example contains two HTML objects that are returned to the user in the HTTP response.

Server push uses a variant of the multipart/mixed MIME type, the multipart/x-mixed-replace MIME type. This is an experimental MIME type created by Netscape for server push. The difference between this MIME type and the standard multipart/mixed MIME type is that multipart/x-mixed-replace replaces previous data blocks with the subsequent data blocks. The format for the multipart/x-mixed-replace MIME type is identical to the above multipart/mixed example. Simply change the first line to

```
Content-type: multipart/x-mixed-replace;boundary=ThisRandomString
```

The major drawback with server push is that the HTTP communications channel remains open until the Web server is finished sending all the data. This means that your Web server must dedicate a TCP/IP port to the user's Web browser for the duration of the server push. When you use server push, you can keep this channel open indefinitely, sending data down whenever you want. Because all systems have a limited number of TCP/IP ports, this might overload your Web server. For this reason, you should use server push with discretion, especially if your Web server machine has limited TCP/IP ports.

THE PUSHED GUIDED TOUR

Using server push, you can redo the guided tour script to push down the modified pages instead of having the Web browser pull down the pages. This makes your guided tour script much simpler, because it does not have to receive any input about the current page to display. The script is only executed once for the entire guided tour instead of once for each Web page as with the client pull guided tour. The script just has to loop over the @pages array and send down the proper header and modified Web page for each element in the @pages array. Listing 8.9 contains the Perl code for the server push guided tour. To run this guided tour, place the code in a file called push-guided.pl (or p-guide.pl if you are restricted to an eight-character file name) and use the same three HTML pages from the client pull guided tour, as shown in Listings 8.4, 8.5, and 8.6. All users need to make the specified change to the path variable. Also, Windows users need to remove the first line and change the file names in both open statements, as noted in the comments.

Listing 8.9: The push-guided.pl File

```perl
#!/usr/local/bin/perl

# All users need to change the path to a valid path for
# their machine. Windows users need a path in the form
# $path="c:\\robertm\\guided";
$path = "/users/robertm/guided";
@pages = ("home.html", "downloads.html", "tech-support.html");
%page_names =
  ( "home.html", "Home Page",
    "downloads.html", "Software Downloads Page",
    "tech-support.html", "Technical Support Page", );
%guide_text =
  ( "home.html", "This is the Educational Software home page. " .
                 "It includes announcements about new and upcoming " .
                 "software releases.",
    "downloads.html", "From this page, you can download the freeware " .
                 "software. There are versions available for both " .
                 "Macintosh and windows machines. To download, just " .
                 "click on the software title under your machine's type.",
    "tech-support.html", "Use this feedback form to send us messages when " .
                 "you have technical problems with our software.", );
$|=1;

print "Content-type: multipart/x-mixed-replace;boundary=ThisRandomString\n\n";

foreach (@pages) {

  print "--ThisRandomString\n";
  print "Content-type: text/html\n\n";

  $guide = "<CENTER><HR>$guide_text{$_}<HR></CENTER>";

  # Windows users need to change the string "$path/$_" to
  # "$path\\$_"
  open(TEMPLATE, "$path/$_") || die "Content-type: text/html\n\nCannot open HTML
files!";
  @template = <TEMPLATE>;
  close(TEMPLATE);

  $template[2] = "<TITLE>Guided Tour - $page_names{$_}</TITLE>\n";
  splice(@template, 5, 0, $guide);

  print @template;

  print "\n\n";
  sleep 30;
}

print "--ThisRandomString\n";
```

Listing 8.9: The push-guided.pl File (Continued)

```
print "Content-type: text/html\n\n";

# Windows users need to change the string "$path/home.html" to
# "$path\\home.html"
open(TEMPLATE, "$path/home.html") || die "Content-type: text/html\n\nCannot open
 HTML files!";
@template = <TEMPLATE>;
close(TEMPLATE);

print @template;
print "\n\n";

print "--ThisRandomString--\n\n";
```

The first thing you should notice in Listing 8.9 is the line

```
$|=1;
```

This is a special Perl variable that, when set to a nonzero value, forces a flush of the output stream (standard output in this example) after every print statement. In other words, it keeps the output stream from being buffered. If you don't include this line in all your server push scripts written in Perl, the output will be buffered and sent to the browser all at once. For this example, buffering the output would result in all four HTML pages (the three modified for the guided tour, and the home page) being sent to the browser after 90 seconds. To the user, it would appear as though only the home page was reloaded.

The next lines in Listing 8.9 output the multipart/x-mixed-replace parsed header to the Web browser and start the foreach loop, which loops over each element in the @pages array. The body of the foreach loop is executed once for each element in the @pages array. First, the body of the foreach loop prints the parsed header for that block of data. The next lines should look familiar from the client pull guided tour example. The explanatory text is placed in the $guide variable, the file is opened and read into the @template array, the file is closed, the contents of the @template array are modified, and the modified contents are then returned to the user's Web browser. Notice how the variable $_ is used in the following lines from Listing 8.9:

```
$guide = "<CENTER><HR>$guide_text{$_}<HR></CENTER>";
open(TEMPLATE, "$path/$_") || die "Content-type: text/html\n\nCannot open HTML
 files!";
$template[2] = "<TITLE>Guided Tour - $page_names{$_}</TITLE>\n";
```

The $_ variable is a special Perl variable that in this context takes on the value of the current array element from the @pages array. For example, in the first iteration of the foreach loop, the $_ variable is equal to home.html. In the second iteration it is equal to downloads.html, and in the final iteration it is equal to tech-support.html. At the end of the body of the foreach loop, the extra blank line is appended to the data object and the program sleeps for 30 seconds. This is the delay time to allow the user time to read the contents of the current page that was just sent.

Following the foreach loop, one more body of data is sent with the lines

```
print "--ThisRandomString\n";
print "Content-type: text/html\n\n";

# Windows users need to change the string "$path/home.html" to
# "$path\\home.html"
open(TEMPLATE, "$path/home.html") || die "Content-type: text/html\n\nCannot open
 HTML files!";
@template = <TEMPLATE>;
close(TEMPLATE);

print @template;
print "\n\n";
```

Then the ending boundary is sent to signal the end of the data being sent. After the last data block is sent, the guided tour returns the user to the home page at the end of the tour. The home.html file is opened, the contents are read into the @template array, and then the contents of the @template array are sent to the user's Web browser. Running the server push guided tour produces HTML pages that look the same as those shown in Figures 8.9, 8.10, and 8.11.

SIMPLE ANIMATION

One nice feature of server push is that you can use it for single images instead of entire documents. If you place the call to the server push CGI script within the <IMG> tag, the server can push down new images that replace the previous image. This creates a flip-book style animation. Flip books are small books that contain one image per page. The image on each page is only slightly different than the image on the previous page. When you flip through the book, the images seem to move; you see a rudimentary animation.

Using this feature of server push, you can create animations for your Web pages. You just have to create the image files, place an <IMG> tag in your Web page to call your animation CGI script, and create a CGI script that pushes down the image files. For this example, you use the 13 images shown in Figure

8.12. These smiley faces are characters used in the Palace chat software distributed by Time Warner. To learn more about the Palace software, or to download a free copy of the Shareware, visit their Web site at http://www.thepalace.com.

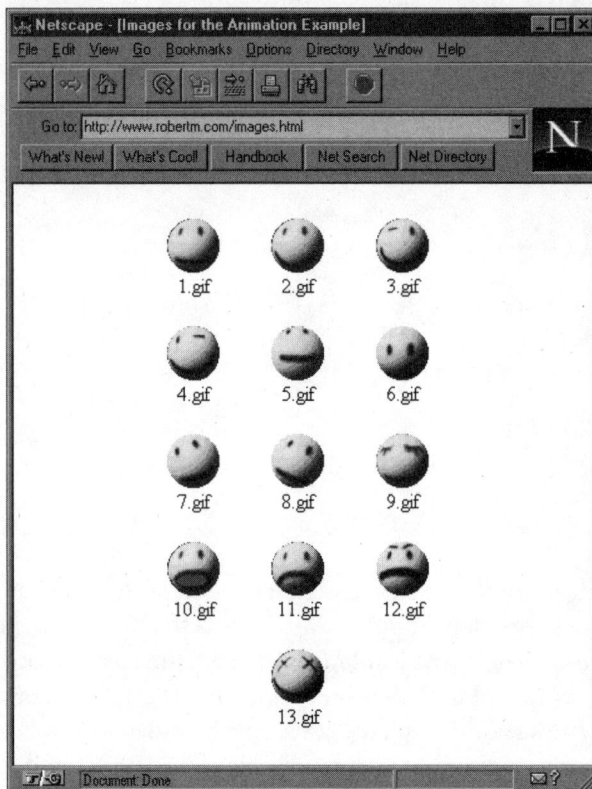

Figure 8.12: The Images for the Animation example

After creating all the image files for your animation, you can create the HTML page in which the animation will be played. Listing 8.10 contains the HTML code for the animation.html file (animate.htm if your system limits you to an eight-character file name and a three-character extension). Notice how the CGI script is being called from within the <IMG> tag.

With the images created and the HTML file ready, you just need to create the animate.pl script file. As with the server push guided tour, the script first needs to send the multipart/x-mixed-replace header to the Web browser. You do this with the line

```
print "Content-type: multipart/x-mixed-replace;boundary=ThisRandomString\n\n";
```

Listing 8.10: The animation.html File

```
<HTML>
<HEAD>
<TITLE>Animation Example</TITLE>
</HEAD>
<BODY BGCOLOR="#FFFFFF">
This animation shows the 13 facial expressions the Palace's default
avatar can use. An avatar is a graphical representation of yourself in
a graphical social environment. The Palace is a 2D graphical social
environment that works on the Internet. For more information about the
Palace, visit their Web site, http://www.thepalace.com.
<CENTER>
<IMG HEIGHT=44 WIDTH=44 SRC="/cgi-bin/animate.pl">
</CENTER></BODY>
</HTML>
```

Next you need a loop to send the header and data body for each image that is being sent. Because there are 13 images, you can use a for loop that will execute 13 times. Here is the for loop for the animation script:

```
for($i=1  $i<=$num_images; $i++) {

  print "--ThisRandomString\n";
  print "Content-type: image/gif\n\n";

  # Windows users need to change the string
  # "$path/$i.gif" to "$path\\$i.gif"
  open(GIF, "$path/$i.gif") || die;
  (undef, undef, undef, undef, undef, undef,, undef,
   $filesize, undef, undef, undef, undef, undef) = stat(GIF);
  sysread(GIF, $image, $filesize);
  close(GIF);
  syswrite(STDOUT, $image, $filesize);

  print "\n\n";
  sleep 1;
}
```

The statement

```
for($i=1  $i<=$num_images; $i++) {
```

is composed of three parts, the initialization of the loop variable, $i=1; the loop conditional, $i<=$num_images; and the incrementation of the loop variable, $i++. The for loops execute until the conditional statement is no longer true. For this example, the loop variable $i will start at one and be incremented by one each time the loop executes until it is greater than the value stored in the $num_images variable. This variable will be set at the beginning of the animation script file, and will contain the number of images to be used. Listing 8.11 shows where this variable is set.

Inside the body of the for loop, the header and data body for each image file is sent to the user's Web browser and the script then sleeps for 1 second. The two lines

```
print "--ThisRandomString\n";
print "Content-type: image/gif\n\n";
```

print the header for the image being sent to the browser. The lines

```
# Windows users need to change the string
# "$path/$i.gif" to "$path\\$i.gif"
open(GIF, "$path/$i.gif") || die;
(undef, undef, undef, undef, undef, undef,, undef,
 $filesize, undef, undef, undef, undef, undef) = stat(GIF);
sysread(GIF, $image, $filesize);
close(GIF);
syswrite(STDOUT, $image, $filesize);
```

open the image file, read the contents of the image file into the $image variable, close the image file, and output the contents of the $image variable to the user's Web browser. After sending the body of the data, you need to send the extra blank line and tell the script to sleep for a second. You do so with the following two lines:

```
print "\n\n";
sleep 1;
```

Listing 8.11 contains all the code for the animate.pl script. Notice that the variables have been set at the beginning and that the ending boundary is sent to the user's Web browser at the end. You need to change the $path variable to be valid for your system. Also, Windows users should remove the first line of the code and change the string in the open statement. Figure 8.13 shows how the Web page appears in Netscape at the end of the animation loop.

Listing 8.11: The animate.pl Script

```
#!/usr/local/bin/perl

# All users need to change the $path variable to a valid
# path for their system. Windows users need to use a
# path in the form $path = "c:\\robertm\\gifs";
```

Listing 8.11: The animate.pl Script (Continued)

```perl
$path = "/users/robertm/gifs";
$num_images = 13;
$|=1;

print "Content-type: multipart/x-mixed-
replace;boundary=ThisRandomString\n\n";

for($i=1  $i<=$num_images; $i++) {

  print "--ThisRandomString\n";
  print "Content-type: image/gif\n\n";

  # Windows users need to change the string
  # "$path/$i.gif" to "$path\\$i.gif"
  open(GIF, "$path/$i.gif") || die;
  (undef, undef, undef, undef, undef, undef,, undef,
   $filesize, undef, undef, undef, undef, undef) = stat(GIF);
  sysread(GIF, $image, $filesize);
  close(GIF);
  syswrite(STDOUT, $image, $filesize);

  print "\n\n";
  sleep 1;
}

print "--ThisRandomString--\n\n";
```

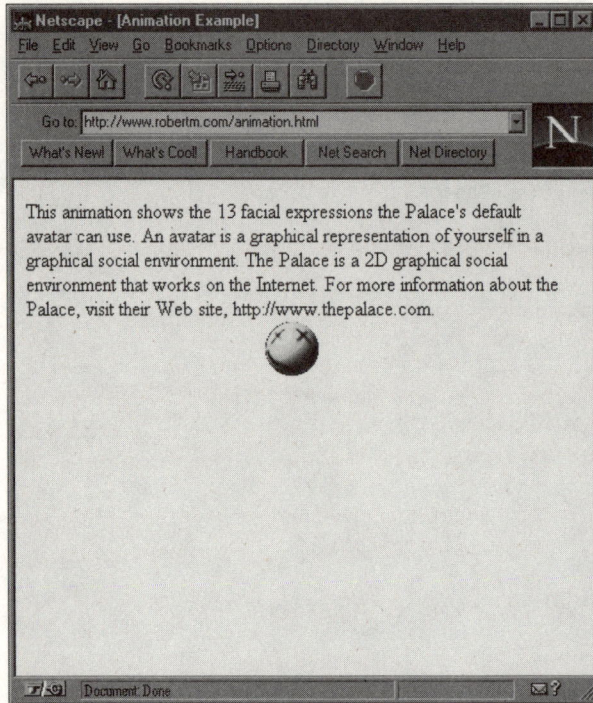

Figure 8.13: The Animation page

Creating Bulletin Boards

CREATING A SIMPLE CGI MESSAGE BOARD

INTERACTING WITH NNTP NEWS SERVERS

Y ou have probably seen traditional bulletin boards or message boards at supermarkets, offices, and college campuses. People usually post messages on these bulletin boards by pinning or stapling them onto the board. Often these boards are not highly organized, to put it mildly. They are used for announcements or for distributing information and do not typically let you post questions and receive responses.

Unlike these traditional bulletin boards, the electronic bulletin boards or (message boards) on the Internet provide a means for reading and posting messages and replies. Most message boards on the Internet are called newsgroups. A *newsgroup* is a bulletin board—usually devoted to a specific subject—that is implemented using the Network News Transfer Protocol (NNTP). NNTP is just another protocol used on the Internet. Newsgroups are distributed, which means that messages posted on one server are propagated to many other NNTP servers on the Internet. Using these bulletin boards, people all over the world can see and respond to messages, or post entirely new messages.

Electronic bulletin boards are also usually organized into message threads. A *message thread* is a single main message and all the related replies to that main message (or the replies to other replies). A single bulletin board has many message threads, which are usually represented as bulleted lists of messages with bulleted lists of replies indented underneath the main message. Figure 9.1 shows how these bulleted lists appear.

Because newsgroups operate under a different protocol than the World Wide Web, you cannot just have a NNTP newsgroup appear in your Web pages. To set up a bulletin board on your Web site, you must either create your

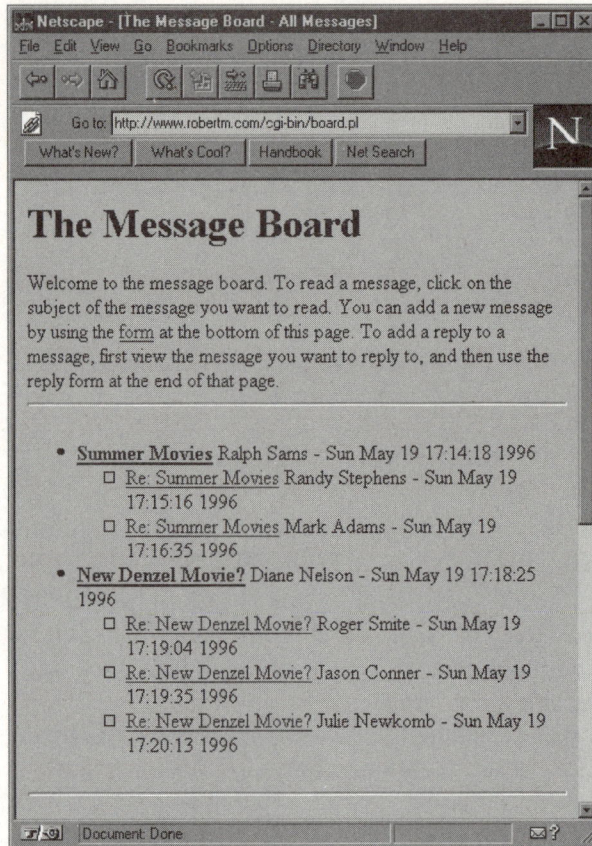

Figure 9.1: The message list

own bulletin board system using text files and CGI scripts, as demonstrated in this chapter, or you must write a CGI script to interface with a NNTP news server. Writing code to interface with an NNTP server would be close to creating a news reader program. A news reader program is the program you use to view the messages in a newsgroup and to post replies and new messages. If you created this style of news reader within your Web pages, the only thing your CGI script would not need to do that other news reader programs do is create an interface to display the news articles for the user. You would be using the user's Web browser as the interface to display the news articles. Creating a NNTP gateway script is much more difficult than creating a text-based bulletin board. The former would require some knowledge of NNTP headers and commands, whereas you can do the latter by creating one CGI script and a few text files.

In this chapter, you develop this text file based bulletin board CGI script that enables you to have a bulletin board on your Web site. Your bulletin board will display a list of all messages that have been posted and will allow visitors to your Web site to read any message simply by clicking on its subject. When the user clicks on the message subject, your bulletin board script formats the messages into HTML code for display in the user's Web browser. Visitors can also add new messages or reply to other messages using HTML form interfaces you create. When a user posts a new message or a reply, the bulletin board script saves the message in a text file. Also, your bulletin board script automatically deletes messages when they have been posted for longer than a specified number of days.

CREATING A SIMPLE CGI MESSAGE BOARD

For this example, you set up a bulletin board where users can post messages about movies. Each message will contain fields for the user's name, e-mail address, message subject, message date, and message contents. So the bulletin board is easy to read and navigate, the user will only see two kinds of pages: a Web page that lists all the messages that have been posted and a Web page that displays one of the messages from the bulletin board.

To reduce the number of HTML tags you need in your bulletin board CGI, you will create HTML template files that hold most of the HTML code for your Web bulletin board pages. An HTML template file is just a file containing text and HTML tags. It is a template file because it is not directly displayed to the user. Instead, your bulletin board CGI script reads in the contents of the template file, makes some changes, and then returns the altered contents to the user's Web browser. Your bulletin board script only requires two template files, one for displaying the headers from all the messages and one for displaying an entire message.

THE HTML TEMPLATES

The first Web page the user sees on your movie bulletin board is a list of headers from all posted messages. For this bulletin board, the header for a single message contains the subject field, the posting user's name, and the date the message was posted. The subject of each message is an HTML link that, when clicked, loads an HTML page containing the entire message. The messages are listed in the order in which they were received, with the most recent at the bottom. Replies to messages are also listed in the order in which they are received, but are indented under the message they are in response to. For example, in Figure 9.1 the messages are the postings by Ralph Sams and Diane Nelson. The postings by Randy Stephens and Mark Adams are replies to the message posted by Ralph Sams. All the other messages are replies to the posting by Diane Nelson.

At the bottom of the list of message headers will be an HTML form to let the user viewing your Web page post a new message. This form is for new messages only. If your users want to reply to a message, they need to use a different form. The HTML code for this form, along with the rest of the HTML code for the first template file, is shown in Listing 9.1. The file name for this template file is message-list.tmpl. (Name the file m-list.tml if your system restricts you to an eight-character file name and a three-character extension.) Figure 9.1 already showed what the message list looks like. Figure 9.2 shows how Netscape displays the new message form that the user uses to post a new message to your bulletin board. Figures 9.1 and Figure 9.2 both display the same HTML page; Figure 9.2 is the bottom part of the page whereas Figure 9.1 is the top part of the page. Notice that the message headers are added between the two <HR> tags. You develop the Perl code for doing this in the next section, "Displaying the Message List."

Listing 9.1: The message-list.tmpl File

```
<HTML>
<HEAD>
<TITLE>The Message Board - All Messages</TITLE>
</HEAD>
<BODY>
<H1>The Message Board</H1>
Welcome to the message board. To read a message, click on the subject
of the message you want to read. You can add a new message by using
the <A HREF="#form">form</A> at the bottom of this page. To add a
reply to a message, first view the message you want to reply to, and
then use the reply form at the end of that page.
<HR>
<HR>
<A NAME="form"><H1>New Message Form</H1></A>
Use this form to add a new message to the message board. Do not use
this form if you want to reply to one of the previous messages.
<FORM METHOD=POST ACTION="/cgi-bin/board.pl">
<TABLE>
<TR>
<TD><B>Name</B></TD>
<TD><INPUT NAME="name" SIZE=42></TD>
</TR>
<TR>
<TD><B>E-mail Address</B></TD>
<TD><INPUT NAME="email" SIZE=42></TD>
</TR>
<TR>
```

Listing 9.1: The message-list.tmpl File (Continued)

```
<TD><B>Subject</B></TD>
<TD><INPUT NAME="subject" SIZE=42></TD>
</TR>
<TR>
<TD COLSPAN=2><B>Comments</B><BR><TEXTAREA NAME="comments" ROWS=5
COLS=38></TEXTAREA></TD>
</TR>
<TR>
<TD COLSPAN=2><INPUT TYPE="submit" NAME="submit" VALUE="Post Message">
<INPUT TYPE="reset" VALUE="Clear"></TD>
</TR>
</TABLE>
</FORM>
</BODY>
</HTML>
```

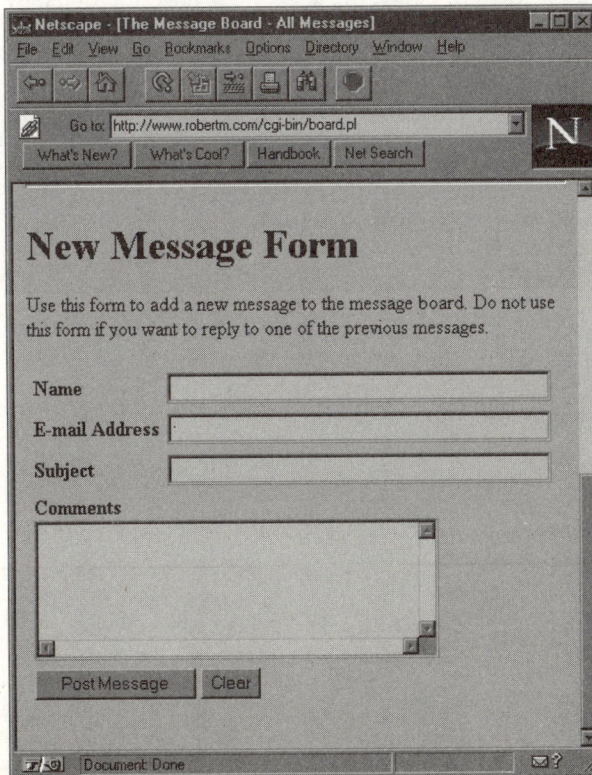

Figure 9.2: The New Message form

You need another HTML template file for displaying an entire message to the user. The message list displays only the header information for each message. To see the entire message, the user needs to click on the message subject. This link loads a page that displays the entire message along with a reply form for posting a new reply. Because each message is stored in a separate text file, your bulletin board script can easily display the selected message by reading in the contents of the text file, inserting it into a template of HTML code, and outputting the results to the user's Web browser. Listing 9.2 contains the HTML code for displaying the messages and replies. Notice how the lines

```
<TITLE>The Message Board - XXXX</TITLE>
<TD><INPUT NAME="subject" VALUE="YYYY" SIZE=42></TD>
```

contain the strings XXXX and YYYY. These are placeholders for real data that will be inserted by your bulletin board script. You will develop the code for displaying messages and replies in the section "Displaying Messages" later in this chapter. Figure 9.3 shows how the Netscape browser displays a sample message and Figure 9.4 shows the Reply form in which the user enters the data for a new reply. Like Figures 9.1 and 9.2, Figures 9.3 and 9.4 are two parts of the same HTML page.

Listing 9.2: The message.tmpl File

```
<HTML>
<HEAD>
<TITLE>The Message Board - XXXX</TITLE>
</HEAD>
<BODY>
<HR>
<A NAME="form"><H1>Reply Form</H1></A>
Use this form to add a reply under this subject heading. Do not use
this form if you want to post a new message.
<FORM METHOD=POST ACTION="/cgi-bin/board.pl">
<TABLE>
<TR>
<TD><B>Name</B></TD>
<TD><INPUT NAME="name" SIZE=42></TD>
</TR>
<TR>
<TD><B>E-mail Address</B></TD>
<TD><INPUT NAME="email" SIZE=42></TD>
</TR>
<TR>
<TD><B>Subject</B></TD>
<TD><INPUT NAME="subject" VALUE="YYYY" SIZE=42></TD>
</TR>
```

Listing 9.2: The message.tmpl File (Continued)

```
<TR>
<TD COLSPAN=2><B>Comments</B><BR><TEXTAREA NAME="comments" ROWS=5
COLS=38></TEXTAREA></TD>
</TR>
<TR>
<TD COLSPAN=2><INPUT TYPE=hidden NAME="list" VALUE="ZZZZ"><INPUT
TYPE="submit" NAME="submit" VALUE="Post Reply"> <INPUT TYPE="reset"
VALUE="Clear"></TD>
</TR>
</TABLE>
</FORM>
</BODY>
</HTML>
```

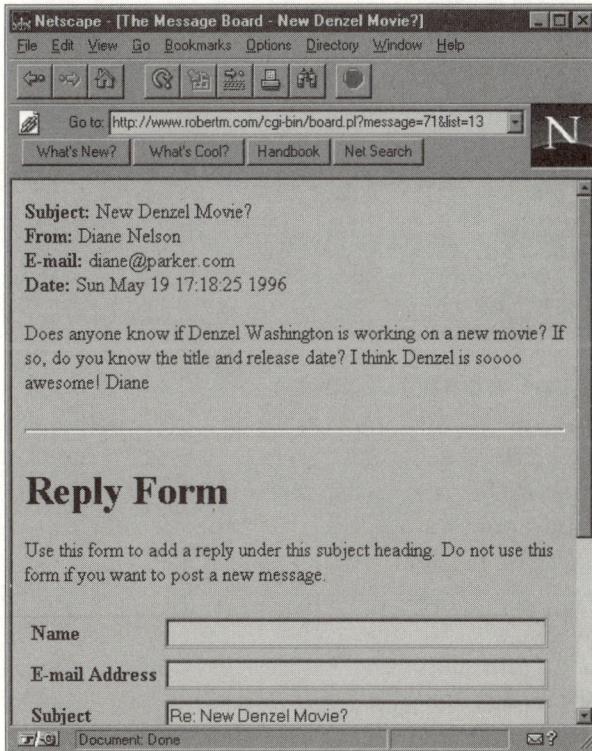

Figure 9.3: A sample message

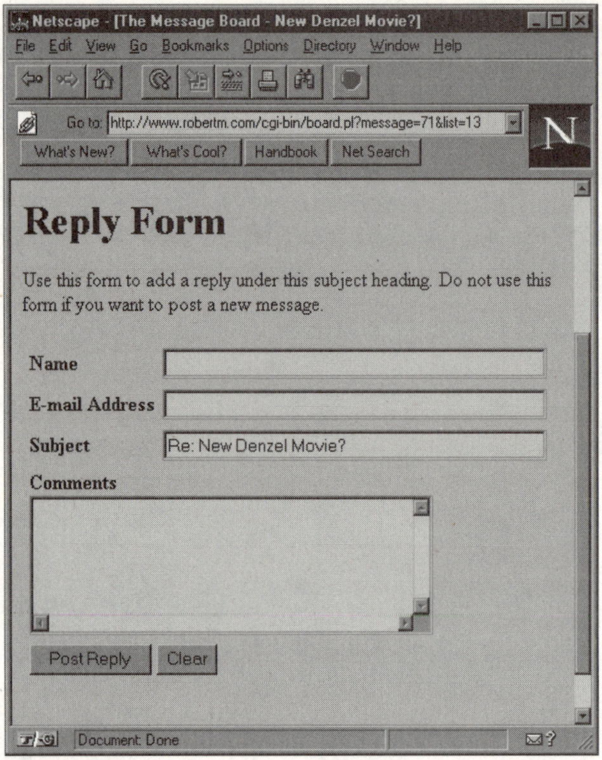

Figure 9.4: The Reply form

THE BULLETIN BOARD SCRIPT

Now that you have the HTML templates for displaying both the message list and the messages, you need to create the bulletin board script. Your script has to display the message list, display messages and replies, and post messages and replies. To make your script file easy to read, you can create subroutines for each of these tasks. The subroutines for the bulletin board script are Display_Message_Lists, Display_Message, Add_New_Message, and Add_Reply. You develop the code for each of these subroutines in the sections that follow.

You also create a fifth subroutine, Expires, that deletes messages that have been posted for over a certain number of days. This subroutine handles the most time consuming administrative chore associated with your bulletin board: deleting old messages. If you place the code for deleting old messages in a separate subroutine, you can easily change your bulletin board script to either expire or not expire old messages simply by either calling or not calling the Expires subroutine. You learn how to do this in the section "The Complete Bulletin Board Script" later in this chapter. There you also discover how to set the number of days messages remain on your bulletin board.

Before writing the five subroutines for the bulletin board script, you should create the files and directories in which the message lists, messages, and replies will be stored. You need two subdirectories, message-lists and messages. (If your operating system restricts you to eight-character directory names, change the directory name message-lists to m-lists and change message-lists to m-lists for the value assigned to the $list_dir variable in Listing 9.8 in the section "The Complete Bulletin Board Script.")

The message-lists directory will hold all the list files. For this example, list files store the headers for a single message and all the replies to that message. There can be numerous list files. The header information for each line in the list file will be in the form

```
name::message subject::date message was posted::file name of message file
```

The message-lists directory also contains the count.dat file. This file stores a number that represents the name of the last list file that was created. For example, when a user posts the first message to your bulletin board, the list file containing the header for that message is named 1 and the count.dat file contains the single digit 1. The headers for all the replies to that first message is appended to the 1 file. When the second message is posted to your bulletin board, the header for that message is placed in the list file 2, and the value in the count.dat file is incremented to 2.

The messages directory is where you place all the text files containing the entire posting for both messages and replies. The files in this directory are also named with digits, such as 1, 2 and 3, and another count.dat file in this directory keeps track of the last file name used in this directory. There is no distinction between message files and reply files in the messages directory. This distinction is made by the configuration of the list files. The header information for the first entry in a list file always refers to the main message for that group. All other lines in the list file contain header information that refer to replies.

With the directories and the two count.dat files created, you can now begin writing the subroutines for your bulletin board script. You start with the Display_Message_Lists subroutine, which is called whenever a user wants to see the header lines for all the messages that have been posted in your bulletin board.

Displaying the Message List   The Display_Message_Lists subroutine needs to create a single list of messages and replies from all the list files in the message-lists directory. To create this single list from the multiple files, you loop over all the files and read in the contents from each file. Then you take the header information you get from each line in the list files and format it with HTML tags. Because the message list only contains header information from each of the messages, the user needs a link to click on to display the entire message or reply. Also, for easy viewing, you should indent the header lines for all replies underneath the main message. You can do this by using the <UL> and <LI> HTML tags. The <UL> tag creates an unordered or bulleted list. Each list item is preceded by an <LI> tag. Finally, remember that most of the HTML code for the message list Web page is stored in the message-list.tmpl file. So, you also need to open this file, read in the contents of the template, add the message headers to the template, and return the modified contents of the template to the user's Web browser.

Start by opening the count.dat file and getting the file name of the last list file that was created. These three lines of Perl

```
open(LISTS,"$list_count") || die "Content-type: text/html\n\nCannot open list
count!";
$num_lists = <LISTS>;
close(LISTS);
```

open the count.dat file and read in the contents—the number used for the last file name. The first line opens the count.dat file for input. The path and file name of the count.dat file are stored in the $list_count variable, which is set at the beginning of the bulletin board script (shown in Listing 9.8 later in this chapter). Then a die statement terminates the program and outputs the contents of the string. The || operator between the open and die statements is the logical or operator. When you place this operator between the two statements, the Perl interpreter first tries to execute the open statement. If the open is successful, the Perl interpreter moves on to the next line of code. However, if the file cannot be opened, the Perl Interpreter executes the die statement. This is a common way to verify that a file is successfully opened and to terminate the Perl program if it is not.

The second line of Perl code reads in the contents of the first line in the count.dat file from the input stream <LISTS> and places it in the $num_lists variable. After the contents of the count.dat file have been read into the $num_lists variable, you can close the input stream <LISTS> by using the close command, as in the third line of code.

Now that the name of the last list file that was created is stored in the $num_lists variable, you can loop over all the list files. The loop is controlled by the for expression, as demonstrated here:

```
for ($i=1; $i<=$num_lists; $i++) {
```

This statement is composed of three parts: the initialization of the loop variable, $i=1, the loop conditional, $i<=$num_lists, and the incrementation of the loop variable, $i++. For loops execute until the conditional statement is no longer true. In this example, the loop variable $i starts at one and is incremented by one each time the loop executes until it is greater than the value stored in the $num_lists variable. So, the body of this loop is executed once for every list file.

Inside the body of the for loop, you need to do many things. First, you need to open the current list file and read in all the contents of that file. You do this with an open statement similar to the open statement you saw a moment ago:

```
open(LIST, "$list_dir/$i") || next;
@list_contents = <LIST>;
close(LIST);
```

The first line opens the file whose path is $list_dir/$i. The $list_dir variable is set at the beginning of your bulletin board script and contains the path to the message-lists subdirectory on your machine. (Listing 9.8 contains the code showing where this variable is set.) The $i variable is the loop variable that contains the name of the current list file. Notice that the die statement has been replaced with the next statement on the right side of the || operator. The next operator, if executed, advances the loop to the next iteration. For a for loop, this means the loop variable is incremented, the conditional is checked, and the loop body starts over. You use the next statement instead of the die operator so that the loop continues even if the list file cannot be opened. If the list file cannot be opened, you assume that it has been deleted by the Expires subroutine, which you will develop in the section "Expiring Messages" later in this chapter. Also notice that the second line uses an array, @list_contents on the left side of the assignment to the <LIST> stream. This reads all the lines from the list file into the @list_contents array, one line per element in the array.

If the body of the for loop continues to execute, the list file must have been successfully opened and the contents of the list file are in the @list_contents array. If the list file exists, there must be header information for the main message on the first line of the list file, which is now in the first element of the @list_contents array. So, you can split apart the header information for the main message, format the individual fields with HTML tags, and store them in a variable to be added to the HTML template. Remember that all header lines are in the format

```
name::message subject::date message was posted::file name of message file
```

So, you can use the Perl split statement to split each element into a separate variable. The following lines split the header information stored in the first element of the @list_contents array and place each field in a variable.

```
($name, $subject, $message_date, $message_file) = split(/::/, $list_contents[Ø]);
chop $message_file;
```

The first line does the actual split by separating the header line at all double colons. Because the $message_file variable receives all the remaining contents of the header information following the last double colon, it also contains a new line character. The second line uses the Perl chop operator to remove this new line character from the end of the $message_file variable.

With the header information split into the appropriate variables, you can now add HTML codes to properly format the information within the user's Web browser.

The following lines of Perl add HTML codes to the values stored in the header information variables and store the corresponding values in the $header variable:

```
unless (-e "$message_dir/$message_file") {
  $header = "<LI><B>$subject</B> $name -  $message_date";
} else {
  $header = "<LI><A HREF=\"/cgi-bin/board.pl?message=$message_file&list=$i\">";
  $header .= "<B>$subject</B></A> $name -  $message_date";
}
```

These lines contain an unless...else conditional, which is similar to an if...else conditional except that the statements under the unless section are executed when the conditional expression is false. In an if...else conditional, in contrast, the statements under the if section are executed when the conditional expression is true. In the first line of code, the conditional expression is contained within the parentheses. It contains the Perl operator -e, which is a file check operator. This conditional expression evaluates to true if the file $message_dir/$message_file exists, and false if it does not.

Remember that the $message_file variable was just set in the split statement. So, it contains the file name of the message file for the main message of the list file. If you plan to enable the Expires subroutine for your bulletin board script, the list file may contain the header information for a main message even after the corresponding message file has been deleted. This situation occurs only when there are replies to the main message that have not yet expired. When there are existing replies, you still want to display them indented under the header for the main message. However, you do not want to create a link to the main message's message file because it has already been deleted. That is what this unless...else conditional does: It checks whether the message file has already been deleted. If so, it formats the header without using the <A> tag (the single expression right after the unless line). If the file does exist, the else portion of the conditional is executed, and the message's subject is made a link to the message file (see in the two lines under the preceding else expression).

The preceding lines of code properly format the header line for the main message. Now you need to properly format the header lines for any existing replies. First, you can easily determine whether there are any replies by checking the length of the @list_contents array. Remember that the header information for the main message is always in the first element of the @list_contents array. Therefore, if the array has more than one element there are replies to the main message. So, you use an if statement to execute a block of code only when the @list_contents array is greater than one. Here is the Perl code for this if block:

```
if (@list_contents > 1) {
  $replies = "<UL>\n";
  for ($j=1; $j<@list_contents; $j++) {

    # Split each message header from the message list file.
    ($name, $subject, $message_date, $message_file) =
            split(/::/, $list_contents[$j]);
    chop $message_file;

    # Format the replies for display in the user's Web browser.
    $replies .= "<LI><A HREF=\"/cgi-
bin/board.pl?message=$message_file&list=$i\">";
    $replies .= "$subject</A> $name - $message_date";
  }

  # Append the replies after the main message.
  $header .= "\n$replies</UL>\n";
}
```

The first line contains the if statement and the conditional expression. Once inside the if block, you begin to format the replies by placing the HTML tag <UL> in the $replies variable. Following this line, another for loop loops over the remaining elements in the @list_contents array. Because Perl arrays are indexed beginning at 0, this loop begins at the second element of the @list_contents array at index 1. Next you use the split statement again to break apart the header information taken from the list file. Notice that this time you use the index $j in the $list_contents[$j] expression. Because $j is the loop variable, it also has the value of the current array element, so you can use it for the index of the array. At the end of the body of the loop, the reply's header is formatted with HTML tags and appended to the $replies variable. In this case, you do not need to check whether the reply's message file exists: If it did not, the reply's header information would not be in the list file. This will become clear when you develop the code for the Expires subroutine. Finally, after the loop has finished executing, all the replies are in the $replies variable, which is then appended to the $header variable along with the ending </UL> bulleted list tag.

Keep in mind that all the code segments up to the line with the for statement containing the $i loop variable are going to be in the body of that for loop. So, all these preceding lines are executed for every list file. You just need one more line to finish the body of this for loop:

```
push(@lists, $header);
```

This line uses the Perl push statement to append the contents of the $header variable to the @lists array. This way, when the for loop is finished, all of the properly formatted messages and replies are in the @lists array, ready for insertion into the HTML template.

When the for loop has completed, you need to add two more HTML tags to the contents of the @lists array to finish formatting it. These are beginning and ending bulleted list tags, <UL> and </UL>. Remember that you already entered these tags for the replies. By adding them around all the messages, you create a bulleted list of main messages with bulleted lists of replies (if there are any) indented under each main message. Refer back to Figure 9.1 for an example of these bulleted lists. Because your bulletin board may contain no messages—either when no one has posted any message yet or when all the messages have expired—the @lists array could be empty. Therefore, you should check whether it contains any messages before adding the <UL> and </UL> tags. If it is empty, place a message in the @lists array that is displayed in the Web page informing the user that there are currently no messages in your bulletin board. The following if...else statement checks the length of the @lists array. If it is not zero (empty), the <UL> and </UL> tags are added. Otherwise, the no messages statement is placed in the first element of the array.

```
# If there are any messages in the @lists array, finish formatting with HTML
if (@lists) {
  unshift(@lists, "<UL>\n");
  push(@lists, "</UL>\n");
} else {

  # No messages exist.
  $lists[0] = "<H2>Currently No Messages</H2>";
}
```

Now your Display_Message_List subroutine just needs to read in the HTML template from the template file, insert the contents of the @lists array into the template, and return the modified contents of the template to the user's Web browser. All this is done in the following lines of Perl:

```
open(TEMPLATE,"$list_template") || die "Content-type: text/html\n\nCannot open
template!";
@template = <TEMPLATE>;
close(TEMPLATE);

# Put the message headers in the template, and send to the user's Web browser.
splice(@template, 8, 0, @lists);

print "Content-type: text/html\n\n";
print @template;
```

You should recognize the open statement from earlier. Here it opens the message list template whose file and path name are stored in the $list_template variable. The contents of the file are then stored in the @template array. The next line uses the Perl splice statement to insert the contents of the @lists array into the @template array before index 8 in the @template array. Remember that index 8 corresponds to the ninth element in the array. Listing 9.1 shows that the ninth element in the @template array is the second of the two <HR> tags. This splice statement inserts the contents of the @lists array between the two <HR> tags. Finally, the last two lines of code output the required parsed header and the modified contents of the @template array to the user's Web browser.

Listing 9.3 contains the complete code for the Display_Message_Lists subroutine. Besides the sub Display_Message_Lists line, the only lines that have been added are the declarations of local variables at the beginning. The local statement is used to declare the arrays and variables as local to the Display_ Message_Lists subroutine. Remember, a local variable exists only within a portion of your Perl code, usually within a subroutine. If a variable with the same name existed outside the subroutine, Perl would consider it a different variable than the one that is declared local within the subroutine. Declaring your subroutine's variables as local helps to keep your subroutines from overwriting values of global variables. A global variable is one that is accessible throughout the entire Perl program, including any subroutines in the same Perl file. In Listing 9.3, the variables $list_count, $list_dir, $message_dir, and $list_template are global variables.

Listing 9.3: The Display_Message_Lists Subroutine

```
sub Display_Message_Lists {
  local (@template, @lists, @list_contents, $num_lists,
         $i, $j, $name, $subject, $message_date, $message_file,
         $header, $replies);

  open(LISTS,"$list_count") || die "Content-type: text/html\n\nCannot open list
count!";
  $num_lists = <LISTS>;
  close(LISTS);

  # Loop over all the message list files and add the contents to the message list
  # which is displayed to the user.
  for ($i=1; $i<=$num_lists; $i++) {

    # Open the message list file. If it cannot be
    # opened, assume it has been deleted and go
    # to the next message list.
    # Windows users need to change the string "$list_dir/$i" to
    # "$list_dir\\$i"
    open(LIST, "$list_dir/$i") || next;
    @list_contents = <LIST>;
    close(LIST);

    # Split the message header from the message list file.
    ($name, $subject, $message_date, $message_file) =
            split(/::/, $list_contents[0]);
    chop $message_file;

    # Format the header depending on whether the message file
    # exists
    # Windows users need to change the string "$message_dir/$message_file"
    # to "$message_dir\\$message_file"
    unless (-e "$message_dir/$message_file") {
      $header = "<LI><B>$subject</B> $name -  $message_date";
    } else {
      $header = "<LI><A HREF=\"/cgi-
bin/board.pl?message=$message_file&list=$i\">";
      $header .= "<B>$subject</B></A> $name -  $message_date";
    }

    # If the header file has more than one line, it contains header lines for
replies.
    if (@list_contents > 1) {
      $replies = "<UL>\n";
      for ($j=1; $j<@list_contents; $j++) {

        # Split each message header from the message list file.
        ($name, $subject, $message_date, $message_file) =
                split(/::/, $list_contents[$j]);
```

Listing 9.3: The Display_Message_Lists Subroutine (Continued)

```perl
        chop $message_file;

        # Format the replies for display in the user's Web browser.
        $replies .= "<LI><A HREF=\"/cgi-
bin/board.pl?message=$message_file&list=$i\">";
        $replies .= "$subject</A> $name - $message_date";
      }

      # Append the replies after the main message.
      $header .= "\n$replies</UL>\n";
    }

    # Put the header and replies (if any) in the @lists array.
    push(@lists, $header);

  }

  # If there are any messages in the @lists array, finish formatting with HTML
  if (@lists) {
    unshift(@lists, "<UL>\n");
    push(@lists, "</UL>\n");
  } else {

    # No messages exist.
    $lists[0] = "<H2>Currently No Messages</H2>";
  }

  open(TEMPLATE,"$list_template") || die "Content-type: text/html\n\nCannot open
template!";
  @template = <TEMPLATE>;
  close(TEMPLATE);

  # Put the message headers in the template, and send to the user's Web browser.
  splice(@template, 8, 0, @lists);

  print "Content-type: text/html\n\n";
  print @template;

}
```

Displaying Messages   Recall from the code in the previous section that the message subject for each header is a link to the message file. The actual HTML looks like this:

```
<A HREF="/cgi-bin/board.pl?message=$message_file&list=$i"><B>$subject</B></A>
```

where $message_file is the file containing the entire message, $i is the list file, and $subject is the message's subject. Notice how the link calls the CGI script board.pl. This is the name of your bulletin board script file. So, each link calls the bulletin board script again and passes two parameters, the message file name and the list file name. In this section, you develop the Display_Message subroutine, which takes these two parameters and displays the corresponding message file.

Your Display_Message subroutine first needs to open the message file, the message's list file, and the message template file. Once these files are opened, their contents is read into three arrays: @message, @list, and @template. This is done with the following lines of Perl code, which are similar to open statements used in the previous section:

```
open(TEMPLATE,"$message_template") || die "Content-type: text/html\n\nCannot open
template!";
@template = <TEMPLATE>;
close(TEMPLATE);

open(MESSAGE,"$message_dir/$data{\"message\"}") || die "Content-type:
text/html\n\nCannot open message!";
@message = <MESSAGE>;
close(MESSAGE);

open(LIST,"$list_dir/$data{\"list\"}") || die "Content-type: text/html\n\nCannot
open message!";
@list = <LIST>;
close(LIST);
```

The message's list file is opened so that the message's subject can be obtained easily. Recall from the section "The HTML Templates" that the message's subject is placed in the title of the Web page and as the default text in the subject field of the Reply form at the bottom of the Page (as shown earlier in Figure 9.4). To get the header information of the current message, you need to loop over all the contents of the list file until you find the line containing the correct header. Because the @list array contains the contents of the list file, you can just loop over the array until you find the correct element. To accomplish this, you use Perl's foreach statement, which loops over each element of the array. Here is the entire foreach statement and body:

```
foreach (@list) {
  # Split each message header from the message list file.
  (undef, $subject, undef, $message_file) =
          split(/::/);
  chop $message_file;

  # Exit the loop when the message has been found.
```

```
    last if $message_file == $data{'message'};
}
```

The first lines in the body of the foreach loop split the header information, as you did in the Display_Message_Lists subroutine. But here the split statement does not specify an argument to split. In Perl, when there is no argument for the split statement, the contents of the $_ variable are split. This is a special variable that, in the context of the preceding foreach loop, is set to the current element in the @list array for each iteration of the loop. Finally, the last statement in the body of the foreach loop compares the value of the $message_file variable, which was just obtained from the header information in the @list array, with the value of the message file that was passed to the script as an argument. The data passed to your bulletin board script is URL decoded and placed into the %data associative array with the User_Data subroutine you have used throughout this book. If the values of these two variables match, the current element of the @list array is the correct header line for the message the user selected for display. So, the last statement at the beginning of the line causes the loop to exit when the conditional is true.

Now that you have obtained the subject from the list file's header information and have read in the entire message from the message file, you can insert the information into the HTML template file and send the modified template back to the user's Web browser. You do this with the following lines of Perl:

```
$template[2] =~ s/XXXX/$subject/ge;

unless ($subject =~ /^re:/i) {
    substr($subject, 0, 0) = "Re: ";
}

$template[20] =~ s/YYYY/$subject/ge;
$template[26] =~ s/ZZZZ/$data{'list'}/ge;

splice(@template, 4, 0, @message);

print "Content-type: text/html\n\n";
print @template;
```

The first line places the message's subject in the HTML line that contains the <TITLE> tags. Recall from Listing 9.2 that this is the third line of the file, which when read into the @template array corresponds to index 2. The unless conditional checks whether the subject already begins with the letters re:, ignoring case. The check is performed by using the regular expression /^re:/i, which is true if the first three characters of the $subject variable are re:,

Re:, rE:, or RE:. If they are not, the string Re: is placed at the beginning of the contents of the $subject variable. Then the modified subject is substituted for the YYYY placeholder. Remember that this placeholder was for the default value of the subject field in the Reply form at the bottom of the Web page the user will see. Next, the list file name is placed into the hidden field of the Reply form, replacing the ZZZZ placeholder. The splice statement, which you used in the Display_Message_List subroutine, inserts the contents of the message into the beginning of the HTML template. Finally, the modified version of the template is sent to the user's Web browser along with the required parsed header.

You can now create the Display_Message subroutine by placing all the code you have developed so far within a subroutine body. You also need to add the declarations of the local variable. Listing 9.4 contains the complete code for the Display_Message subroutine.

Listing 9.4: The Display_Message Subroutine

```
sub Display_Message {
  local (%data) = @_;
  local (@template, @list, @message, $subject, $message_file);

  # Open and read in the template
  open(TEMPLATE,"$message_template") || die "Content-type:
text/html\n\nCannot open template!";
  @template = <TEMPLATE>;
  close(TEMPLATE);

  # Open and read in the message file
  # Windows users need to change the string
"$message_dir/$data{\"message\"}"
  # to "$message_dir\\$data{\"message\"}"
  open(MESSAGE,"$message_dir/$data{\"message\"}") || die "Content-
type: text/html\n\nCannot open message!";
  @message = <MESSAGE>;
  close(MESSAGE);

  # Open and read in the list file
  # Windows users need to change the string
"$list_dir/$data{\"list\"}" to
  # "$list_dir\\$data{\"list\"}"
  open(LIST,"$list_dir/$data{\"list\"}") || die "Content-type:
text/html\n\nCannot open message!";
  @list = <LIST>;
  close(LIST);
```

Listing 9.4: The Display_Message Subroutine (Continued)

```perl
# Find the subject for the message to be displayed.
foreach (@list) {
  # Split each message header from the message list file.
  (undef, $subject, undef, $message_file) =
          split(/::/);
  chop $message_file;

  # Exit the loop when the message has been found.
  last if $message_file == $data{'message'};
}

# Put the subject in the <TITLE> line of the template.
$template[2] =~ s/XXXX/$subject/ge;

# Format the subject line for the Reply form at the end of the page.
unless ($subject =~ /^re:/i) {
  substr($subject, 0, 0) = "Re: ";
}

# Insert the subject and list into the template.
$template[20] =~ s/YYYY/$subject/ge;
$template[26] =~ s/ZZZZ/$data{'list'}/ge;

# Insert the message into the template and send it to the user's Web
browser.
  splice(@template, 4, 0, @message);

  print "Content-type: text/html\n\n";
  print @template;

}
```

Adding New Messages You now have subroutines for displaying a list of the headers and the actual contents of all the messages and replies that have been posted to your bulletin board. The next step is to create subroutines that will handle postings to the bulletin board. You have already created both the forms for posting messages and replies. In this section, you develop the Add_New_Message subroutine, which is called when the user posts a message with the form on the bottom of the message list Web page. This form was shown in Figure 9.2.

With the Add_New_Message subroutine, the user creates a new message. You need to create a new list file for the header information for this new message and any replies that may be posted at a later time. To create a new list file, you first need to read in the value stored in the count.dat file. Remember, this value is the file name of the last list file your bulletin board script created. So, once you read in the value, you need to increment it by one and store the new value back in the count.dat file. You do this with the following lines:

```
open(LISTS,"$list_count") || die "Content-type: text/html\n\nCannot open list
count!";
$num_lists = <LISTS>;
close(LISTS);

$num_lists++;

open(LISTS,">$list_count") || die "Content-type: text/html\n\nCannot open list
count!";
print LISTS $num_lists;
close(LISTS);
```

The first open statement works just like the open statement you used in the Display_Message_Lists subroutine to open the count.dat file. The line immediately following these three lines—that is, the line containing $num_lists++;—increments the value in the $num_lists variable. The ++ operator is a Perl operator that takes the current value in the variable ($num_lists in this case), adds one to it, and stores it back in the variable. Following the incrementation of the $num_lists variable, the count.dat file is once more opened and the incremented value is printed to the file. Notice that the operator > precedes the $list_count variable in the second open statement. This operator specifies to open the file for output, overwriting the file if it already exists.

You now have the value to use for the file name of the new list file you are going to create. You also need the file name for the new message file you will create. As with the list file, the file names for the message files are stored in the count.dat file. The only difference is the directory in which the count.dat file is located. For the message file, you need to use the count.dat file in the messages subdirectory you created earlier. The following lines of Perl are similar to the earlier ones for retrieving, incrementing, and saving the list file name value. The only difference is that the following lines retrieve, increment, and save the message file name value.

```
open(MESSAGES,"$message_count") || die "Content-type: text/html\n\nCannot open
message count!";
$num_messages = <MESSAGES>;
close(MESSAGES);

$num_messages++;
```

```
open(MESSAGES,">$message_count") || die "Content-type: text/html\n\nCannot open
message count!";
print MESSAGES $num_messages;
close(MESSAGES);
```

Now that you have the file names for both the new list file and the new message file, you are ready to create these files. First, you can create the new message file. The following lines open the new file for output and print the contents of the data received from the user:

```
open(NEWMESSAGE,">$message_dir/$num_messages") || die "Content-type:
text/html\n\nCannot create new message!";
print NEWMESSAGE "<B>Subject:</B> $data{\"subject\"}<BR>\n";
print NEWMESSAGE "<B>From:</B> $data{\"name\"}<BR>\n";
print NEWMESSAGE "<B>E-mail:</B> $data{\"email\"}<BR>\n" if $data{'email'};
print NEWMESSAGE "<B>Date:</B> $date<P>\n";
print NEWMESSAGE "$data{\"comments\"}<P>\n";
close(NEWLIST);
```

Remember that using the > operator before the file name in the open statement causes the file to be created if it doesn't already exist. You can create the new list file in a similar manner using the following lines of Perl code:

```
open(NEWLIST,">$list_dir/$num_lists") || die "Content-type: text/html\n\nCannot
create new list!";
print NEWLIST "$data{\"name\"}::$data{\"subject\"}::${date}::$num_messages\n";
close(NEWLIST);
```

Notice that the header information is formatted in the file. Each field is separated by two colons, which is the format you worked with in the Display_Message_Lists and Display_Message subroutines.

Listing 9.5 contains all of the code for the Add_New_Message subroutine. This listing contains a couple of lines that weren't discussed in this section, in addition to the subroutine and local variable declarations. The first new section is immediately after the local variable declarations. It consists of a die statement and an unless conditional. This code makes the subroutine exit if the user did not supply values for the Name, Subject, and Comments fields. Your bulletin board script does not have to have this code, but it helps to keep empty postings from appearing on your bulletin board. The other line that is was not discussed previously is the final line, which calls the Display_Message_Lists subroutine. After the user's message is added to the bulletin boards, it makes sense for your script to redisplay the message list, which will now contain the user's new message.

Listing 9.5: The Add_New_Message Subroutine

```
sub Add_New_Message {
  local (%data) = @_;
  local ($num_lists, $num_messages);

  # Verify the user entered the required fields
  die "Content-type: text/html\n\nYou must enter data for every field
except the E-mail address."
        unless ($data{'name'} && $data{'subject'} &&
$data{'comments'});

  # Get the last list number
  open(LISTS,"$list_count") || die "Content-type: text/html\n\nCannot
open list count!";
  $num_lists = <LISTS>;
  close(LISTS);

  # Increment the number
  $num_lists++;

  # Save the current list number to the file
  open(LISTS,">$list_count") || die "Content-type: text/html\n\nCannot
open list count!";
  print LISTS $num_lists;
  close(LISTS);

  # Get the last message number
  open(MESSAGES,"$message_count") || die "Content-type:
text/html\n\nCannot open message count!";
  $num_messages = <MESSAGES>;
  close(MESSAGES);

  # Increment the number
  $num_messages++;

  # Save the current message number to the file
  open(MESSAGES,">$message_count") || die "Content-type:
text/html\n\nCannot open message count!";
  print MESSAGES $num_messages;
  close(MESSAGES);

  # Create the new message
  # Windows users need to change the string
">$message_dir/$num_messages"
  # to ">$message_dir\\$num_messages"
```

Listing 9.5: The Add_New_Message Subroutine (Continued)

```
  open(NEWMESSAGE,">$message_dir/$num_messages") || die "Content-type:
text/html\n\nCannot create new message!";
  print NEWMESSAGE "<B>Subject:</B> $data{\"subject\"}<BR>\n";
  print NEWMESSAGE "<B>From:</B> $data{\"name\"}<BR>\n";
  print NEWMESSAGE "<B>E-mail:</B> $data{\"email\"}<BR>\n" if
$data{'email'};
  print NEWMESSAGE "<B>Date:</B> $date<P>\n";
  print NEWMESSAGE "$data{\"comments\"}<P>\n";
  close(NEWLIST);

  # Create the new list
  # Windows users need to change the string ">$list_dir/$num_lists" to
  # ">$list_dir\\$num_lists"
  open(NEWLIST,">$list_dir/$num_lists") || die "Content-type:
text/html\n\nCannot create new list!";
  print NEWLIST
"$data{\"name\"}::$data{\"subject\"}::${date}::$num_messages\n";
  close(NEWLIST);

  &Display_Message_Lists;

}
```

Adding Replies   In this section, you develop the other subroutine needed for posting messages to your bulletin board. The Add_New_Message subroutine you developed in the previous section is used only for adding new messages to the bulletin board, not for replying to existing messages. For this, you develop the Add_Reply subroutine. The Add_Reply subroutine is very similar to the Add_New_Message subroutine. The only difference is that it does not create a new list file. Instead, the header for the new reply is added to the list file containing the header information for the message the reply references.

The lines for retrieving, incrementing, and saving the new message count file name as well as the lines for creating the new message file are exactly the same as those in the Add_New_Message subroutine. However, the addition of the header information to the list file is different. The following lines of Perl code open the existing list file and append the new header information to it:

```
open(LIST,">>$list_dir/$data{\"list\"}") || die "Content-type:
text/html\n\nCannot open list!";
print LIST "$data{\"name\"}::$data{\"subject\"}::${date}::$num_messages\n";
close(LIST);
```

Notice that the file name in the open statement is preceded by the >> operator. This operator indicates that the file will be opened for output and the output will be appended to the file rather than overwriting it.

Listing 9.6 contains the complete Add_Reply subroutine. As with the Add_New_Message subroutine, the Name, Subject, and Comments fields are checked for values, and the subroutine exists if they do not contain any. Also, the Display_Message_Lists subroutine is called after the user's reply has been posted to the bulletin board.

Listing 9.6: The Add_Reply Subroutine

```
sub Add_Reply {
  local (%data) = @_;
  local ($num_lists, $num_messages);

  # Verify the user entered the required fields
  die "Content-type: text/html\n\nYou must enter data for every field
except the E-mail address."
        unless ($data{'name'} && $data{'subject'} &&
$data{'comments'});

  # Get the last message number
  open(MESSAGES,"$message_count") || die "Content-type:
text/html\n\nCannot open message count!";
  $num_messages = <MESSAGES>;
  close(MESSAGES);

  # Increment the number
  $num_messages++;

  # Save the current message number to the file
  open(MESSAGES,">$message_count") || die "Content-type:
text/html\n\nCannot open message count!";
  print MESSAGES $num_messages;
  close(MESSAGES);

  # Create the new message
  # Windows users need to change the string
">$message_dir/$num_messages" to
  # ">$message_dir\\$num_messages"
  open(NEWMESSAGE,">$message_dir/$num_messages") || die "Content-type:
text/html\n\nCannot create new message!";
  print NEWMESSAGE "<B>Subject:</B> $data{\"subject\"}<BR>\n";
  print NEWMESSAGE "<B>From:</B> $data{\"name\"}<BR>\n";
```

Listing 9.6: The Add_Reply Subroutine (Continued)

```
  print NEWMESSAGE "<B>E-mail:</B> $data{\"email\"}<BR>\n" if
$data{'email'};
  print NEWMESSAGE "<B>Date:</B> $date<P>\n";
  print NEWMESSAGE "$data{\"comments\"}<P>\n";
  close(NEWLIST);

  # Add message header to the list
  # Windows users need to change the string
">>$list_dir/$data{\"list\"}"
  # to ">>$list_dir\\$data{\"list\"}"
  open(LIST,">>$list_dir/$data{\"list\"}") || die "Content-type:
text/html\n\nCannot open list!";
  print LIST
"$data{\"name\"}::$data{\"subject\"}::${date}::$num_messages\n";
  close(LIST);

  &Display_Message_Lists;

}
```

Expiring Messages   You could set up a working bulletin board with the four subroutines you have created. However, eventually, your bulletin board will contain messages that are very old. Of course, you could always delete the message files yourself, but then you would also need to modify the list files, removing the header information for any message files you deleted. Handling the expiration of messages is a job better left to your bulletin board script. It can easily check messages for expiration, removing all reference to them in the list files when deleting them. It can also regularly check for expiration, keeping your bulletin board fresh for everyone who uses it.

The Expires subroutine you develop in this section checks the date when each message file was last modified. Because the message files are only modified when they are created, this is the date the file was created. If the number of days since the file was created is greater than a number you specify, the Expires subroutine deletes the message file and removes the header information from the list file, unless the header information is for the main message (the first message in the list file) and there are headers for replies in the same file. If the main message is the only file in the list file, and its message file has expired or no longer exists (if it had previously expired but the header was not removed because of replies), the list file is also deleted.

Your Expires subroutine is similar in structure to the Display_Message_Lists subroutine. The Expires subroutine starts by looping over all of the message list files, opening each one and reading in all the lines containing message and reply header information. If there are any reply headers, an inner loop breaks apart each reply header, checking whether the corresponding message file has expired. If it has, the message file is deleted and the reply header is removed from the file. Once the inner loop has completed, the header for the main message is split apart, and the corresponding message file is checked for expiration (or to see whether it even exists).

As in the Display_Message_Lists subroutine, you use for loops for both the inner and outer loop. The outer loop needs to be executed once for every list file. So, you once again open the count.dat file in the message-lists subdirectory and use that value as the upper bounds for your outer for loop. The following four lines of Perl code open the count.dat file, retrieve the number that was last used for a list file name, and start the outer loop:

```
open(LISTS,"$list_count") || die "Content-type: text/html\n\nCannot open list count!";
$num_lists = <LISTS>;
close(LISTS);


for ($i=1; $i<=$num_lists; $i++) {
```

Once inside the body of the outer loop, you need to open the list file and read in all the contents of the file. To do so, you use the following three lines of Perl, which are identical to the lines you used to open and read in the contents of the list file in the Display_Message_Lists subroutine:

```
open(LIST, "$list_dir/$i") || next;
@list_contents = <LIST>;
close(LIST);
```

Next, you need to initialize a new array, one that you did not use in the Display_Message_Lists subroutine. You do this with the Perl statement

```
@new_list_contents = ($list_contents[0]);
```

This new array stores the contents for the new list file that replaces the old list file. Because you will remove header lines from the @list_contents array when the message file for the reply expires, you need to create a new list file that reflects these deletions. To do this, you use the @new_list_contents array. In the preceding line, you initialize the array to contain only the header for the main message. During the inner loop that you will develop in a moment, you append to the @new_list_contents array the header information for all replies that have not expired.

You now need to begin the inner loop, which will loop over the reply header lines in the @list_contents array. First, you should check whether there are any reply headers. Because the first element in the @list_contents array always contains the header information for the main message, you can check for the existence of any replies by checking the size of the @list_contents array. If the length of the @list_contents array is greater than 1, it contains reply headers. So, you can surround your inner for loop with an if conditional that checks the length of the @list_contents array. The following lines of Perl contain the if conditional and the inner for loop for the Expires subroutine:

```
if (@list_contents > 1) {

  for ($j=1; $j<@list_contents; $j++) {

    ($name, $subject, $message_date, $message_file) =
       split(/::/, $list_contents[$j]);
    chop $message_file;

    if (-M "$message_dir/$message_file" > $expires) {
      unlink "$message_dir/$message_file";
    } else {
      push(@new_list_contents, $list_contents[$j]);
    }

  }

  open(LIST, ">$list_dir/$i") || die "Content-type: text/html\n\nCannot open list
file for output!";
  print LIST @new_list_contents;
  close(LIST);
}
```

The first several lines should look familiar. They are identical to lines from the Display_Message_Lists subroutine. But the second if statement is different. The conditional expression for this if statement checks whether the number of days since the message file (which you just got from the splitting the header information in the previous lines) was last modified is greater than the value in the $expires variable. The -M is a special Perl file operator that, when given a file name as a parameter, returns the number of days since the file was last modified. The $expires variable is a global variable that you set at the beginning of your bulletin board script. For this example, you will set this variable to 90. So, when the Expires subroutine is called, it deletes any files and header lines for messages and replies that are over 90 days old. By modifying the value you assign to the $expires variable, you can control how long messages remain on your bulletin board.

If the conditional expression in the inner if statement evaluates to true—meaning the file is older than 90 days—the message file is deleted with the Perl unlink statement. If the file is not older than 90 day, the header information is placed in the last element of the @new_list_contents array. This if statement is evaluated for each of the reply headers in the @list_contents array. After the for loop has finished, you have the new contents for your list file stored in the @new_list_contents array. So, the next few lines after the for loop open the list file for output and replace the old list contents with the new list contents.

At this point in the Expires subroutine, you have only expired replies to the main message. You have not yet checked whether the main message itself has expired. This is left until last so you already know whether there are still any unexpired replies. If not, and the main message file has expired, you will also delete the message list file, because you no longer have any messages or replies for that message list.

To finish the Expires subroutine, you need to check the message file for the main message for expiration. Before doing so, you need to split apart the header information for the main message. You do this with the following lines of Perl code:

```
($name, $subject, $message_date, $message_file) =
  split(/::/, $list_contents[0]);
chop $message_file;
```

Next, you should check whether there are any replies. Remember that you placed any unexpired reply headers in the @new_list_contents array. Also remember that you initialized the @new_list_contents array with the header information for the main message before you entered the inner loop. Because you already placed at least one element in the @new_list_contents array, if the length is not equal to 1, you know there are reply headers in the @new_list_contents array. Otherwise, there is just the header information for the main message. You use the following if...else block to check the main message file for expiration:

```
if (@new_list_contents == 1) {

  if (-e "$message_dir/$message_file") {

    unlink "$list_dir/$i", "$message_dir/$message_file"
      if (-M "$message_dir/$message_file" > $expires);

  } else {
```

```
    unlink "$list_dir/$i";
  }

} else {

  unlink "$message_dir/$message_file"
    if ( (-e "$message_dir/$message_file") &&
         (-M "$message_dir/$message_file" > $expires) );
}
```

The preceding if...else block uses a conditional that is true when the @new_list_contents array only contains the header information for the main message. That is, the lines of code under the if portion of the if...else are only executed when there are no unexpired reply headers, whereas the else portion is only executed when there are unexpired reply headers.

The lines of code within the if portion contain another if...else statement block. This if...else uses the -e Perl file operator, which evaluates to true when the specified file (the main message file in this case) exists. You need to check whether the file exists because it could have already expired and been deleted. Remember that the header information for the main message remains as long as there are reply headers in the same file. So, even if the main message file has already been deleted, the main message header information could still exist. This if...else block checks whether the main message file still exists. If it does, the statements under the if portion of the if...else block are executed. These lines use the Perl unlink statement to remove both the main message file and list file if the main message file has expired. Keep in mind that these statements are only executed if there are no replies. So, if the main message file is expired, you no longer need the message list file either. The else portion of this inner if...else block is executed only when the main message file doesn't exist. Again, there are no replies left, so you can delete the message list file.

The lines of code under the else portion of the outer if...else portion are only executed when there is still header information for replies. In this case, you only need to delete the main message file if it has expired. Whether or not you delete the main message file, you still keep the message list file because it contains the headers for replies. You use the Perl unlink statement to delete the message file if it both exists and is expired.

You now have all the code you need for the Expires subroutine. Listing 9.7 puts together all the code you have developed. The only new lines are the subroutine and local variable declarations.

Listing 9.7: The Expires Subroutine

```
sub Expires {
  local (@lists, @list_contents, @new_list_contents,
         $num_lists, $i, $j, $name, $subject, $message_date,
         $message_file, $header, $replies);

  open(LISTS,"$list_count") || die "Content-type: text/html\n\nCannot open list
count!";
  $num_lists = <LISTS>;
  close(LISTS);

  for ($i=1; $i<=$num_lists; $i++) {

    # Open the message list file. If it cannot be
    # opened, assume it has been deleted and go
    # to the next message list.
    # Windows users need to change the string "$list_dir/$i" to
    # "$list_dir\\$i"
    open(LIST, "$list_dir/$i") || next;
    @list_contents = <LIST>;
    close(LIST);

    # Start the creation of the new header file list by placing the main message
in
    # the first element of the @new_list_contents array
    @new_list_contents = ($list_contents[0]);

    # If the header file only contains 1 message, there are no replies.
    if (@list_contents > 1) {

      # The message list contains replies, so check to
      # see if they have expired.
      for ($j=1; $j<@list_contents; $j++) {

        # Split each message header from the message list file.
        ($name, $subject, $message_date, $message_file) =
                split(/::/, $list_contents[$j]);
        chop $message_file;

        # This checks to see if the associated message file has expired. If so
        # the message file is deleted.
        # Windows users need to change the "$message_dir/$message_file" strings
        # below to "$message_dir\\$message_file"
        if (-M "$message_dir/$message_file" > $expires) {
          unlink "$message_dir/$message_file";
        } else {

          # The message file has not expired, so add the header line to
          # the new contents of the header file stored in the @new_list_contents
array.
```

Listing 9.7: The Expires Subroutine (Continued)

```
        push(@new_list_contents, $list_contents[$j]);
    }

  }

  # Create the new header file.
  # Windows users need to change the string "$list_dir/$i" to
  # "$list_dir\\$i"
  open(LIST, ">$list_dir/$i") || die "Content-type: text/html\n\nCannot open
list file for output!";
  print LIST @new_list_contents;
  close(LIST);
}

# Split each message header from the message list file.
($name, $subject, $message_date, $message_file) =
      split(/::/, $list_contents[0]);
chop $message_file;

# Check to see if the main message has expired.
if (@new_list_contents == 1) {

  # The list only contains the original message (no replies)

  # Windows users need to change the string "$message_dir/$message_file" to
  # "$message_dir\\$message_file"
  if (-e "$message_dir/$message_file") {

    # If the message has expired delete the message file
    # and the list file.

    # Windows users need to change the "$list_dir/$i" and
    # "$message_dir/$message_file" strings below to
    # "$list_dir\\$i" and $message_dir\\$message_file"
    unlink "$list_dir/$i", "$message_dir/$message_file"
      if (-M "$message_dir/$message_file" > $expires);

  } else {

    # The original message file does not exist, so delete
    # the list.
    # Windows users need to change the string "$list_dir/$i"
    # to "$list_dir\\$i"
    unlink "$list_dir/$i";
  }

} else {

  # The list contains the original message and replies. Delete only the main
```

Listing 9.7: The Expires Subroutine (Continued)

```
# message file if it exists and has expired.
# Windows users need to change the "$message_dir/$message_file" strings
# below to "$message_dir\\$message_file"
unlink "$message_dir/$message_file"
  if ( (-e "$message_dir/$message_file") &&
       (-M "$message_dir/$message_file" > $expires) );


  }

 }

}
```

The Complete Bulletin Board Script   Now that you have completed the five subroutines for your bulletin board script, you can put them all together into a single file called board.pl. Listing 9.8 contains the complete code for the bulletin board script. At the beginning of the board.pl file are several variable assignments. This is where the global variables mentioned in the previous sections are set. Also notice that the subroutines User_Data and No_SSI are both included in the board.pl file. You developed these subroutines earlier in this book. User_Data retrieves and URL decodes any data received from the user's Web browser. No_SSI eliminates any Server Side Include statements the user may have included in a message or reply.

Every time your bulletin board script is called, the line

```
$ENV{"REQUEST_METHOD"} eq "POST" ? &Which_Post : &Which_Get;
```

is executed. This line checks which method was used to call the board.pl script. If it was the POST method, which is used when a user posts a new message or a reply, the Which_Post subroutine is called. If it was the GET method, which is used when the user asks to view the message list or a specific message or reply, the Which_Get subroutine is called.

The Which_Post subroutine performs two main actions. First, it calls both the User_Data and No_SSI subroutines. This properly formats the user-supplied data into the %data_received associative array. Then it calls the proper subroutine, either Add_New_Message or Add_Reply, depending on which push button the user pressed. Recall from Listing 9.1 that the value for the submit button sent to the bulletin board script when the user posts a new message is Post Message. Also, from Listing 9.2, you see that the value for the submit button is Post Reply. So, you can call the correct subroutine by checking the value stored in the $data_received{'submit'} array element.

The Which_Get subroutine is called to display both the message list and messages and replies. Like Which_Post, Which_Get calls both the User_Data and No_SSI subroutines to retrieve any user data and place it in the %data_ received associative array. Then, an if...else statement block is used to distinguish which subroutine should be called, the Display_Message or Display_ Message_Lists subroutine. The conditional expression checks whether there is a value for the $data_received{'list'} array element. This element only has a value when the user asks to view a message or reply. In other words, the code under the if portion of the if...else statement calls the Display_Message subroutine. If the $data_ received{'list'} element does not contain a value, the message list is displayed to the user. Immediately before the Display_Message_Lists subroutine is called, the Expires subroutine can be called. If you place the subroutine call here, the message lists are updated every time any user requests the message list page. This keeps the message list fresh and current for every user. If you do not want your bulletin boards messages and replies to expire, just comment out the Expires subroutine by adding a pound sign (#) at the beginning of the line.

Listing 9.8: The board.pl File

```perl
#!/usr/local/bin/perl

# All users need to change the values of the $path variable
# to the valid path for their machine. Windows users need to
# use a path in the form $path = "c:\\robertm";
$path = "/users/robertm";

# Windows users need to change all the slashes (/) in the following lines
# to double backslashes (\\). For example, $list_template would be
# $list_template = $path . "\\message-list.tmpl";
$list_template = $path . "/message-list.tmpl";
$list_dir = $path . "/message-lists";
$list_count = $list_dir . "/count.dat";
$message_template = $path . "/message.tmpl";
$message_dir = $path . "/messages";
$message_count = $message_dir . "/count.dat";

# All users need to change the value of $expires to the amount
# of days before you want messages on your bulletin board to expire.
# If you don't want messages to expire, comment out the line
# &Expires;
# in the Which_Get subroutine below.
$expires = 90;
$date = localtime(time);

$ENV{"REQUEST_METHOD"} eq "POST" ? &Which_Post : &Which_Get;
```

Listing 9.8: The board.pl File (Continued)

```perl
sub Which_Post {
  %data_received = &User_Data();
  &No_SSI(%data_received);

  &Add_New_Message(%data_received) if $data_received{'submit'} eq "Post Message";
  &Add_Reply(%data_received) if $data_received{'submit'} eq "Post Reply";

}

sub Which_Get {
  %data_received = &User_Data();
  &No_SSI(%data_received);

  if ($data_received{'list'}) {
    &Display_Message(%data_received);
  } else {

    # If you don't want messages on your bulletin board to expire, comment out
    # the &Expires; line below.
    &Expires;
    &Display_Message_Lists;
  }

}

sub Expires {
  local (@lists, @list_contents, @new_list_contents,
        $num_lists, $i, $j, $name, $subject, $message_date,
        $message_file, $header, $replies);

  open(LISTS,"$list_count") || die "Content-type: text/html\n\nCannot open list
count!";
  $num_lists = <LISTS>;
  close(LISTS);

  for ($i=1; $i<=$num_lists; $i++) {

    # Open the message list file. If it cannot be
    # opened, assume it has been deleted and go
    # to the next message list.
    # Windows users need to change the string "$list_dir/$i" to
    # "$list_dir\\$i"
    open(LIST, "$list_dir/$i") || next;
    @list_contents = <LIST>;
    close(LIST);


    # Start creating the new header file list by placing the main message in
    # the first element of the @new_list_contents array
```

Listing 9.8: The board.pl File (Continued)

```perl
    @new_list_contents = ($list_contents[0]);

   # If the header file only contains 1 message, there are no replies.
   if (@list_contents > 1) {

     # The message list contains replies, so check to
     # see if they have expired.
     for ($j=1; $j<@list_contents; $j++) {

       # Split each message header from the message list file.
       ($name, $subject, $message_date, $message_file) =
               split(/::/, $list_contents[$j]);
       chop $message_file;

       # This checks to see if the associated message file has expired. If so
       # the message file is deleted.
       # Windows users need to change the "$message_dir/$message_file" strings
       # below to "$message_dir\\$message_file"
       if (-M "$message_dir/$message_file" > $expires) {
         unlink "$message_dir/$message_file";
       } else {

         # The message file has not expired, so add the header line to
         # the new contents of the header file stored in the @new_list_contents
array.
         push(@new_list_contents, $list_contents[$j]);
       }

     }

     # Create the new header file.
     # Windows users need to change the string "$list_dir/$i" to
     # "$list_dir\\$i"
     open(LIST, ">$list_dir/$i") || die "Content-type: text/html\n\nCannot open
list file for output!";
     print LIST @new_list_contents;
     close(LIST);
   }

   # Split each message header from the message list file.
   ($name, $subject, $message_date, $message_file) =
         split(/::/, $list_contents[0]);
   chop $message_file;

   # Check to see if the main message has expired.
   if (@new_list_contents == 1) {

     # The list only contains the original message (no replies)
```

Listing 9.8: The board.pl File (Continued)

```perl
        # Windows users need to change the string "$message_dir/$message_file" to
        # "$message_dir\\$message_file"
        if (-e "$message_dir/$message_file") {

            # If the message has expired, delete the message file
            # and the list file.

            # Windows users need to change the "$list_dir/$i" and
            # "$message_dir/$message_file" strings below to
            # "$list_dir\\$i" and $message_dir\\$message_file"
            unlink "$list_dir/$i", "$message_dir/$message_file"
                if (-M "$message_dir/$message_file" > $expires);

        } else {

            # The original message file does not exist, so delete
            # the list.
            # Windows users need to change the string "$list_dir/$i"
            # to "$list_dir\\$i"
            unlink "$list_dir/$i";
        }

    } else {

        # The list contains the original message and replies. Delete only the main
        # message file if it exists and has expired.
        # Windows users need to change the "$message_dir/$message_file" strings
        # below to "$message_dir\\$message_file"
        unlink "$message_dir/$message_file"
            if ( (-e "$message_dir/$message_file") &&
                 (-M "$message_dir/$message_file" > $expires) );

    }

  }

}

sub Display_Message_Lists {
  local (@template, @lists, @list_contents, $num_lists,
         $i, $j, $name, $subject, $message_date, $message_file,
         $header, $replies);

  open(LISTS,"$list_count") || die "Content-type: text/html\n\nCannot open list
count!";
  $num_lists = <LISTS>;
  close(LISTS);

  # Loop over all the message list files and add the contents to the message list
```

Listing 9.8: The board.pl File (Continued)

```perl
# which is displayed to the user.
for ($i=1; $i<=$num_lists; $i++) {

  # Open the message list file. If it cannot be
  # opened, assume it has been deleted and go
  # to the next message list.
  # Windows users need to change the string "$list_dir/$i" to
  # "$list_dir\\$i"
  open(LIST, "$list_dir/$i") || next;
  @list_contents = <LIST>;
  close(LIST);

  # Split the message header from the message list file.
  ($name, $subject, $message_date, $message_file) =
          split(/::/, $list_contents[0]);
  chop $message_file;

  # Format the header depending on whether the message file
  # exists
  # Windows users need to change the string "$message_dir/$message_file"
  # to "$message_dir\\$message_file"
  unless (-e "$message_dir/$message_file") {
    $header = "<LI><B>$subject</B> $name -  $message_date";
  } else {
    $header = "<LI><A HREF=\"/cgi-
bin/board.pl?message=$message_file&list=$i\">";
    $header .= "<B>$subject</B></A> $name -  $message_date";
  }

  # If the header file has more than one line, it contains header lines for
replies.
  if (@list_contents > 1) {
    $replies = "<UL>\n";
    for ($j=1; $j<@list_contents; $j++) {

      # Split each message header from the message list file.
      ($name, $subject, $message_date, $message_file) =
              split(/::/, $list_contents[$j]);
      chop $message_file;

      # Format the replies for display in the user's Web browser.
      $replies .= "<LI><A HREF=\"/cgi-
bin/board.pl?message=$message_file&list=$i\">";
      $replies .= "$subject</A> $name - $message_date";
    }

    # Append the replies after the main message.
    $header .= "\n$replies</UL>\n";
  }
```

Listing 9.8: The board.pl File (Continued)

```perl
    # Put the header and replies (if any) in the @lists array.
    push(@lists, $header);

  }

  # If there are any messages in the @lists array, finish formatting with HTML
  if (@lists) {
    unshift(@lists, "<UL>\n");
    push(@lists, "</UL>\n");
  } else {

    # No messages exist.
    $lists[0] = "<H2>Currently No Messages</H2>";
  }

  open(TEMPLATE,"$list_template") || die "Content-type: text/html\n\nCannot open
template!";
  @template = <TEMPLATE>;
  close(TEMPLATE);

  # Put the message headers in the template, and send to the user's Web browser.
  splice(@template, 8, 0, @lists);

  print "Content-type: text/html\n\n";
  print @template;

}

sub Display_Message {
  local (%data) = @_;
  local (@template, @list, @message, $subject, $message_file);

  # Open and read in the template
  open(TEMPLATE,"$message_template") || die "Content-type: text/html\n\nCannot
open template!";
  @template = <TEMPLATE>;
  close(TEMPLATE);

  # Open and read in the message file
  # Windows users need to change the string "$message_dir/$data{\"message\"}"
  # to "$message_dir\\$data{\"message\"}"
  open(MESSAGE,"$message_dir/$data{\"message\"}") || die "Content-type:
text/html\n\nCannot open message!";
  @message = <MESSAGE>;
  close(MESSAGE);

  # Open and read in the list file
  # Windows users need to change the string "$list_dir/$data{\"list\"}" to
  # "$list_dir\\$data{\"list\"}"
```

Listing 9.8: The board.pl File (Continued)

```perl
  open(LIST,"$list_dir/$data{\"list\"}") || die "Content-type:
text/html\n\nCannot open message!";
  @list = <LIST>;
  close(LIST);

  # Find the subject for the message to be displayed.
  foreach (@list) {
    # Split each message header from the message list file.
    (undef, $subject, undef, $message_file) =
          split(/::/);
    chop $message_file;

    # Exit the loop when the message has been found.
    last if $message_file == $data{'message'};
  }

  # Put the subject in the <TITLE> line of the template.
  $template[2] =~ s/XXXX/$subject/ge;

  # Format the subject line for the Reply form at the end of the page.
  unless ($subject =~ /^re:/i) {
    substr($subject, 0, 0) = "Re: ";
  }

  # Insert the subject and list into the template.
  $template[20] =~ s/YYYY/$subject/ge;
  $template[26] =~ s/ZZZZ/$data{'list'}/ge;

  # Insert the message into the template and send it to the user's Web browser.
  splice(@template, 4, 0, @message);

  print "Content-type: text/html\n\n";
  print @template;

}

sub Add_New_Message {
  local (%data) = @_;
  local ($num_lists, $num_messages);

  # Verify the user entered the required fields
  die "Content-type: text/html\n\nYou must enter data for every field except the
E-mail address."
        unless ($data{'name'} && $data{'subject'} && $data{'comments'});

  # Get the last list number
  open(LISTS,"$list_count") || die "Content-type: text/html\n\nCannot open list
count!";
  $num_lists = <LISTS>;
```

Listing 9.8: The board.pl File (Continued)

```perl
  close(LISTS);

  # Increment the number
  $num_lists++;

  # Save the current list number to the file
  open(LISTS,">$list_count") || die "Content-type: text/html\n\nCannot open list
count!";
  print LISTS $num_lists;
  close(LISTS);

  # Get the last message number
  open(MESSAGES,"$message_count") || die "Content-type: text/html\n\nCannot open
message count!";
  $num_messages = <MESSAGES>;
  close(MESSAGES);

  # Increment the number
  $num_messages++;

  # Save the current message number to the file
  open(MESSAGES,">$message_count") || die "Content-type: text/html\n\nCannot open
message count!";
  print MESSAGES $num_messages;
  close(MESSAGES);

  # Create the new message
  # Windows users need to change the string ">$message_dir/$num_messages"
  # to ">$message_dir\\$num_messages"
  open(NEWMESSAGE,">$message_dir/$num_messages") || die "Content-type:
text/html\n\nCannot create new message!";
  print NEWMESSAGE "<B>Subject:</B> $data{\"subject\"}<BR>\n";
  print NEWMESSAGE "<B>From:</B> $data{\"name\"}<BR>\n";
  print NEWMESSAGE "<B>E-mail:</B> $data{\"email\"}<BR>\n" if $data{'email'};
  print NEWMESSAGE "<B>Date:</B> $date<P>\n";
  print NEWMESSAGE "$data{\"comments\"}<P>\n";
  close(NEWLIST);

  # Create the new list
  # Windows users need to change the string ">$list_dir/$num_lists" to
  # ">$list_dir\\$num_lists"
  open(NEWLIST,">$list_dir/$num_lists") || die "Content-type: text/html\n\nCannot
create new list!";
  print NEWLIST "$data{\"name\"}::$data{\"subject\"}::${date}::$num_messages\n";
  close(NEWLIST);

  &Display_Message_Lists;

}
```

Listing 9.8: The board.pl File (Continued)

```perl
sub Add_Reply {
  local (%data) = @_;
  local ($num_lists, $num_messages);

  # Verify the user entered the required fields
  die "Content-type: text/html\n\nYou must enter data for every field except the
E-mail address."
        unless ($data{'name'} && $data{'subject'} && $data{'comments'});

  # Get the last message number
  open(MESSAGES,"$message_count") || die "Content-type: text/html\n\nCannot open
message count!";
  $num_messages = <MESSAGES>;
  close(MESSAGES);

  # Increment the number
  $num_messages++;

  # Save the current message number to the file
  open(MESSAGES,">$message_count") || die "Content-type: text/html\n\nCannot open
message count!";
  print MESSAGES $num_messages;
  close(MESSAGES);

  # Create the new message
  # Windows users need to change the string ">$message_dir/$num_messages" to
  # ">$message_dir\\$num_messages"
  open(NEWMESSAGE,">$message_dir/$num_messages") || die "Content-type:
text/html\n\nCannot create new message!";
  print NEWMESSAGE "<B>Subject:</B> $data{\"subject\"}<BR>\n";
  print NEWMESSAGE "<B>From:</B> $data{\"name\"}<BR>\n";
  print NEWMESSAGE "<B>E-mail:</B> $data{\"email\"}<BR>\n" if $data{'email'};
  print NEWMESSAGE "<B>Date:</B> $date<P>\n";
  print NEWMESSAGE "$data{\"comments\"}<P>\n";
  close(NEWLIST);

  # Add message header to the list
  # Windows users need to change the string ">>$list_dir/$data{\"list\"}"
  # to ">>$list_dir\\$data{\"list\"}"
  open(LIST,">>$list_dir/$data{\"list\"}") || die "Content-type:
text/html\n\nCannot open list!";
  print LIST "$data{\"name\"}::$data{\"subject\"}::${date}::$num_messages\n";
  close(LIST);

  &Display_Message_Lists;

}
```

Listing 9.8: The board.pl File (Continued)

```perl
sub No_SSI {
  local (*data) = @_;

  foreach $key (sort keys(%data)) {
    $data{$key} =~ s/<!--(.|\n)*-->//g;
  }

}


sub User_Data {
  local (%user_data, $user_string, $name_value_pair,
         @name_value_pairs, $name, $value);

  # If the data was sent via POST, then it is available
  # from standard input. Otherwise, the data is in the
  # QUERY_STRING environment variable.
  if ($ENV{"REQUEST_METHOD"} eq "POST") {
    read(STDIN,$user_string,$ENV{"CONTENT_LENGTH"});
  } else {
    $user_string = $ENV{"QUERY_STRING"};
  }

  # This line changes the + signs to spaces.
  $user_string =~ s/\+/ /g;

  # This line places each name/value pair as a separate
  # element in the name_value_pairs array.
  @name_value_pairs = split(/&/, $user_string);

  # This code loops over each element in the name_value_pairs
  # array, splits it on the = sign, and places the value
  # into the user_data associative array with the name as the
  # key.
  foreach $name_value_pair (@name_value_pairs) {
    ($name, $value) = split(/=/, $name_value_pair);

    # These two lines decode the values from any URL
    # hexadecimal encoding. The first section searches for a
    # hexadecimal number and the second part converts the
    # hex number to decimal and returns the character
    # equivalent.
    $name =~
      s/%([a-fA-F0-9][a-fA-F0-9])/pack("C",hex($1))/ge;
    $value =~
      s/%([a-fA-F0-9][a-fA-F0-9])/pack("C",hex($1))/ge;

    # If the name/value pair has already been given a value,
    # as in the case of multiple items being selected, then
    # separate the items with a " : ".
```

Listing 9.8: The board.pl File (Continued)

```
    if (defined($user_data{$name})) {
      $user_data{$name} .= " : " . $value;
    } else {
      $user_data{$name} = $value;
    }
  }
  return %user_data;
}
```

INTERACTING WITH NNTP NEWS SERVERS

Instead of using a text file based bulletin board, you could set up an NNTP news server on your server machine to control the adding and deleting of messages to your bulletin board. You would still need to create a CGI script to interface with the NNTP server. Unless you know quite a bit about the NNTP protocol, this task would be quite difficult. If you intend to take this approach, check script repositories for library routines that handle the NNTP interaction for you. This way you can use the subroutines and functions that others have already created, instead of having to take the time to write and debug them from scratch yourself.

Rodger Anderson created one such library for Perl called NNTPClient, which is available from the CPAN (Comprehensive Perl Archive Network) modules section of the Perl Web site (http://www.perl.com). The NNTPClient module implements a client interface to NNTP, enabling a Perl application (using version 5 or greater) to talk to NNTP news servers. This module contains all the subroutines you need to write a CGI script in Perl to display newsgroups in your Web pages.

Because NNTP news servers store the news articles in plain text files, just like the text based bulletin board example in this chapter, you do not gain much by interfacing with an NNTP server to create your own bulletin board on your Web site. However, if you want to display messages from Internet wide newsgroups in your Web pages, the simple bulletin board example would not be of any use to you. In this case, you would want to create the NNTP gateway script.

QUICK REFERENCE

This Quick Reference section mentions a number of online resources you can turn to if you want to learn more about CGI and related topics such as HTML, Perl, and Netscape Cookies. It's an excellent idea to familiarize yourself with at least some of these resources. Not only can they supply material that didn't fit within the confines of this book, they can also provide the most up-to-date information available.

USEFUL WEB PAGES

This section lists the URLs for Web sites that cover a number of CGI-related topics, including HTTP, HTML, CGI, Perl, Netscape cookies, script archives, gateways, libraries, World Wide Web software, search engines, and directories. If you can't find what you want in this book, these pages should help you track down the information you need.

HTTP

Overview of HTTP
http://www.w3.org/hypertext/WWW/Protocols/

HTTP/1.0 Specification
http://www.ics.uci.edu/pub/ietf/http/draft-ietf-http-v10-spec-03.html

Object Headers
http://www.w3.org/hypertext/WWW/Protocols/HTTP/Object_Headers.html

Secure HTTP
http://www.eit.com/creations/s-http/

Names and Addresses, URIs, URLs, URNs, URCs
http://www.w3.org/hypertext/WWW/Addressing/Addressing.html

Uniform Resource Identifiers (URI) Working Group
http://www.ics.uci.edu/pub/ietf/uri/

Uniform Resource Locators
http://www.w3.org/hypertext/WWW/Addressing/URL/Overview.html

HTML

HTML Quick Reference
http://www.cc.ukans.edu/info/HTML_quick.html

Hypertext Markup Language
http://www.w3.org/pub/WWW/MarkUp/

A Beginner's Guide to HTML
http://www.ncsa.uiuc.edu/General/Internet/WWW/HTMLPrimer.html

An Introduction to SGML
http://www.brainlink.com/~ben/sgml/

Special Characters
http://www.utirc.utoronto.ca/HTMLdocs/NewHTML/entities.html

ISO8859-1 (Latin-1) Table
http://www.uni-passau.de/~ramsch/iso8859-1.html

CGI

The Common Gateway Interface
http://hoohoo.ncsa.uiuc.edu/cgi/

CGI Programmer's Reference
http://www.best.com/~hedlund/cgi-faq/

CGI Applications in AppleScript

http://129.79.157.79/Tutorials/Extending_MacHTTP/CGIScripts.html
W3C httpd CGI/1.1 Script Support
http://www.w3.org/hypertext/WWW/Daemon/User/CGI/Overview.html

Windows CGI 1.1 Description
http://www.city.net/win-httpd/httpddoc/wincgi.htm

PERL

Perl Home Page
http://www.perl.com

Perl Basics
http://briet.berkeley.edu/perl/perl_tutorial.txt

Perl Manual in HTML
http://www.cis.ufl.edu/cgi-bin/plindex

Perl for Win32
http://www.perl.hip.com

University of Florida's Perl Pages
http://www1.cis.ufl.edu/perl/

Index of Perl/HTML archives
http://www.seas.upenn.edu/~mengwong/perlhtml.html

NETSCAPE COOKIES

Netscape's Persistent Cookies documentation
http://home.netscape.com/newsref/std/cookie_spec.html

Malcolm's Guide to Persistent Cookies
http://www.emf.net/~mal/cookiesinfo.html

Andy's Netscape HTTP Cookie Notes
http://www.illuminatus.com/cookie

SCRIPT ARCHIVES, GATEWAYS, AND LIBRARIES

Boutell.com contains many useful Web resources, including gd GIF C
Library and cgic ANSI C-language CGI library.
http://www.boutell.com/

Matt's Script Archive
http://www.worldwidemart.com/scripts/

Selena Sol's CGI Script Archive
http://www2.eff.org/~erict/Scripts/

Digit Mania
http://cervantes.learningco.com/kevin/digits/index.html

C++ CGI Class Library
http://sweetbay.will.uiuc.edu/cgi++/

cgi-lib.pl Perl CGI library
http://www.bio.cam.ac.uk/cgi-lib/

CGI.pm Perl 5 CGI Library
http://www-genome.wi.mit.edu/ftp/pub/software/WWW/cgi_docs.html

Felipe's AppleScript CGI Examples
http://edb518ea.edb.utexas.edu/scripts/cgix/cgix.html

Information Through Programs
http://ecsdg.lu.se/info-prog.html

WDB - A Web interface to SQL Databases
http://arch-http.hq.eso.org/bfrasmus/wdb/wdb.html

Free Database Gateway List
http://cuiwww.unige.ch/~scg/FreeDB/FreeDB.list.html

WWW-DBMS Gateways
http://grigg.chungnam.ac.kr/~uniweb/documents/www_dbms.html

GSQL - a Mosaic-SQL gateway
http://www.ncsa.uiuc.edu/SDG/People/jason/pub/gsql/starthere.html

Oracle/Web Development Tools
http://www.coe.missouri.edu/~pixel/computers/oracle.html

WWW Access to Relational Databases
http://www.w3.org/hypertext/WWW/RDBGate/Overview.html

Yahoo's CGI page
http://www.yahoo.com/Computers_and_Internet/Internet/World_Wide_
Web/CGI___Common_Gateway_Interface/

WORLD WIDE WEB SOFTWARE

Netscape—Navigator (browser), NetSite (server), and more
http://www.netscape.com/

Microsoft—Internet Explorer (browser), Internet Information Server
(server), and more
http://www.microsoft.com

O'Reilly Software's WebSite
http://website.ora.com/

Apache SSL Webserver
http://www.c2.org/apachessl/

NCSA—Mosaic (browser), HTTPD (server), and more
http://hoohoo.ncsa.uiuc.edu/

SEARCH ENGINES AND DIRECTORIES

Yahoo
http://www.yahoo.com/

Infoseek
http://www.infoseek.com/

AltaVista
http://altavista.digital.com/

Excite
http://www.excite.com/

The Lycos A2Z directory

http://a2z.lycos.com/

C|Net's Search.com
http://www.search.com/

IBM's InfoMarket
http://www.infomarket.ibm.com/

Magellan
http://www.mckinley.com/

Open Text Index
http://www.opentext.com/omw/f-omw.html

Point
http://www.pointcom.com/

Starting Point
http://www.stpt.com/

WebCrawler
http://www.webcrawler.com/

Usenet newsgroups and mailing lists

This section lists a number of newsgroups and mailing lists that cover CGI and related topics. Such discussion groups can be excellent places to post messages to which you need a response.

NEWGROUPS

This newsgroup is for messages about CGI scripting.
comp.infosystems.www.authoring.cgi

This newsgroup is for messages about HTML coding.
comp.infosystems.www.authoring.html

This newsgroup is for messages about authoring for the World Wide Web in general.
comp.infosystems.www.authoring.misc

The following newsgroups are for messages pertaining to Web browsers:
comp.infosystems.www.browsers.mac
comp.infosystems.www.browsers.ms-windows
comp.infosystems.www.browsers.x
comp.infosystems.www.browsers.misc

The following groups are for messages pertaining to Web servers:
comp.infosystems.www.servers.mac
comp.infosystems.www.servers.ms-windows
comp.infosystems.www.servers.unix
comp.infosystems.www.servers.misc

Deja News is a service that searches Usenet newsgroups by keywords.
http://www.dejanews.com/

MAILING LISTS

Common Gateway Interface List
To subscribe send e-mail to: listserv@vm.ege.edu.tr. In the body of the
message, type

`subscribe CGI-L Firstname Lastname`

Advanced CGI Discussion List
To subscribe send e-mail to listproc@lists.nyu.edu. In the body of the
message, type

`subscribe ADV-CGI Firstname Lastname`

Advanced HTML Discussion List
To subscribe send e-mail to listserv@ua1vm.ua.edu. In the body of the
message, type

`subscribe ADV-HTML Firstname Lastname`

Index